IMAGES
of America

CLEVELAND COUNTY
PEOPLE AND PLACES

IMAGES
of America

CLEVELAND COUNTY
PEOPLE AND PLACES

Barry E. Hambright
and U.L. "Rusty" Patterson

ARCADIA
PUBLISHING

ISBN-13 978-0-7385-1465-9

Published by Arcadia Publishing
Charleston, South Carolina

Printed in the United States of America

Library of Congress Catalog Card Number: 2002107725

For all general information contact Arcadia Publishing at:
Telephone 843-853-2070
Fax 843-853-0044
E-mail sales@arcadiapublishing.com
For customer service and orders:
Toll-Free 1-888-313-2665

Visit us on the Internet at www.arcadiapublishing.com

Contents

Acknowledgments 6

Introduction 7

1. Shelby: Pre-1940 9
2. Shelby: Mid-Century 35
3. Kings Mountain 77
4. Boiling Springs 93
5. Around the County 105

Acknowledgments

The authors thank those who have helped make this publication possible. Many people throughout the county have graciously and enthusiastically provided photos, names, and background information. Credit has been given at the end of each caption for those postcards and photographs from other collections. Several publications have been instrumental in confirming people, places, names, facts, and timelines, including the following: *The Living Past of Cleveland County* by Lee B. Weathers, *Our Heritage, A History of Cleveland County* by Henry Lee Weathers, *The Heritage of Cleveland County* published by the Cleveland County Historical Association, *Governor O. Max Gardner* by Joseph L. Morrison, and the Shelby newspaper, *The Star*.

We thank Tommy Forney for access to the Lloyd Hamrick collection of photos. The works of professional photographers Floyd Willis and the Ellis Studios have been instrumental in developing the book, as have postcards produced by the T.W. Hamrick Co., Austin and Clontz 5, 10, and 25¢ Store, and the Asheville Postcard Co. We are thankful for the use of photos from Shelby High School and David Allen and the Uptown Shelby Association and Ted Alexander.

We are grateful to Robert Arey Sr., Betsy Brantley, the Alston Bridges family, Severne Budd, Wallace Carpenter, Virginia Coon, Adelaide Austell Craver, Peggy Kuykendall Conlan, Dewey Cooke, Delane Davis, Ralph Dixon, Paul Durst, Dean Floyd, Edwin and Esther Anne Ford, Jean Harry Francis, Joe A. Goforth, Harvey Hamrick Jr., Madge Harris, Boyd Hendrick, the Jack Hughes family, Helen Lackey, Bill Lattimore, David Lynn, the C.J. Mabry Sr. family, Vic McCord, Jane McDaniel, Roger McKee, Tim Moore, the Jack Morgan family, Betty Sue Morris, Reanza Waldrep Murray, Stella Neisler Putnam, R.W. Richardson, Mike Royster, Becky Sain, Joe Southards, Clevie Spangler, Eloise Spangler, Tony Stewart, Bob Still, Dr. John Still, Tommy Tedder, Evan Thompson, Larry Ware, Debbie Bridges Webb, Harvey Whisnant, Tom Wright, Gene and Margaret Yarboro, and H. Fields Young III for their contributions of photos and histories. Thanks to Laura Daniels New at Arcadia Publishing for her technical support. And special thanks to Mary Emma Hambright and to Frankie, Marion, and Margaret Patterson for their love and support.

A reasonable effort has been made to gather accurate information about each image. All of these people helped to make this publication possible. None of them are responsible for the errors, which are the authors' alone.

INTRODUCTION

Two years ago, we compiled our first book on Shelby and Cleveland County. We became aware of people's interest and love of local history, especially those people and places that bring back memories of yesteryear. In every city and town people have pictures from the past that can give a record of the community in which they live. Gradually these images are being lost or discarded by those who do not see their value. Additionally the stories and history that make these images so valuable need to be recorded. Arcadia's *Images of America* series is saving memories of communities across the country. Over 1,000 titles have been published storing valuable views of people and places across the nation.

In our first volume, we collected pictures that were easily available. In this work, we have searched for pictures of people and places that we felt would be significant in the heritage of Cleveland County. We have searched for pictures not in the public domain, and we have tried to put more emphasis on the people either who have built the county in the 20th century or who represent typical people going about their lives as the county grew and modernized.

Our focus is still Cleveland County, which is in the western Piedmont of North Carolina. Cleveland County lies on the South Carolina border with just one county between it and the fast growing Charlotte, which has been North Carolina's largest city for several decades. The county was formed by an act of the North Carolina Legislature on January 11, 1841 from parts of Rutherford and Lincoln Counties. The county was named for Revolutionary War leader Gen. Benjamin Cleaveland. The state legislature changed the spelling to Cleveland in 1887 while Grover Cleveland was President and there was confusion over the two spellings. The site for the county seat was to be established within four miles of the famed Cleveland Springs. The county seat was named Shelby in honor of Col. Issac Shelby who had fought in the 1780 Battle of Kings Mountain.

In this volume, we will seek to show the development of Cleveland County as an agricultural area followed by the rise of the textile industry and small towns that grew around them. In the last half of the century, both agriculture and textiles were in decline but both remain significant to our heritage. The last several decades have resulted in an influx of new industry and the diversification of the county.

This book features people and places in Shelby, which has grown to a city of over 19,000 people. Kings Mountain is now a city of almost 10,000 people in the eastern part of the county along the Gaston County line. Again, we feature Boiling Springs—a fast growing community with nearly 4,000 residents—and Gardner-Webb University with over 3,000 students. We have pictures of leading families, and postcards showing the cities in the early 20th century.

We conclude with a visit to the small towns of Lawndale, Fallston, and Grover. We hope you will not only remember the scenes of the towns and county, but also will see the people as characteristic of bygone eras. Notice the changing styles in everything from clothing to automobiles. Our goal is to preserve memories of the past and give our readers pleasure remembering people and places out of Cleveland County's history.^

One

Shelby
Pre-1940

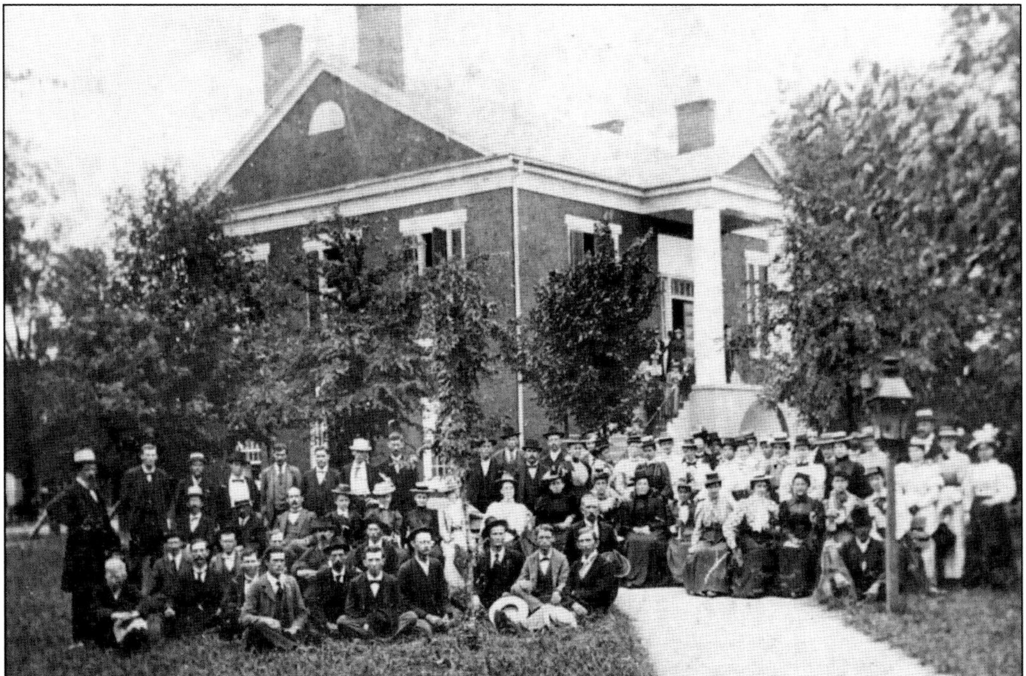

This *c.* 1879 picture shows a meeting of public school teachers from schools throughout the county. Public schools were just beginning to grow after the Civil War. J.A. Anthony served as superintendent of schools during this time. (*The Heritage of Cleveland County.*)

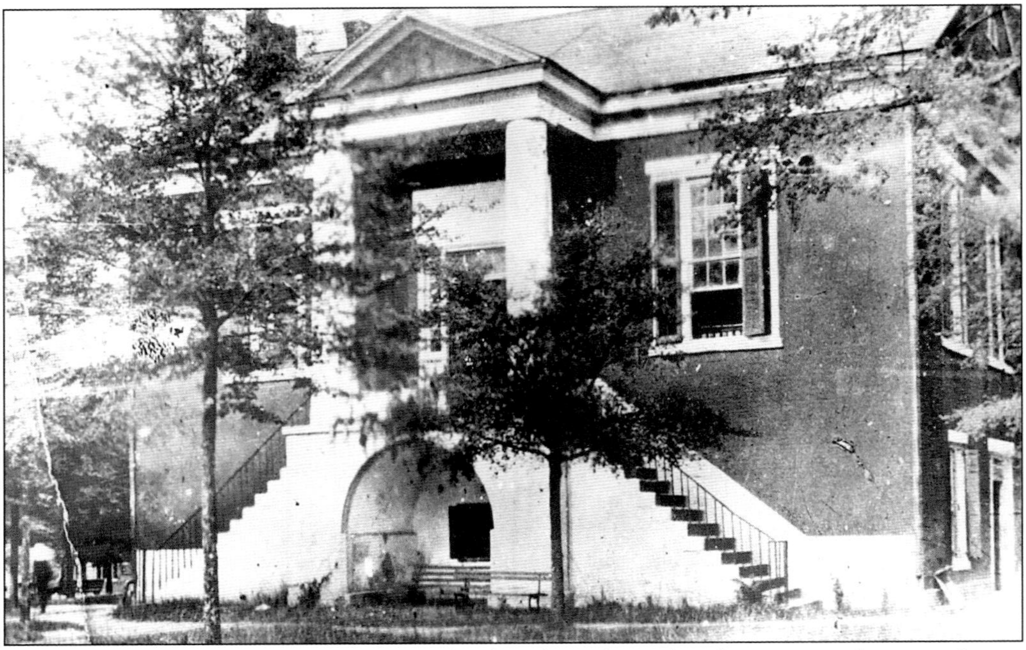

Uptown Shelby has no "main street." The founders planned wide streets with a courthouse built on a large block, which was to be the center of town. The first courthouse on the square was built in 1845 and torn down in 1907. On the four sides, four wide streets were built. Just as the county and city were named for Revolutionary War leaders, these streets were named Washington, Lafayette, Marion, and Warren.

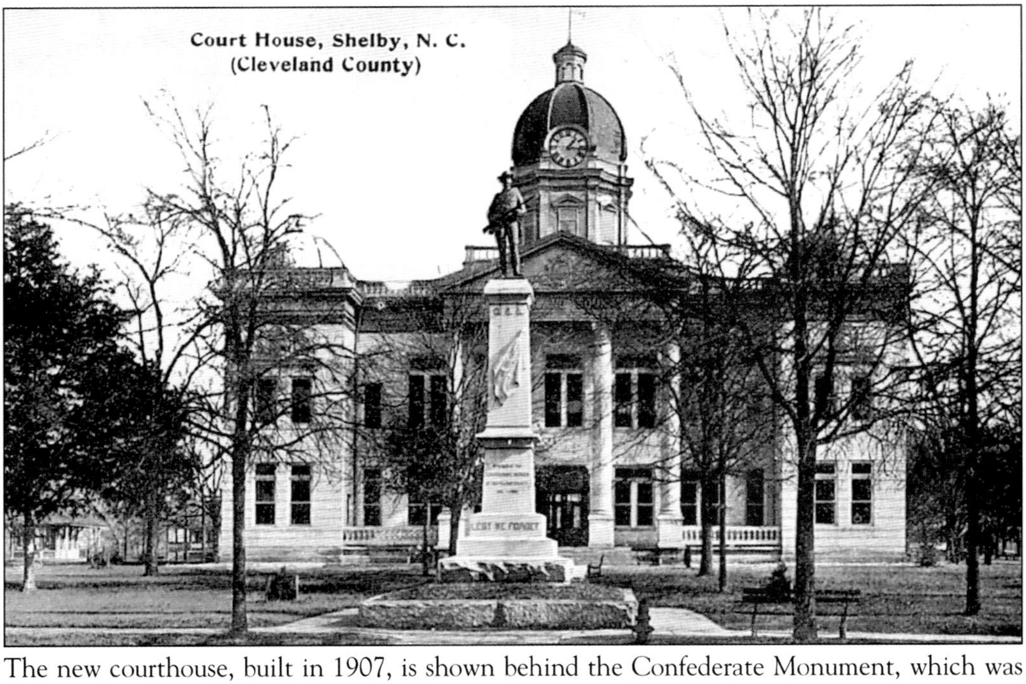

The new courthouse, built in 1907, is shown behind the Confederate Monument, which was dedicated in 1906. At the left is a building on the square where Lithia spring water was pumped for sale. The house between the springhouse and the courthouse was torn down in 1924 to make room for the new Central Methodist Church.

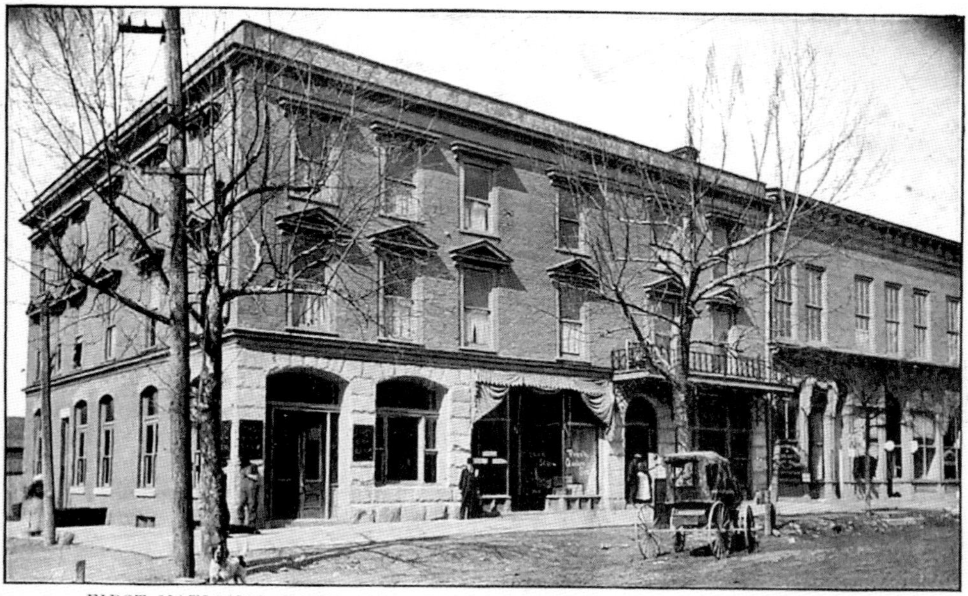

FIRST NATIONAL BANK AND CENTRAL HOTEL BUILDING, SHELBY, N. C.

This image shows the Central Hotel with the First National Bank on the corner. The metal plaques on the front wall of the building indicate the new home for the bank. The hotel would burn in 1928 with a loss of four lives.

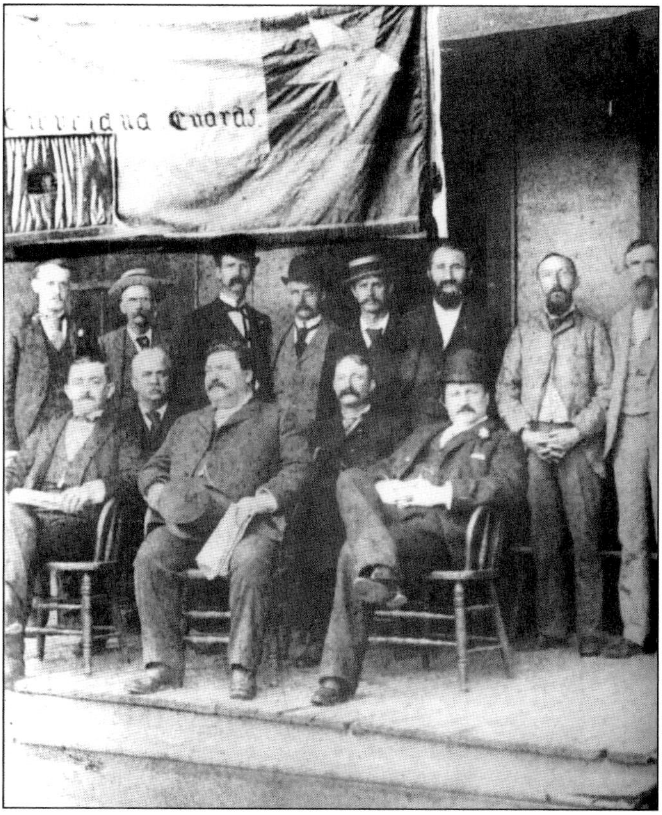

The Civil War was still a part of everyday life in the 1890s, although it had concluded over 25 years before. Veterans of the war were proud and honored men. This photo shows Shelby officials with a delegation from Boston, Massachusetts, who had traveled to Shelby to return a flag of the Cleveland Guards that had been captured in the Civil War. The flag hangs behind them. (*Our Heritage, A History of Cleveland County*.)

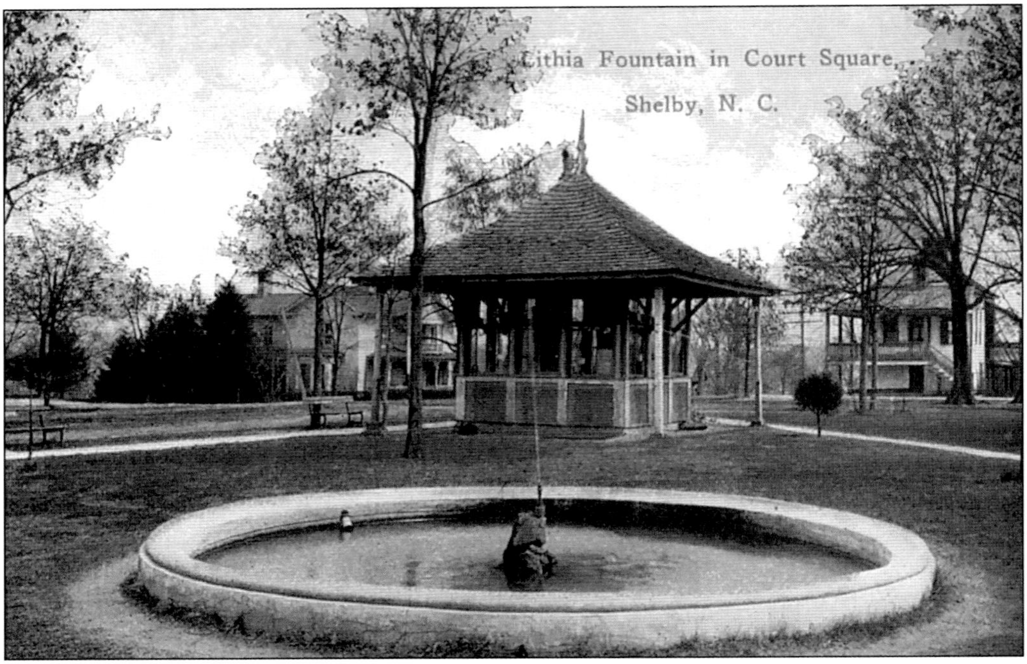

The springhouse and fountain are seen on the northeast corner of the court square. The first house built in Shelby is seen across the street. Central Methodist Church replaced the first house.

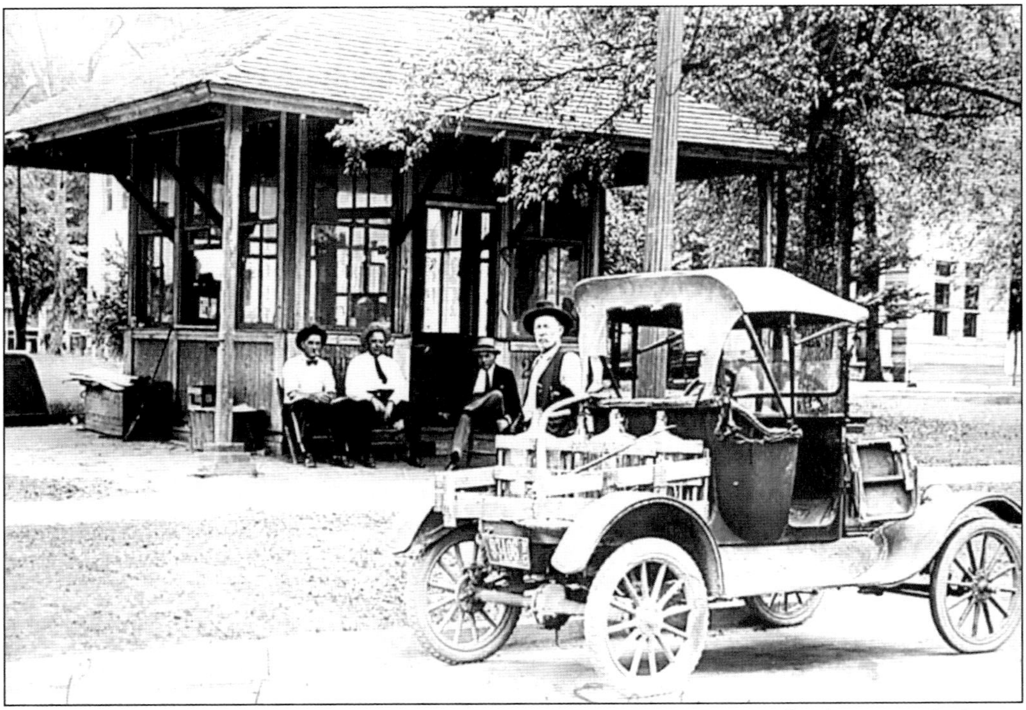

This is a *c.* 1920 postcard view of the springhouse with Beck Quinn in the foreground. Quinn sold water by the glass at the fountain and made home deliveries as seen by the jugs of water loaded on his truck. (Edwin and Esther Anne Ford.)

The Roberts Tabernacle C.M.E. Church of Shelby was organized by a small group of African-Americans in 1884. Their first church was on the corner of West Graham and South Morgan Streets. (Severne Budd.)

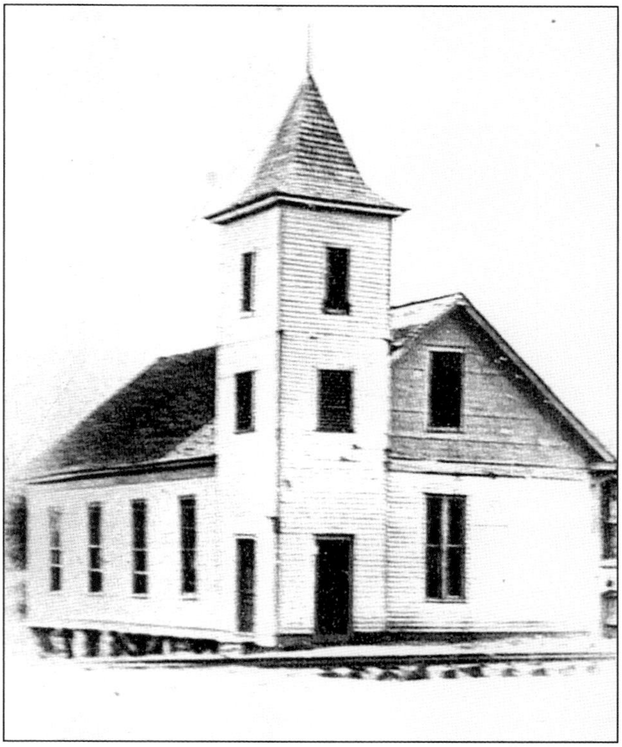

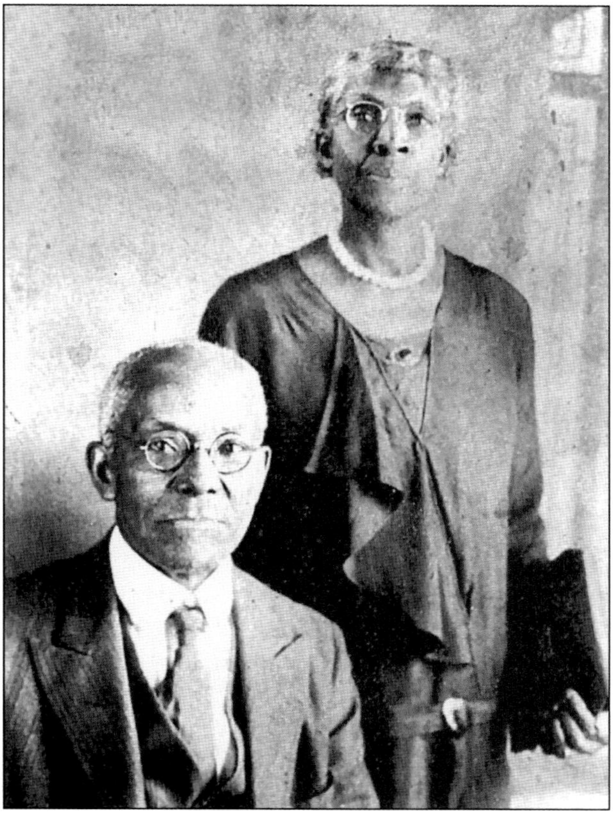

The Roberts Tabernacle C.M.E. Church is named for Rev. John Wesley Roberts. Reverend Roberts is pictured here with his wife Ida. (Severne Budd.)

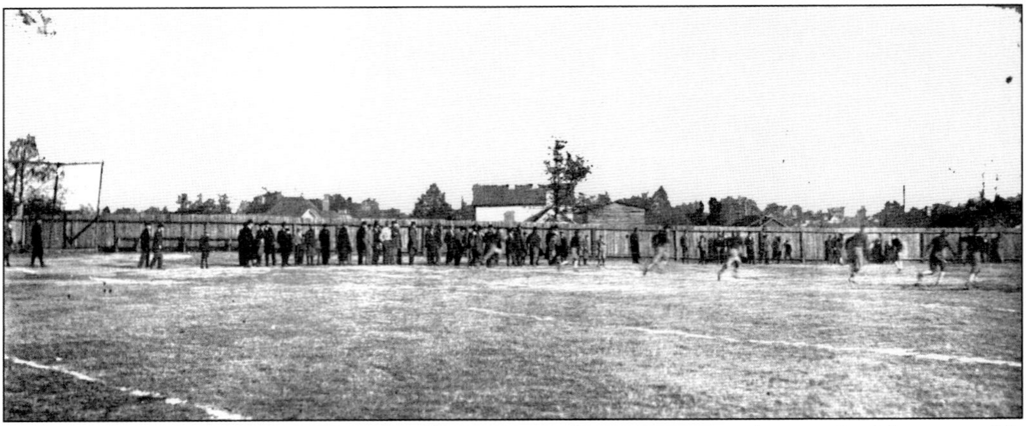

Shelby High School developed a football program in the 20th century that was highly successful. A century makes a big difference—compare the packed stadium on Friday night today with this c. 1910 game in a field on the corner of Martin and West Graham. (*Our Heritage, A History of Cleveland County.*)

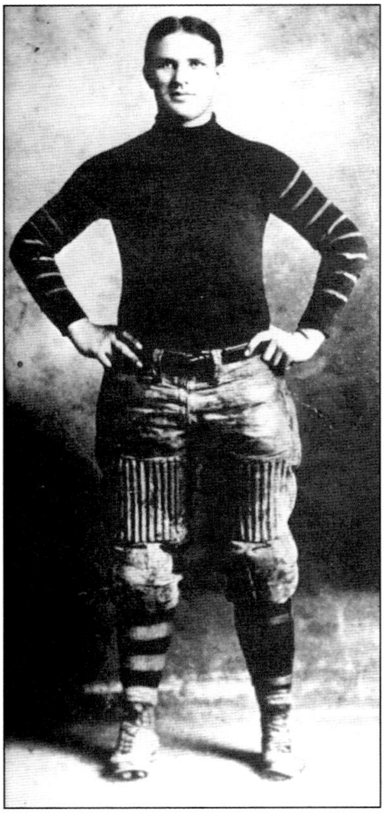

State leaders of the future were beginning to emerge early in the 20th century. A young O. Max Gardner served as captain of the football team at Chapel Hill where he was a law student. Earlier, Gardner had played for North Carolina A&M (NC State). He chose not to play in the 1905 game against his alma mater in Raleigh. (*Gov. O. Max Gardner.*)

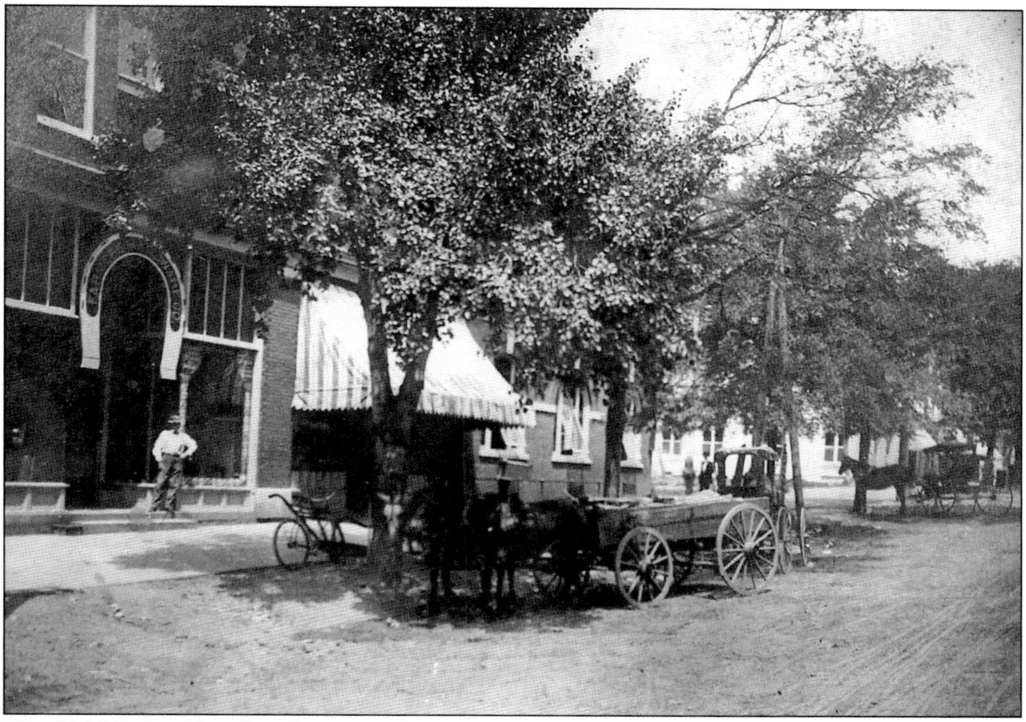

The 200 block of South Lafayette in the era of horse-and-buggies still had dirt streets. The trees provided shade for the horses in front of Farmers Hardware. The bank and hotel building can be seen on the right. (City of Shelby.)

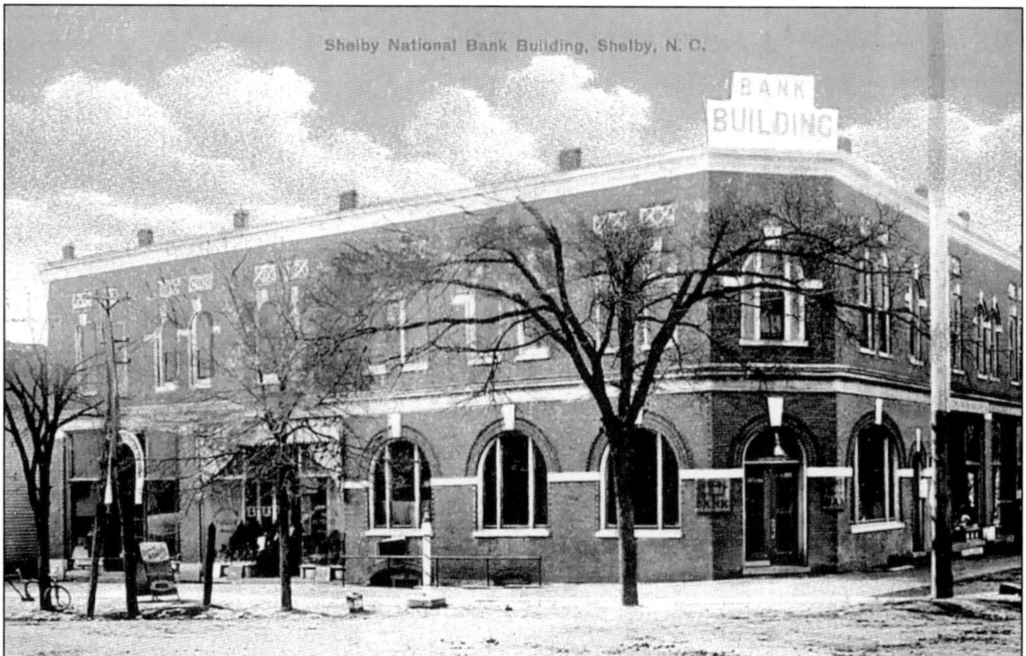

A c. 1915 postcard view shows the side of the bank building across from First National and the court square. The Cleveland Chamber of Commerce occupies this site today.

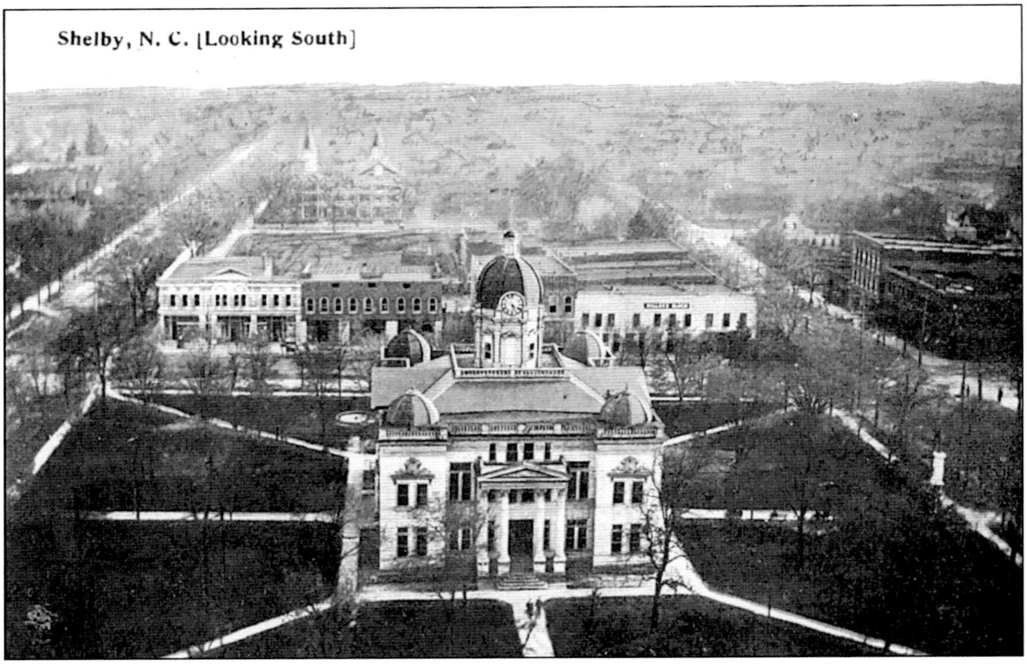

This *c.* 1910 postcard image was taken looking south at the new courthouse built in 1907. The south side of Warren Street was developed. Located one block behind these buildings, the large building on the corner of Washington and Graham was the first Shelby Hospital.

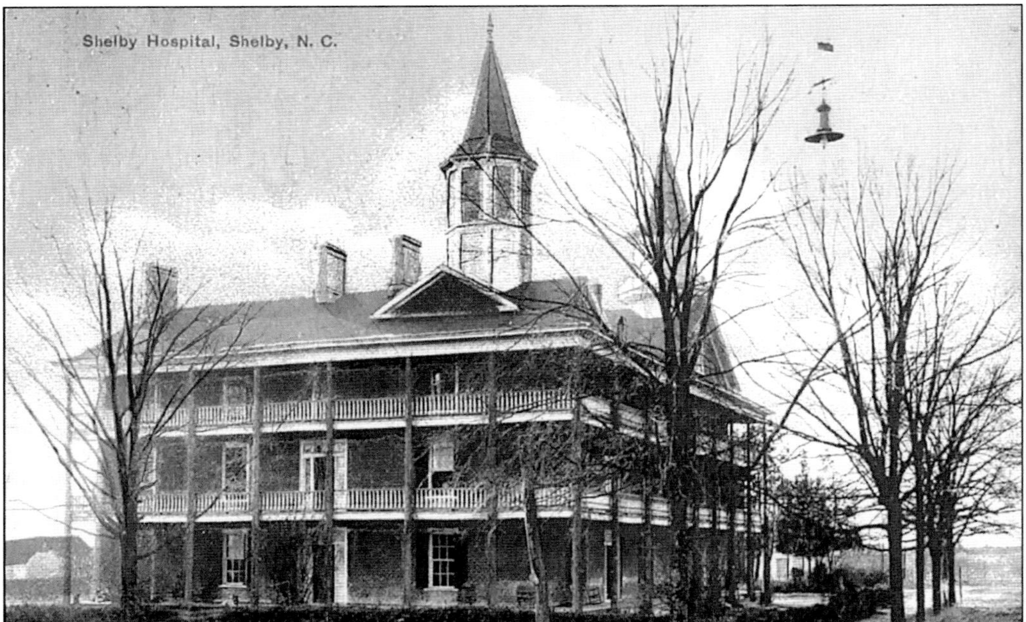

This 1910 postcard shows a close-up view of the hospital. The building had previously been the Shelby Female Academy and a hotel. The building later served again as a hotel before being removed in the 1930s to make room for the new City Hall.

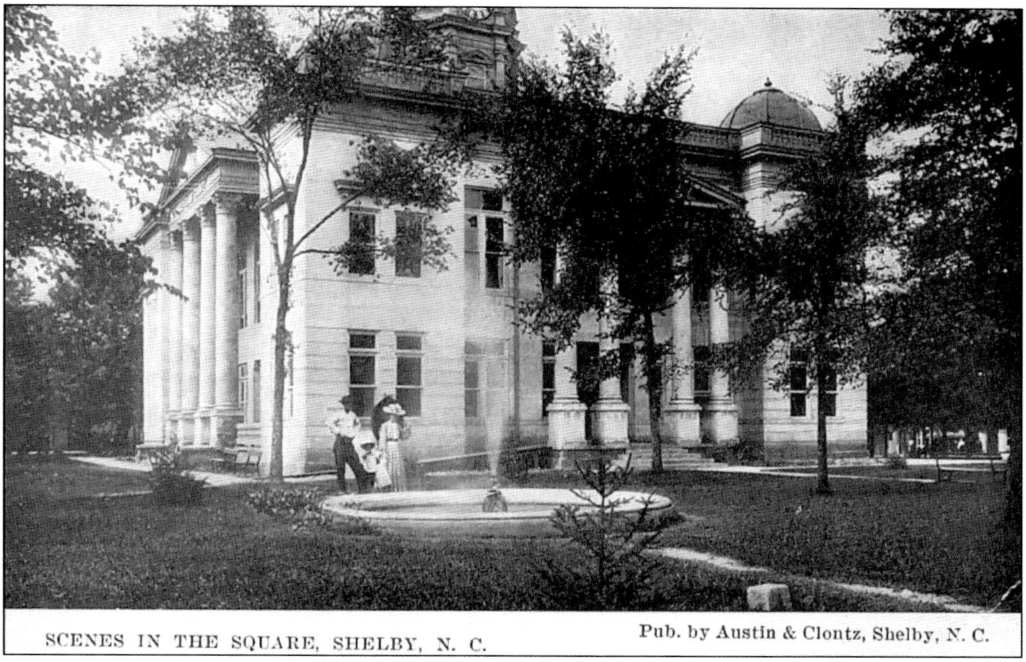

This view of the courthouse shows a couple and their child dressed for an afternoon walk by the fountain. Note the lady has a parasol to shade her from the sun. (Mike Royster.)

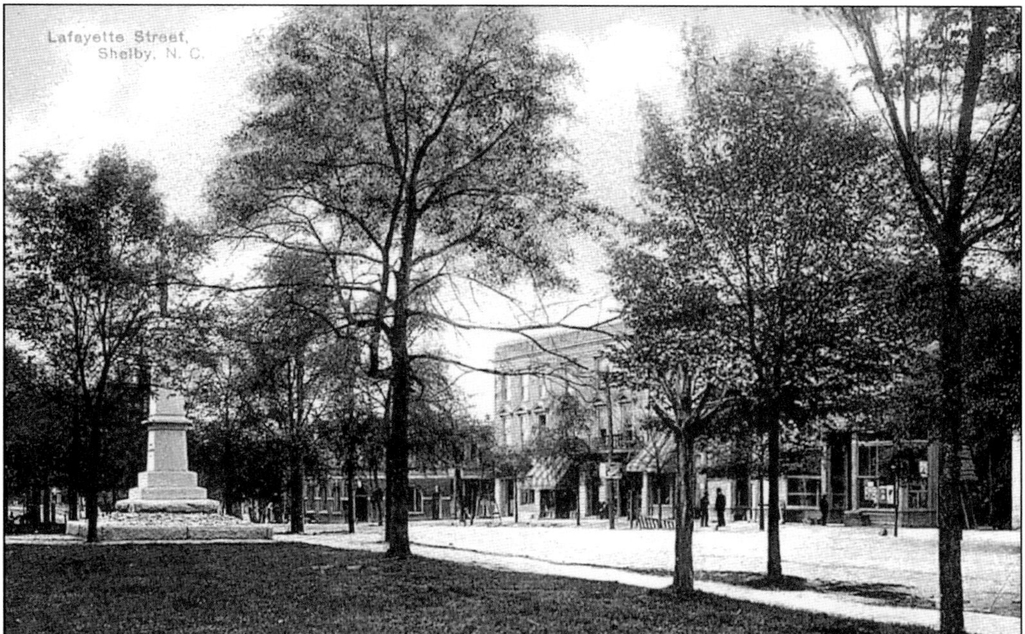

Again we see uptown Shelby from the court square. This postcard view looks southwest. The two banks previously pictured can be seen in the center.

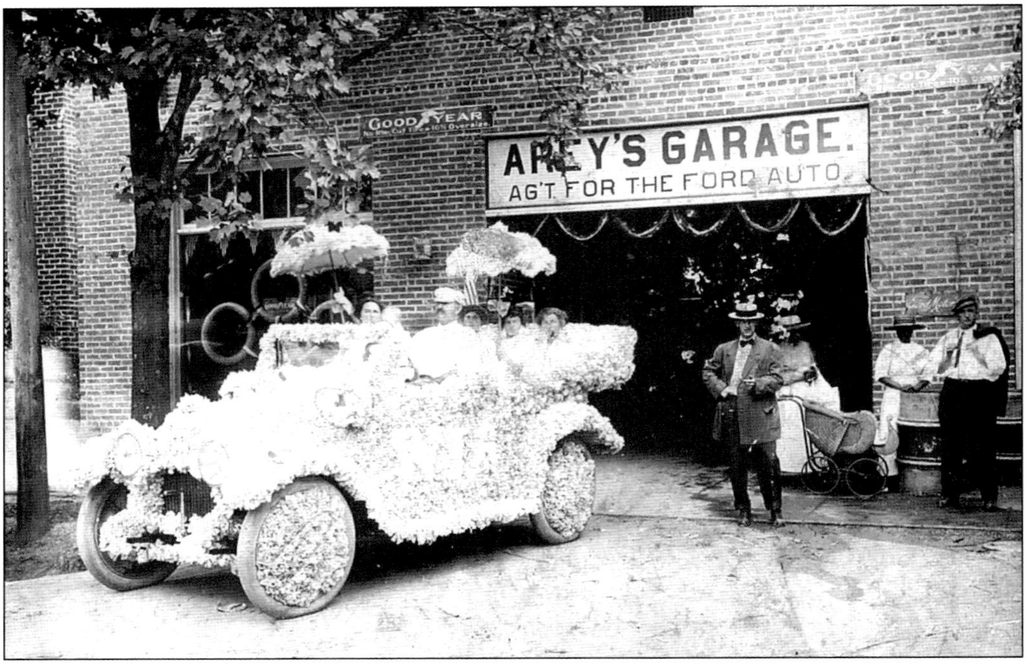

W.J. Arey was the first Ford Agent in Shelby. Arey is leaving his garage preparing for an Independence Day celebration. (Robert Arey Sr.)

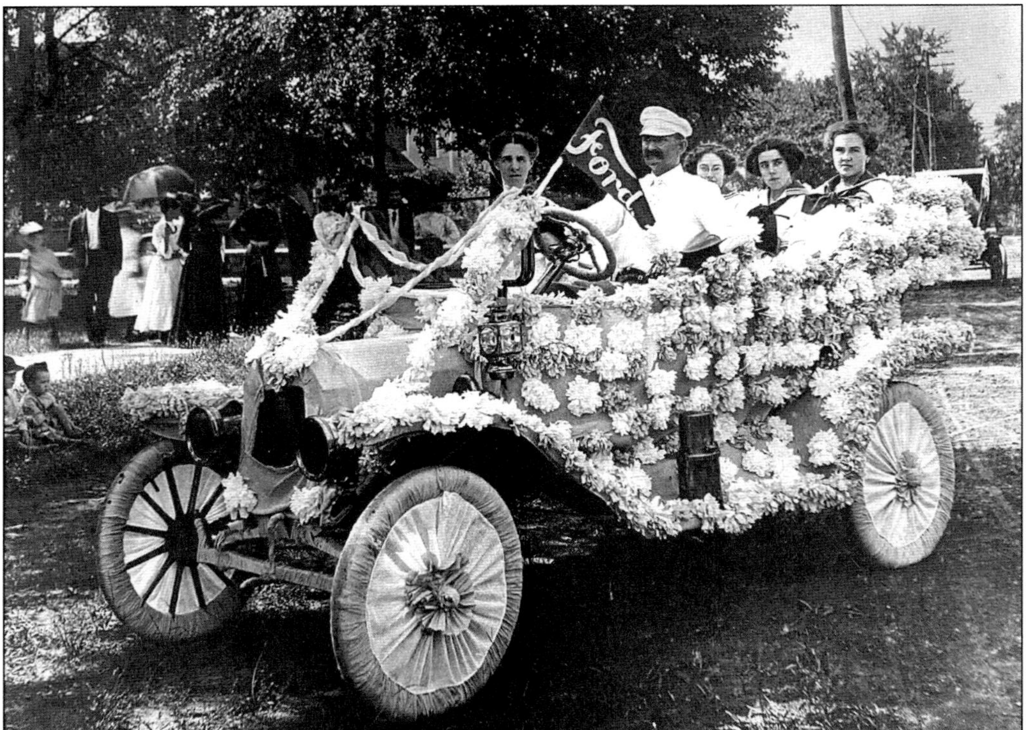

W.J. Arey drives a new Ford in preparation for the Fourth of July Parade in 1916. Mr. and Mrs. Arey are in the front seat and in the back seat are Laura Miller, Helen Miller, and Beth Andrews. (Robert Arey Sr.)

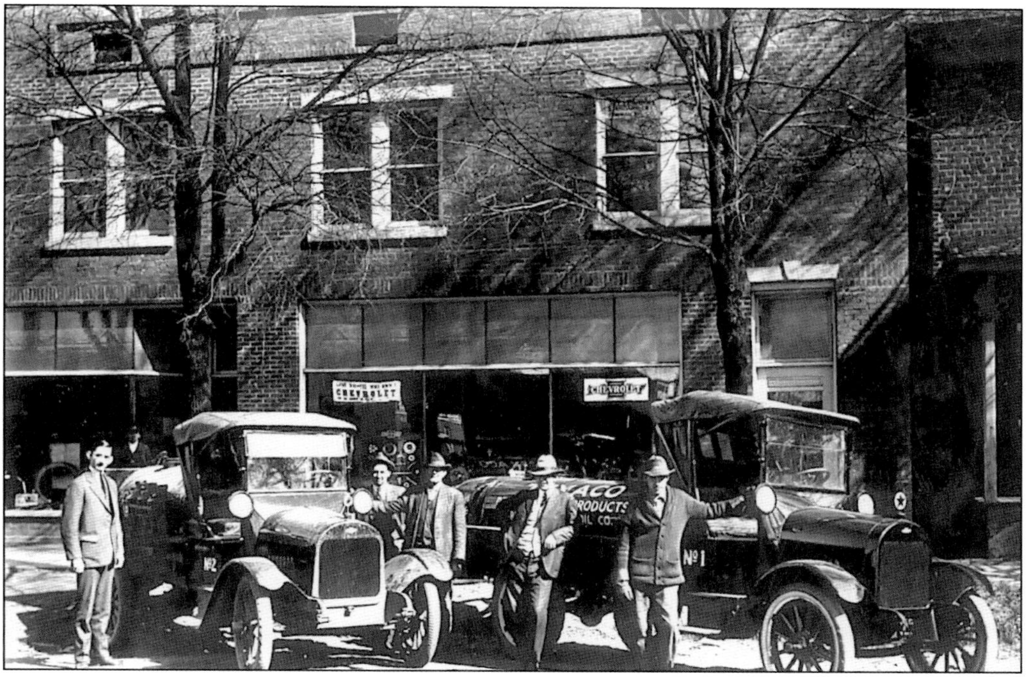

The family of W.J. Arey Sr. has been in business in Shelby for over 90 years. This South Washington Street photo was taken in front of Arey's Chevrolet dealership. He was also a distributor for Texaco Oil. (Robert Arey Sr.)

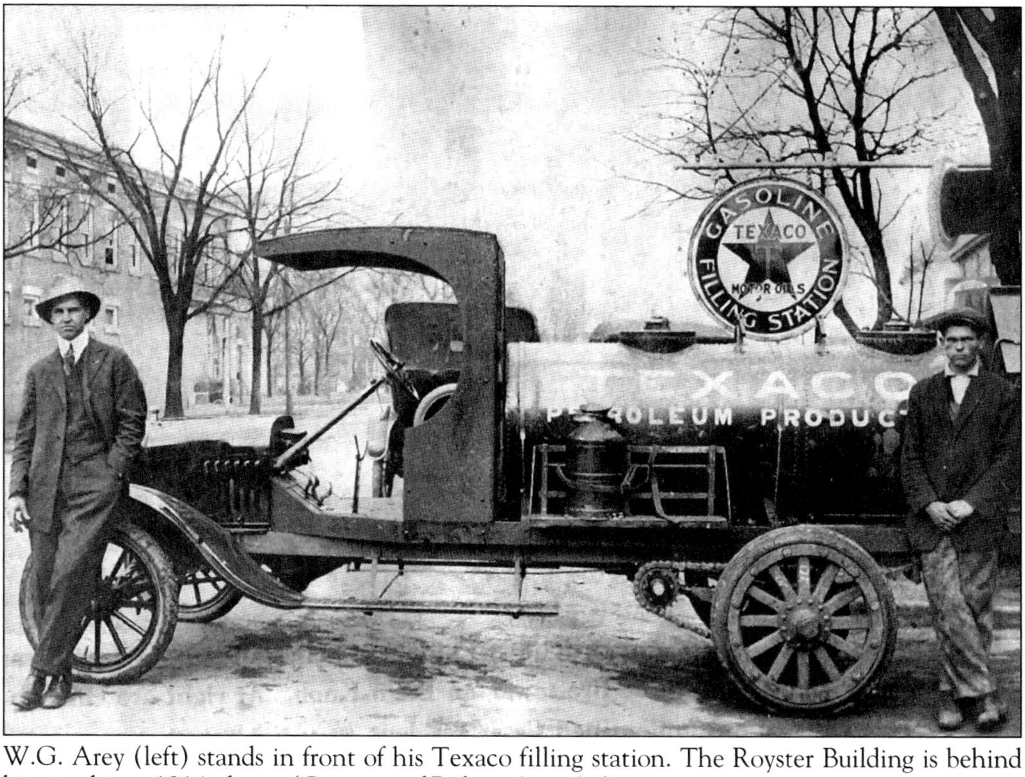

W.G. Arey (left) stands in front of his Texaco filling station. The Royster Building is behind him in this *c.* 1914 photo. (Courtesy of Robert Arey Sr.)

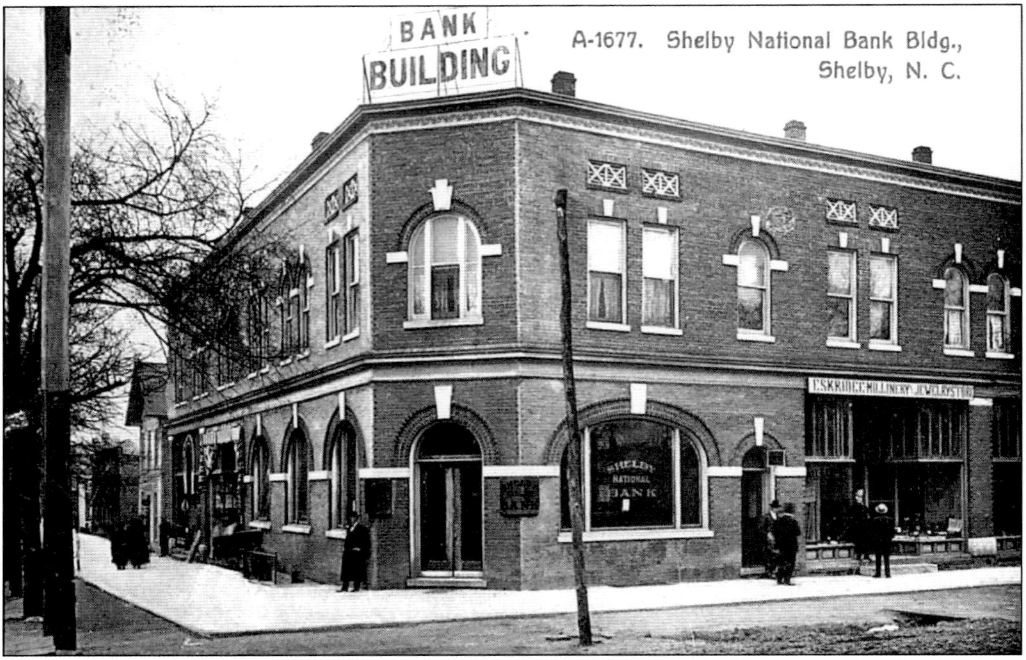

The building on the southwest corner of Lafayette and Warren Streets housed the Shelby National Bank in the early 20th century. The bank later gave way to Messick's Soda Shop and later a music store. The building was one of three destroyed by a tragic fire in 1979.

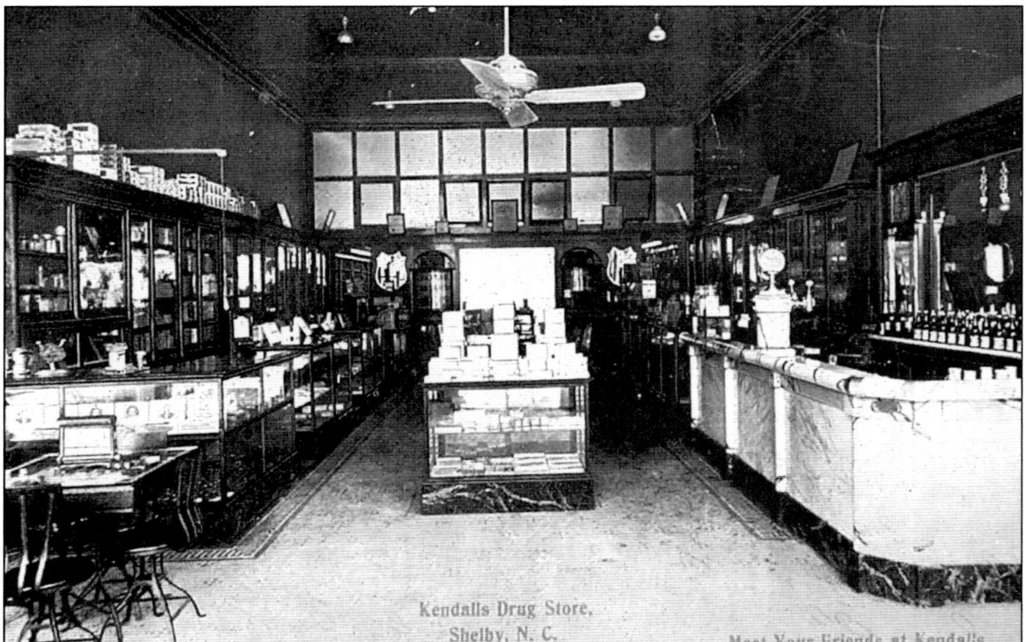

This c. 1915 postcard view of the Kendall Drug Store shows the interior of the store. Kendall's was one of over half a dozen drug stores to operate around the court square. (Mike Royster.)

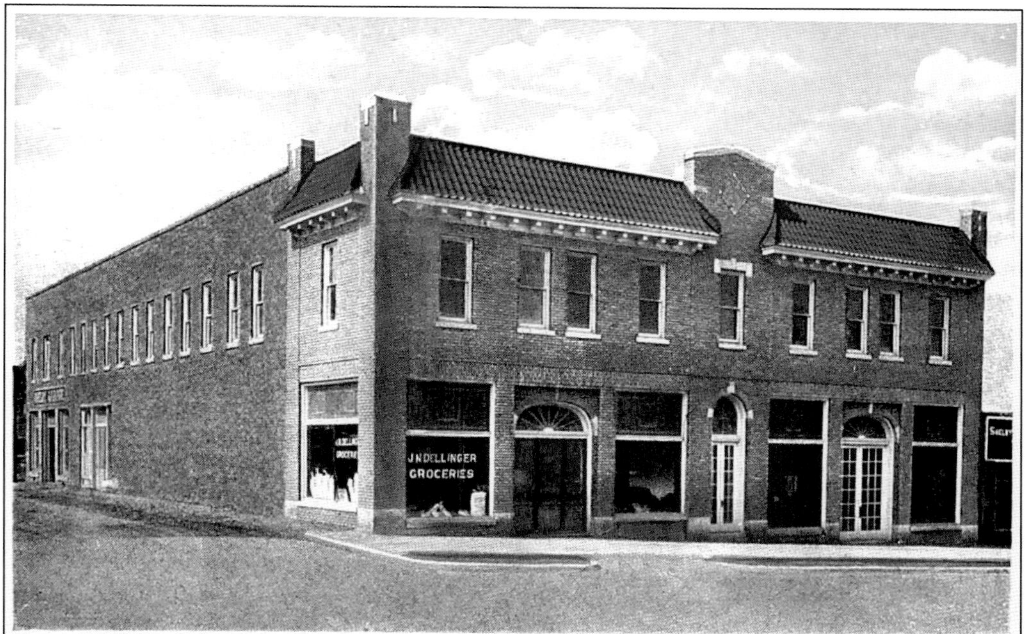

HAMRICK BROS. AND RIVIERE BUILDING, SHELBY, N. C.

This building is half a block from the square on West Marion. Probably few today would know it was called the Hamrick Brothers and Riviere Building. In the 1930s, Bost Bakery began in the back of the building in a cafe. Shelbians from as far back as the 1950s will remember Gilliatt's Florist in the building. (Mike Royster.)

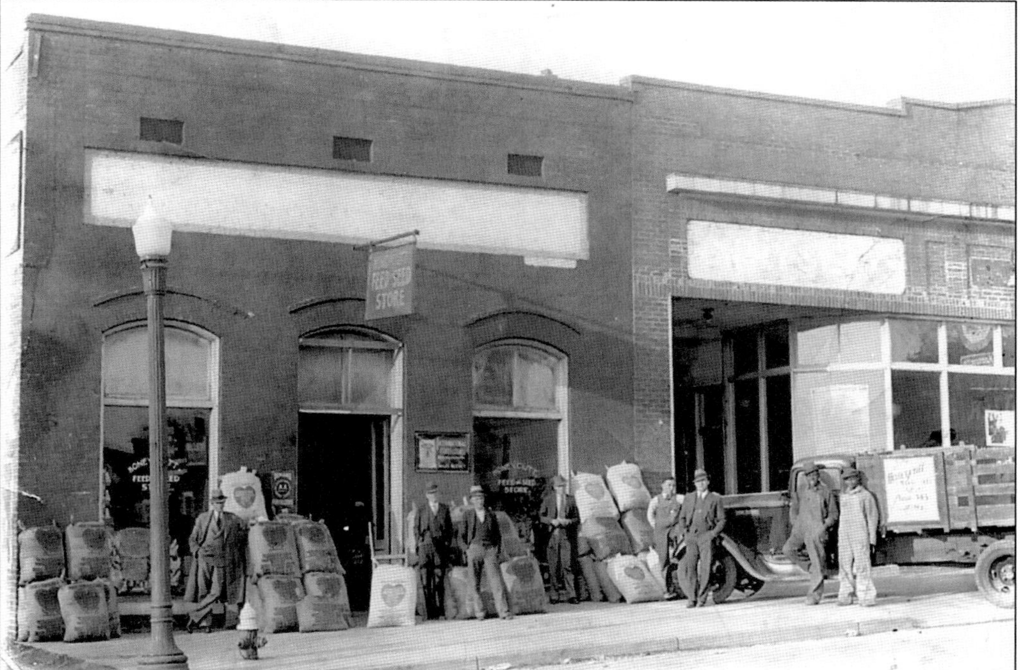

Honeycutt Feed and Seed operated from West Warren Street. O.Z. Morgan would later move the business across the railroad tracks and open Morgan and Co. (Jack Morgan Family.)

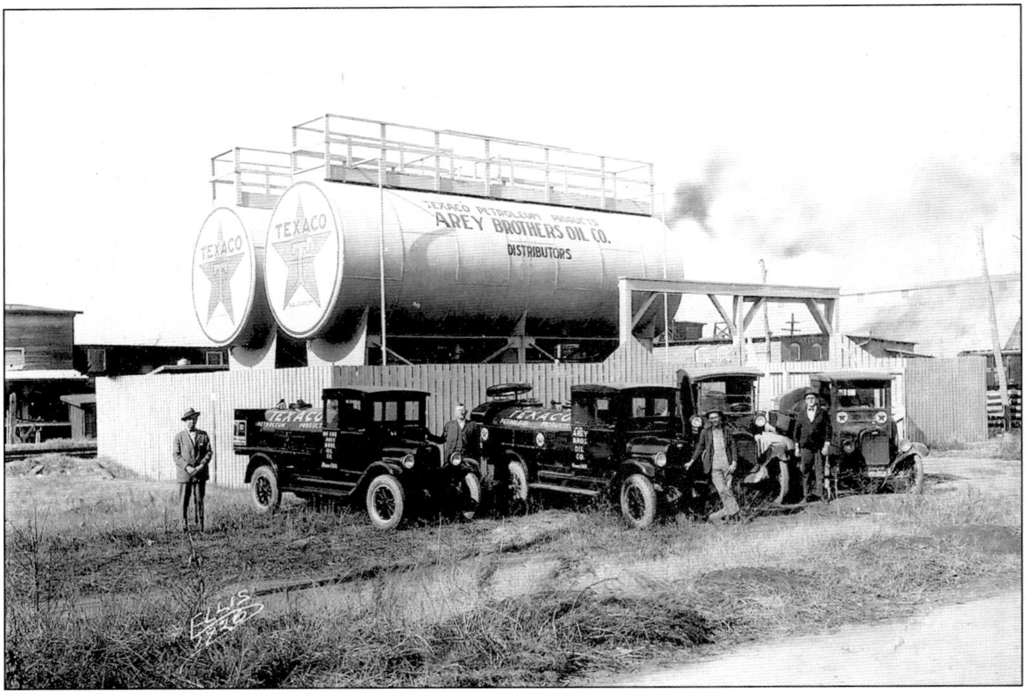

In the 1920s, the Arey Brothers Oil Co. was still selling Texaco products. These delivery trucks supplied a much smaller market of cars. This scene is at the railroad on South Morgan Street. (Robert Arey Sr.)

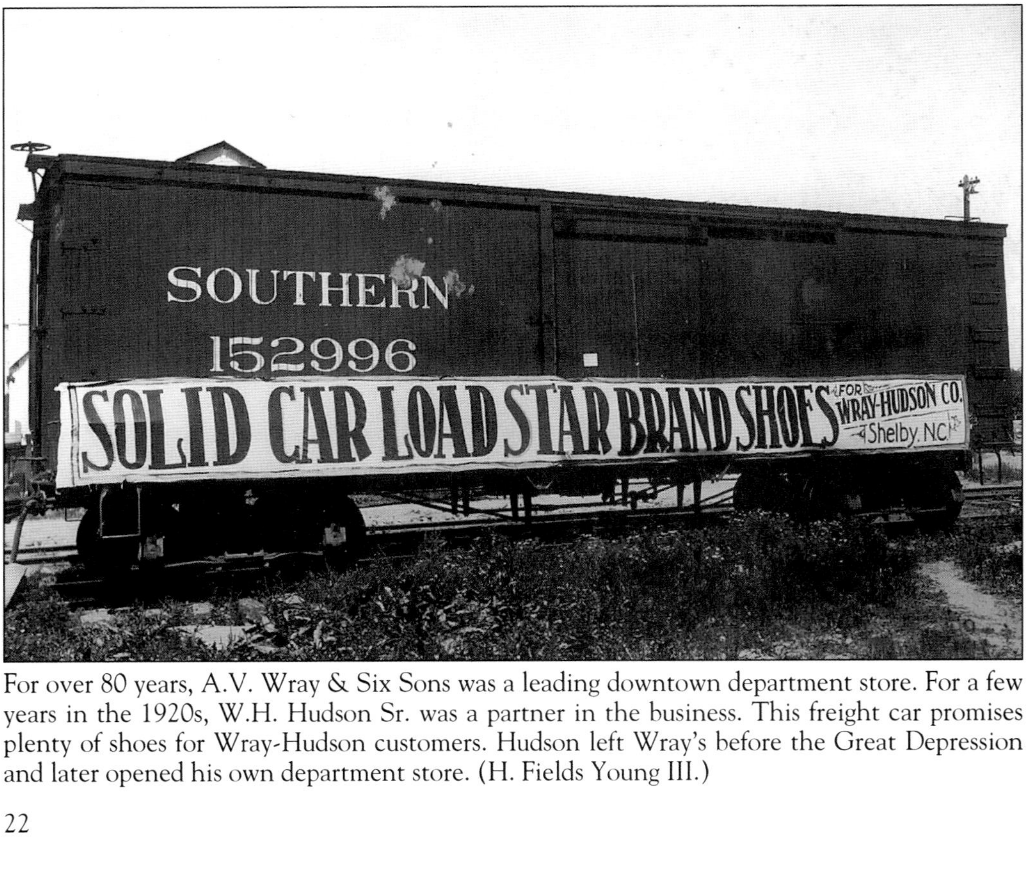

For over 80 years, A.V. Wray & Six Sons was a leading downtown department store. For a few years in the 1920s, W.H. Hudson Sr. was a partner in the business. This freight car promises plenty of shoes for Wray-Hudson customers. Hudson left Wray's before the Great Depression and later opened his own department store. (H. Fields Young III.)

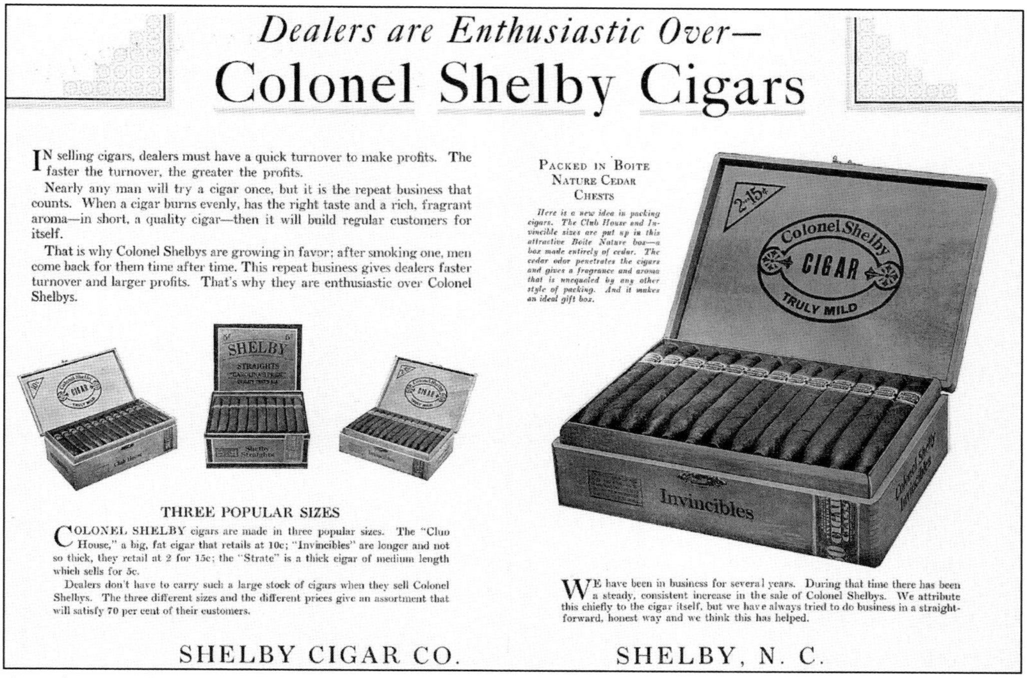

Another product produced in Shelby was the Colonel Shelby Cigar. After several years, the business moved from North Carolina and smokers lost the pleasure of a local cigar.

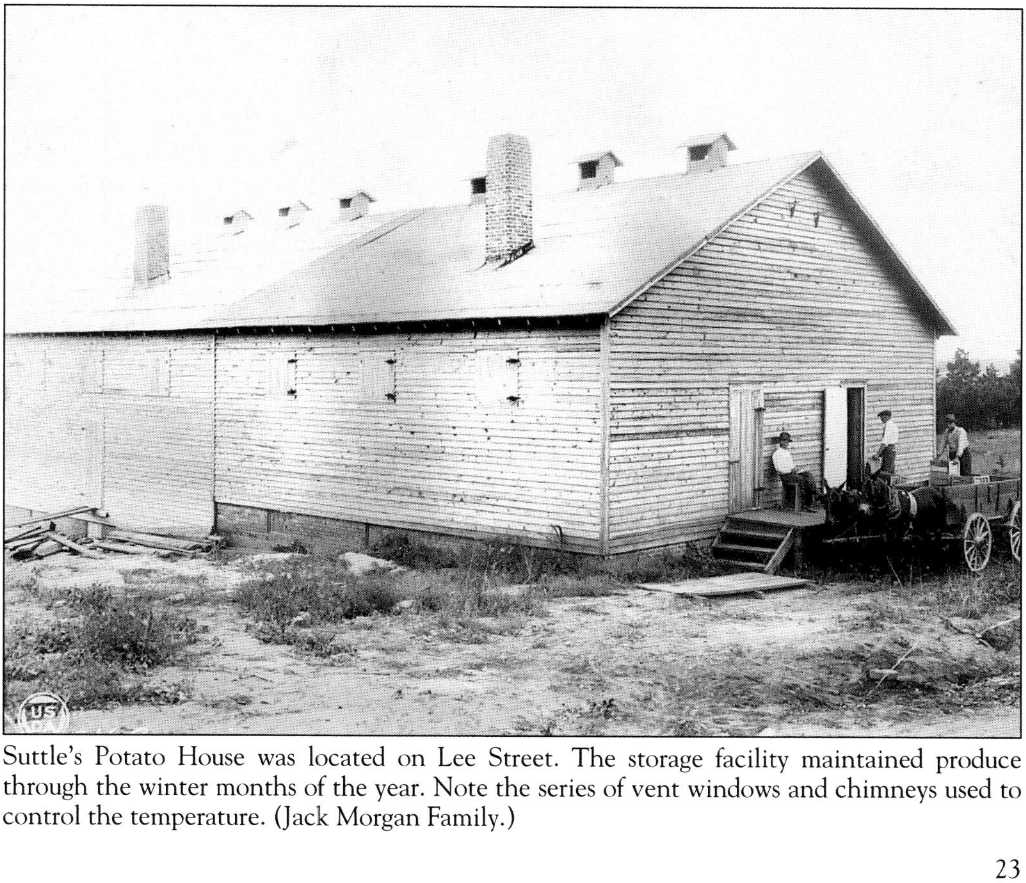

Suttle's Potato House was located on Lee Street. The storage facility maintained produce through the winter months of the year. Note the series of vent windows and chimneys used to control the temperature. (Jack Morgan Family.)

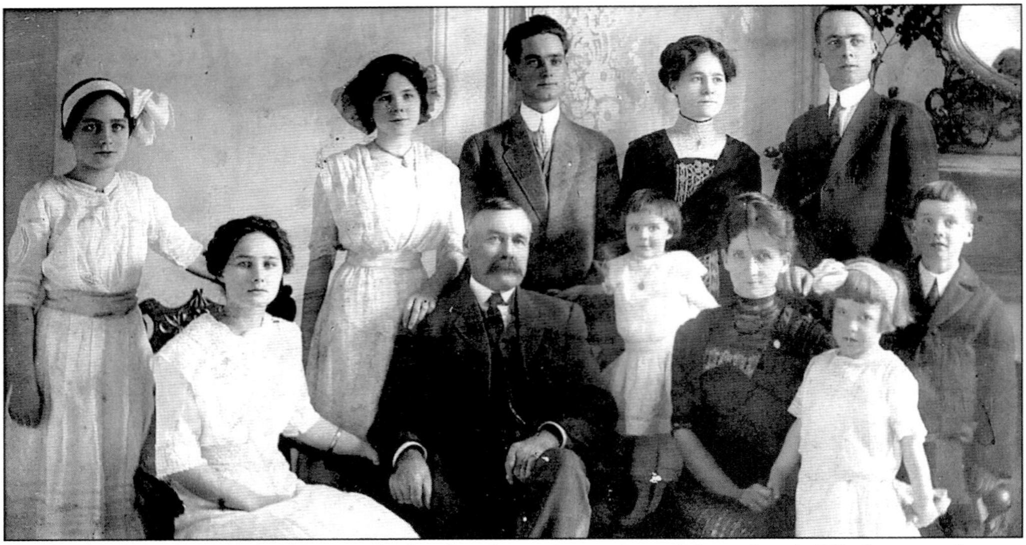

This 1911 photo shows a leading Shelby family in the parlor of their South Washington home. The John R. Dover family included, from left to right, (front row) Lila Dover (Roberts), John R. Dover, Katherine Dover (Chamberlain), Ella Toms Dover, Evelyn (Fox), and Charles Dover; (back row) Dorothy Dover (Laney), Margaret Dover (Love), James T. Dover, Helen Dover (Quinn), and John R. Dover Jr. (Edwin and Esther Anne Ford.)

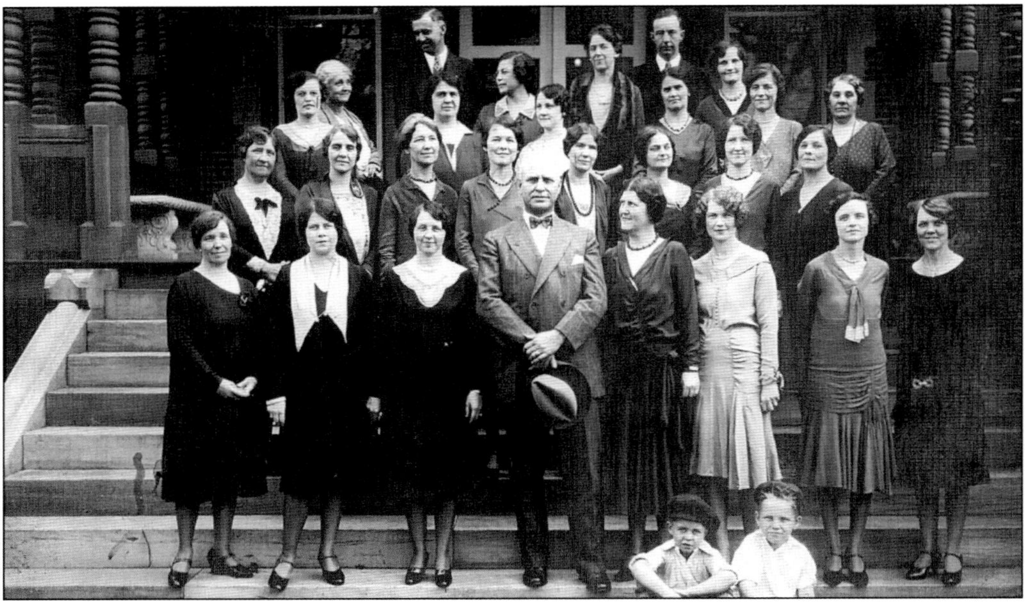

This 1929 picture of the Cecilia Music Club was taken on the steps of the Governor's Mansion in Raleigh. In the center is recently elected Gov. O. Max Gardner and his wife Faye Webb. Seated on the curb are David Royster Jr. and O. Max Gardner Jr. From left to right are (first row) Cleo Whisnant, Beaula Bennett, Viola Lackey, Governor Gardner, Faye Webb Gardner, Eugenia Holland, Mrs. Ben Suttle, and Mrs. Rush Thompson; (second row) Hattie Lattimore, Margaret McMurry, Mrs. George Hoyle, Margaret Dover, Bertha Bostic, Mildred Hamrick, Lily Parrish, and Evelyn Pyle; (third row) Nell Geir, Mae Kendall, Katherine Roberts, Mrs. Thad Ford, Mrs. Dewitt Quinn, and Amos Willis; (fourth row) Bess Hoey, Mabel Quinn, Mrs. P.L. Hennessa, Rosylyn Nix, Will Arey, and Earle Hamrick. (Edwin and Esther Anne Ford.)

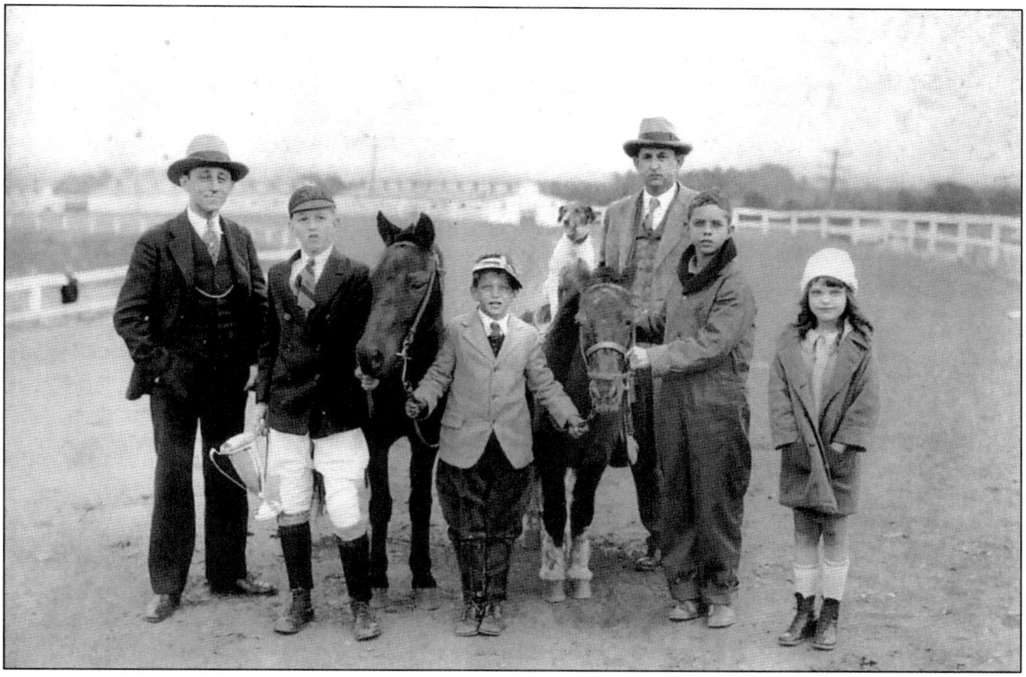

This 1920s photo shows a young Fields Young Jr. receiving a cup for his horse riding skills at the Cleveland County Fairgrounds. At the left is Dr. J.S. Dorton, known as "Mr. Fair." Dorton directed the Cleveland County Fair for almost 40 years. Next to Dorton is Fields Jr. Lamar "Buddy" Young is in the center. H. Fields Young Sr. stands behind his son Carlos and his daughter Eloise. Note the dog on the back of the horse. (Eloise Young Spangler.)

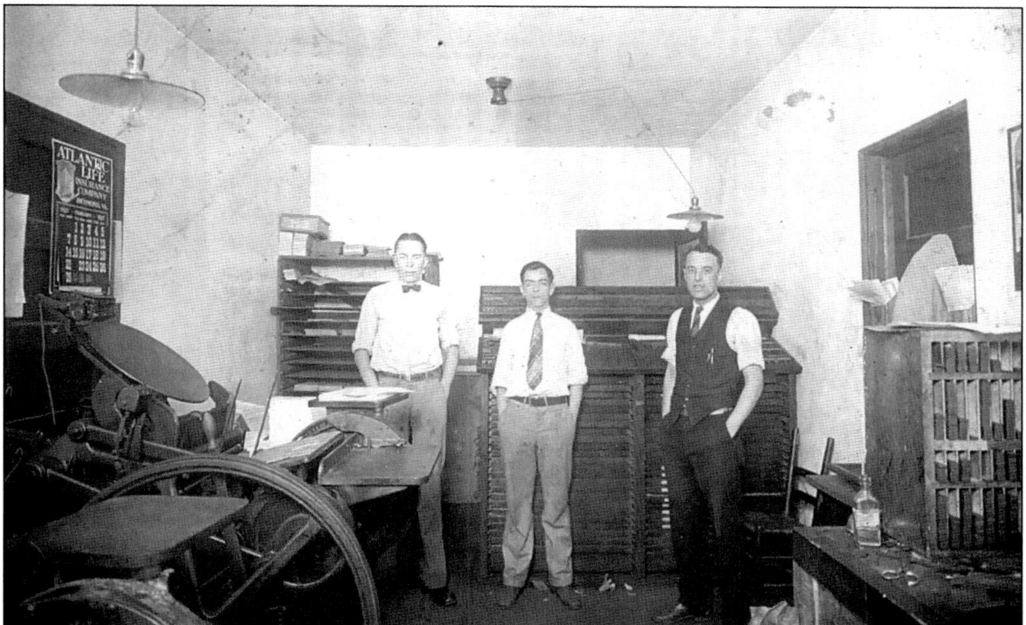

Shelby Printing Co. was established by C.J. Mabry Sr. in 1923. Pictured here in the West Marion Street business are Evan Berry, C.C. McMurray, and C.J. Mabry Sr. (C J. Mabry Sr. Family.)

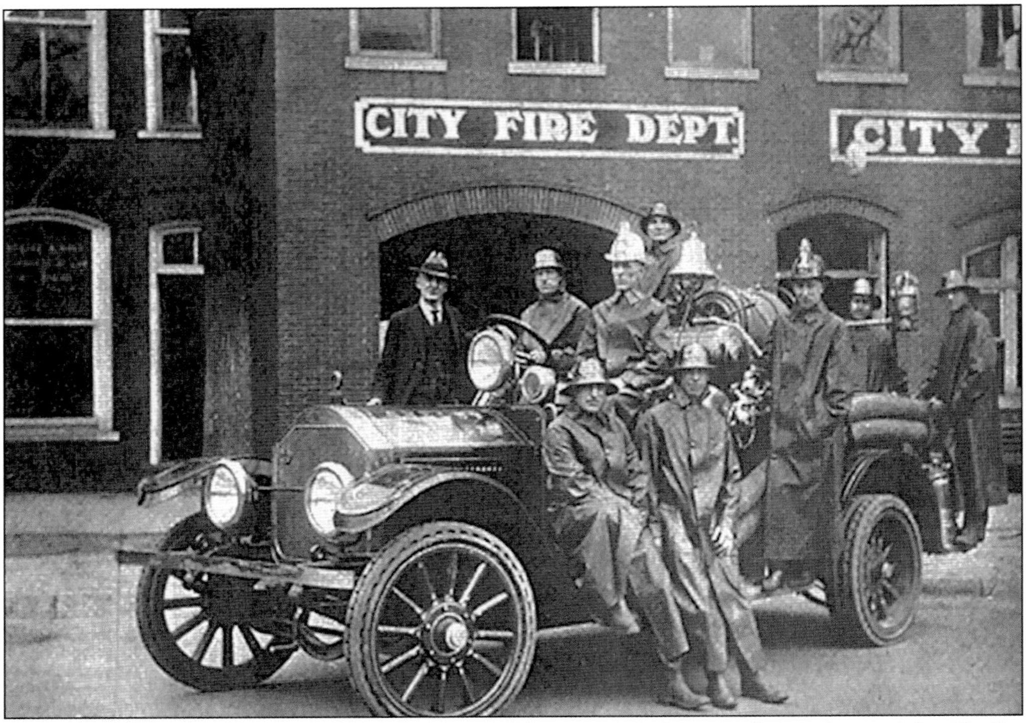

Shelby mayor W.D. Lackey stops by to pose in this *c.* 1919 photo with members of the Shelby Fire Department. Star Publishing operated in the building to the left and printed the weekly *Cleveland Star* newspaper. City Hall was to the left of this East Marion Street site. (*The Star.*)

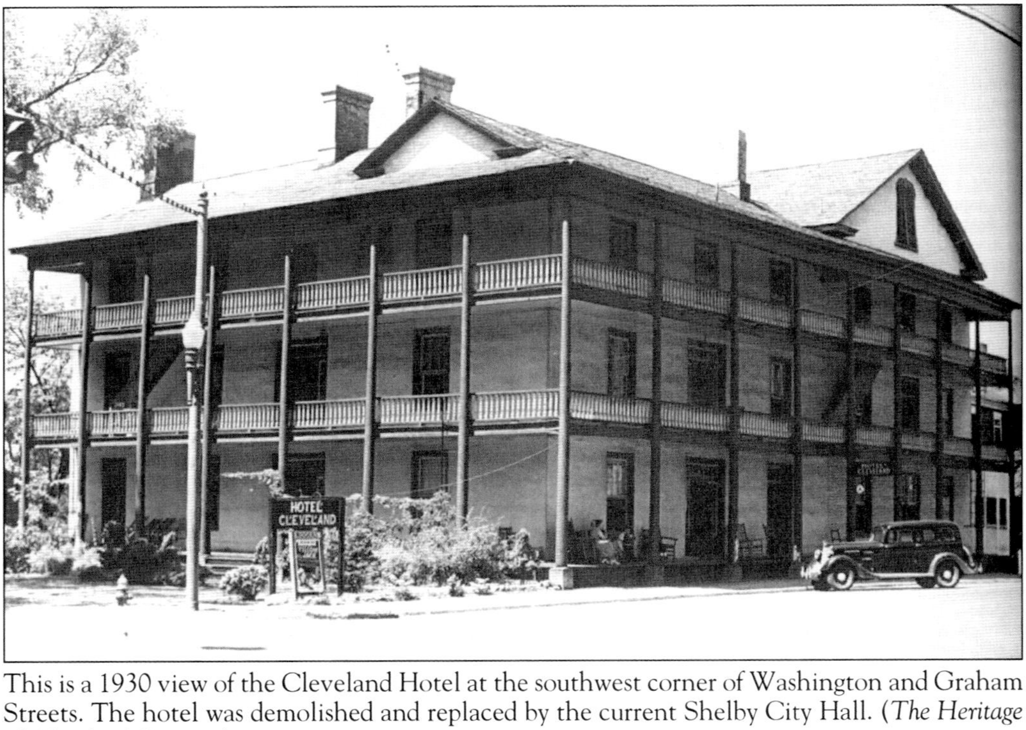

This is a 1930 view of the Cleveland Hotel at the southwest corner of Washington and Graham Streets. The hotel was demolished and replaced by the current Shelby City Hall. (*The Heritage of Cleveland County.*)

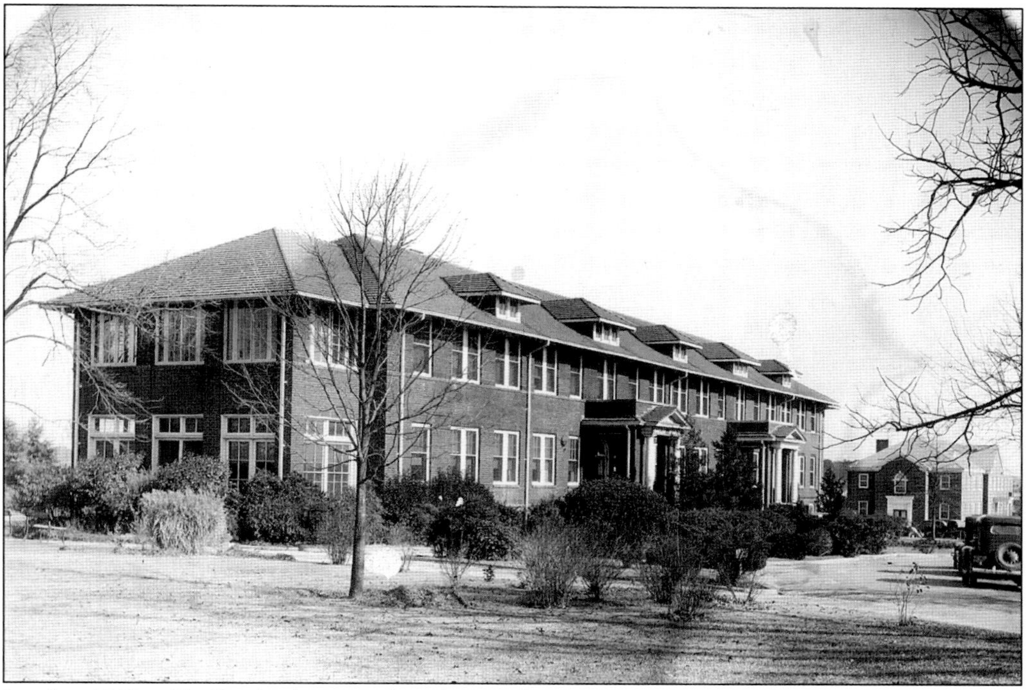

In the 1920s, Shelby built a modern hospital on Grover Street. This facility served the community for years and was gradually expanded. Today the old facility is completely gone and the new Cleveland Regional Medical Center occupies the same location. (Uptown Shelby Association.)

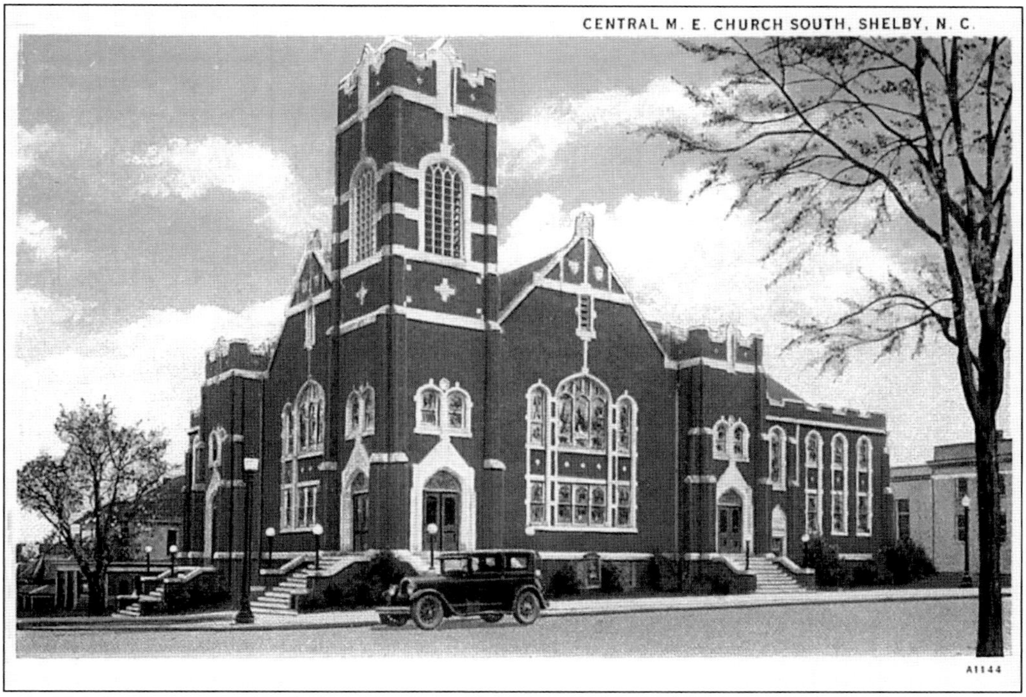

A c. 1939 postcard shows the Central Methodist Church, built in 1924. The building is still in use today. The former post office building can be seen at the right.

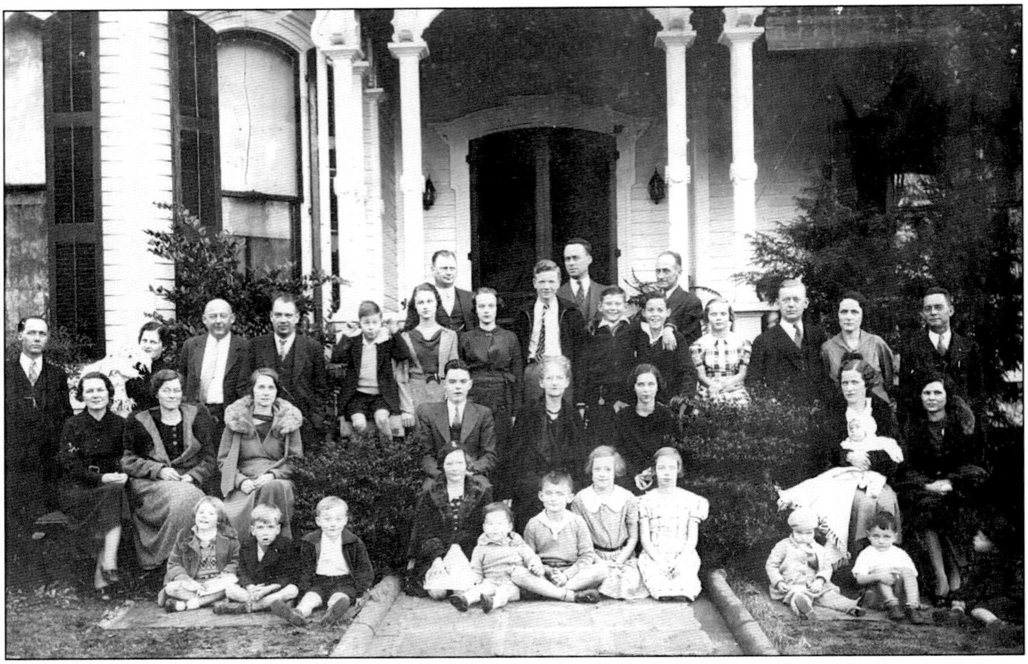

This photo shows the first Dover family reunion in 1938. The home of John R. Dover Sr. was on the southeast corner of Graham and Washington streets. (Edwin and Esther Anne Ford.)

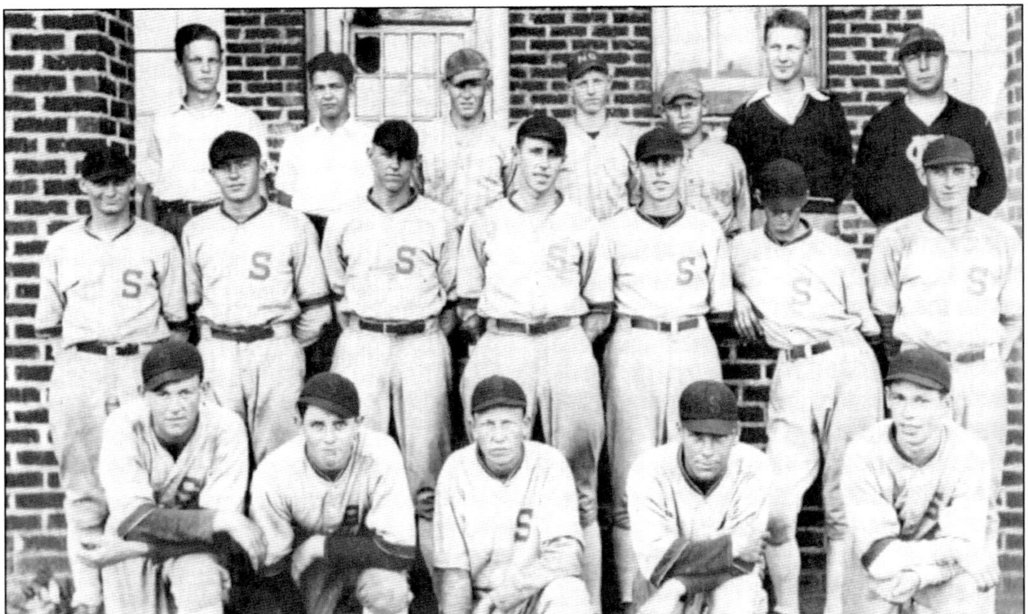

Shelby was very successful in high school sports in the 20th century. This photo shows the 1929 Shelby High School state championship baseball team. From left to right are (front row) Frank Harrelson, Doane Hulick Jr., Palmer McSwain, Carl Queen, and Guy Bridges; (middle row) Thurston Bumgardner, Hal Farris, Marshall "Lefty" Moore, Milton Gold, Sherrill Hamrick, Clay "Mud" Poston, and Cline Own Lee; (back row) Allen Suttle, Charles Switzer, an unidentified player, Sam Dayberry, an unidentified player, manager Ralph Gardner, and Coach R.W. "Casey" Morris. (*Our Heritage*, *A History of Cleveland County*.)

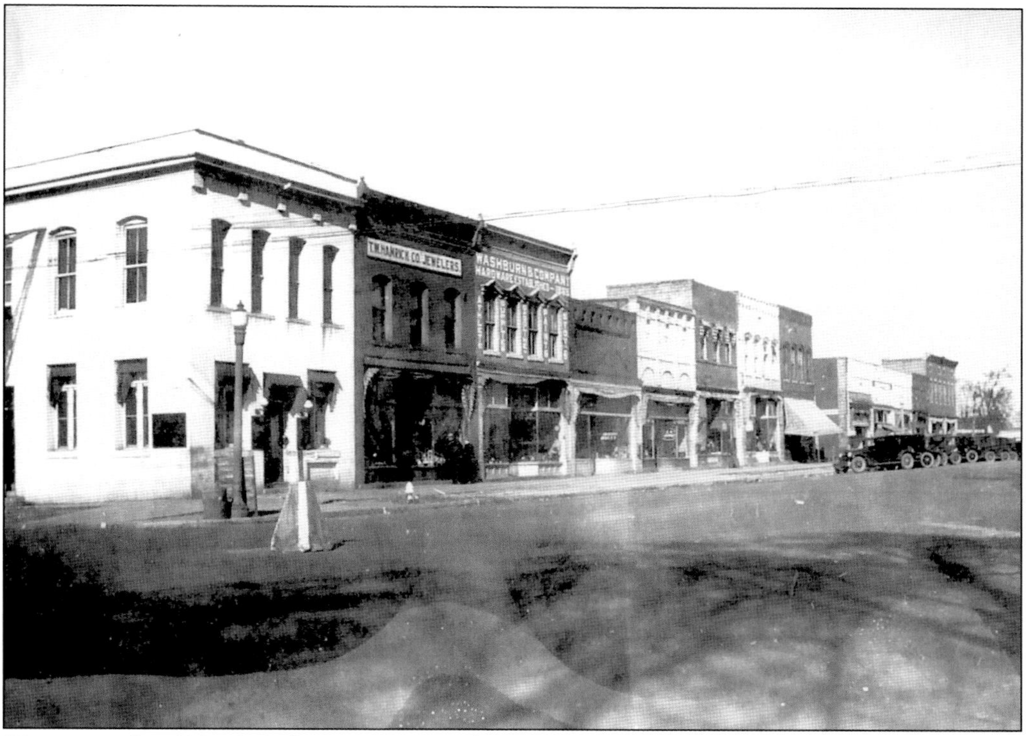

The west side of North Lafayette Street is shown in this 1930s photo. The T.W. Hamrick Co. sold jewelry but also produced postcards of Shelby in the first part of the century. Washburn's Hardware can be seen to the right.

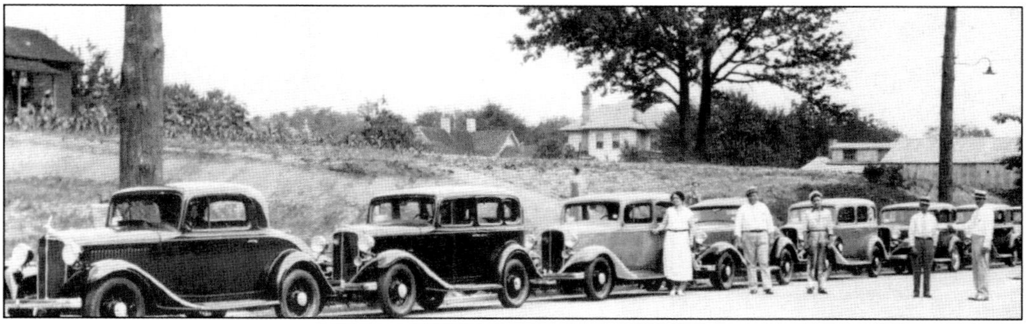

D. "Huss" Cline was the Chevrolet dealer in the early 1930s. These cars were the first train shipment of Chevrolets thus allowing customers to select from actual cars rather than ordering from pictures. The cars are lined on South Morgan Street (now Market Street) near the railroad. (*The Heritage of Cleveland County*.)

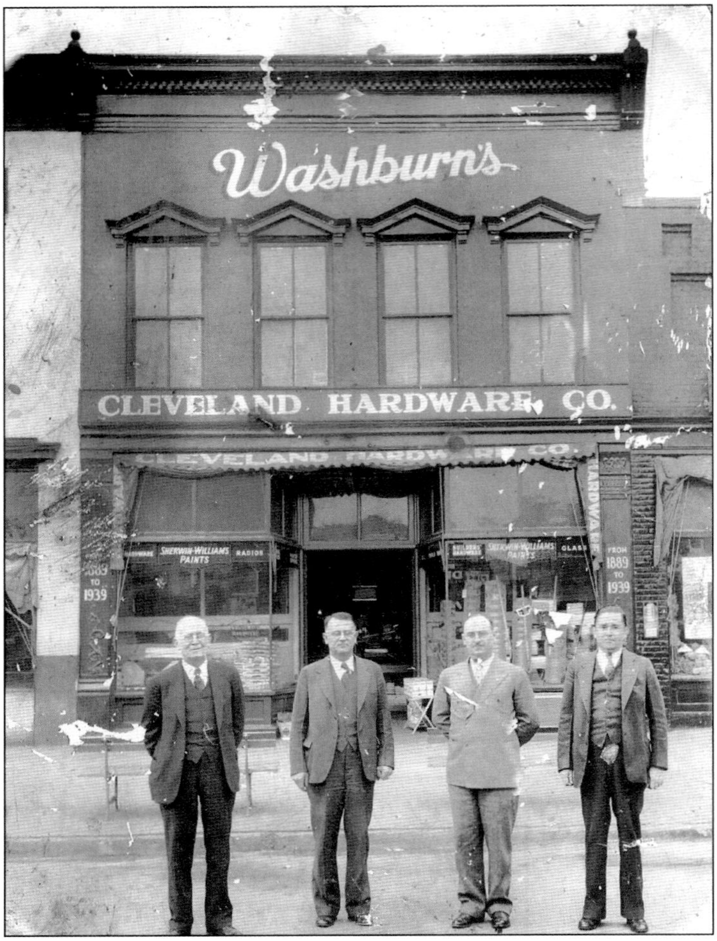

This late 1930s photo shows Washburn's Cleveland Hardware Co. on North Lafayette Street. Pictured, from left to right, are Seaton Washburn and his sons Charlie, George, and Max. (Edwin and Esther Anne Ford.)

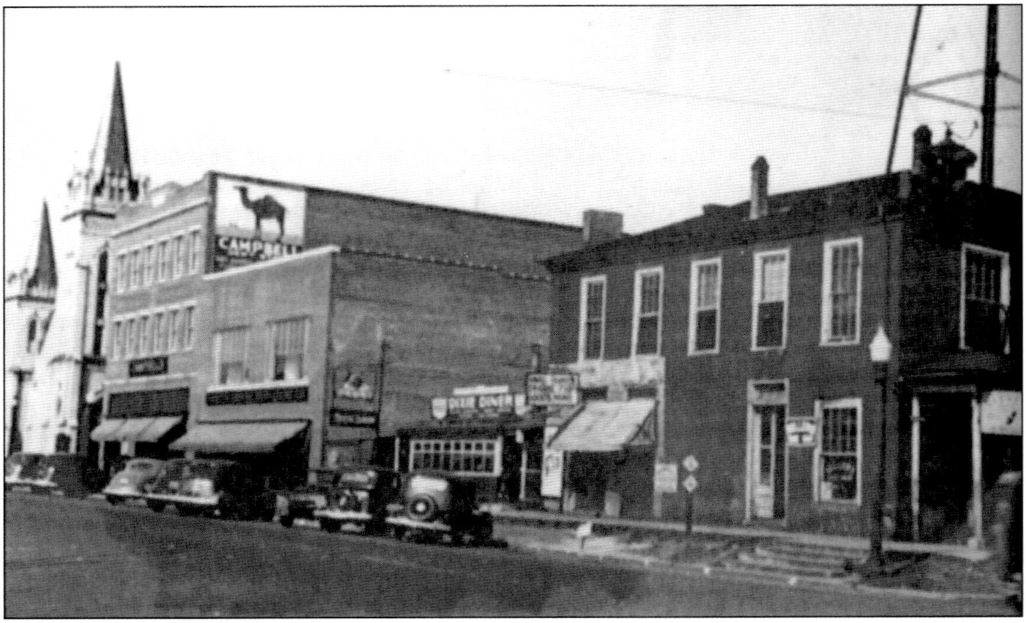

Before Sterchi's Furniture was built in 1939, the Courtview Hotel occupied the northeast corner of Lafayette and Marion Streets. Behind the hotel were the Dixie Diner and Campbell's Department Store. (*Our Heritage, A History of Cleveland County.*)

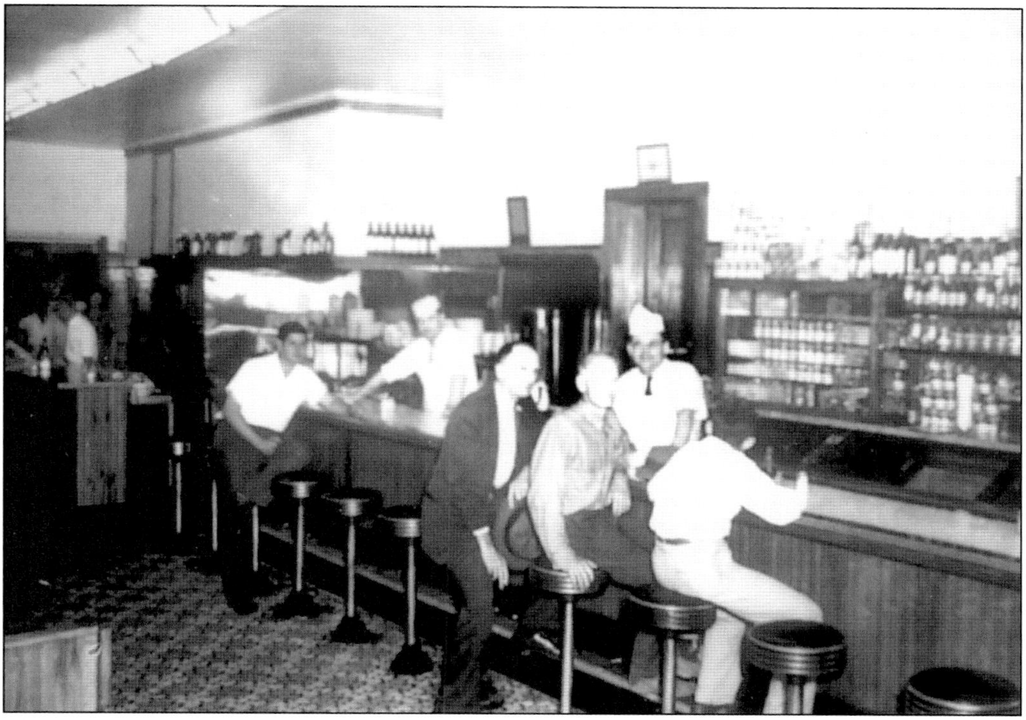

This 1940s interior view shows the Sanitary Lunch on South Lafayette Street. The Sanitary Lunch was a popular spot to meet and eat. (Uptown Shelby Association.)

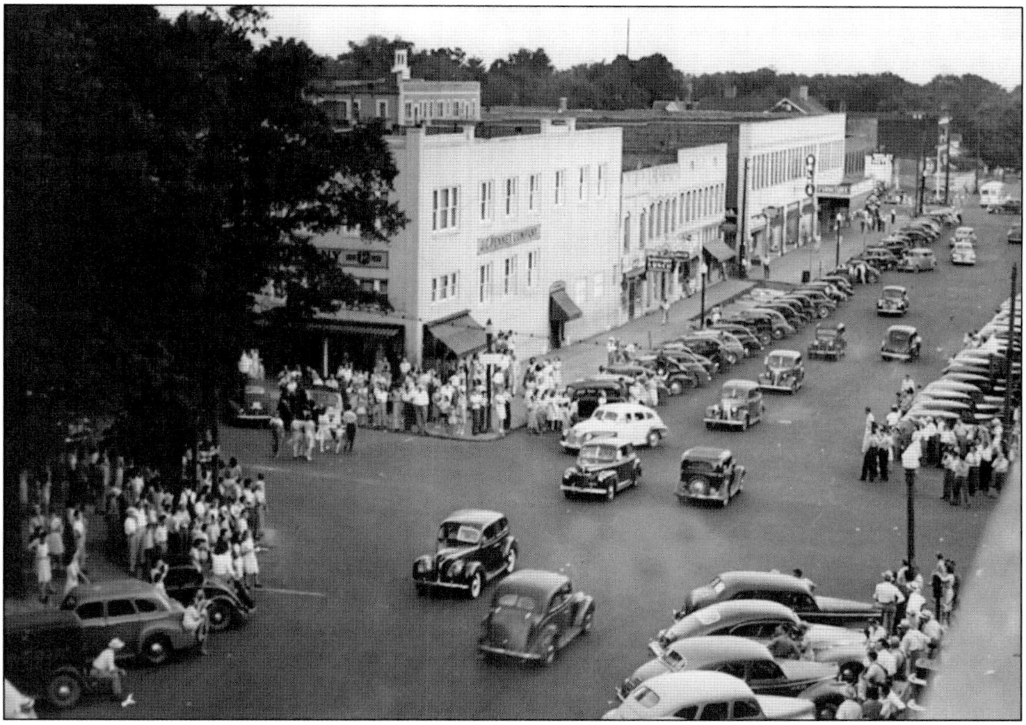

This is a busy day in uptown Shelby *c.* 1940. Looking south on Lafayette, one can see J. C. Penny's and Belk's. Just behind Penny's was the Sanitary Lunch. (City of Shelby.)

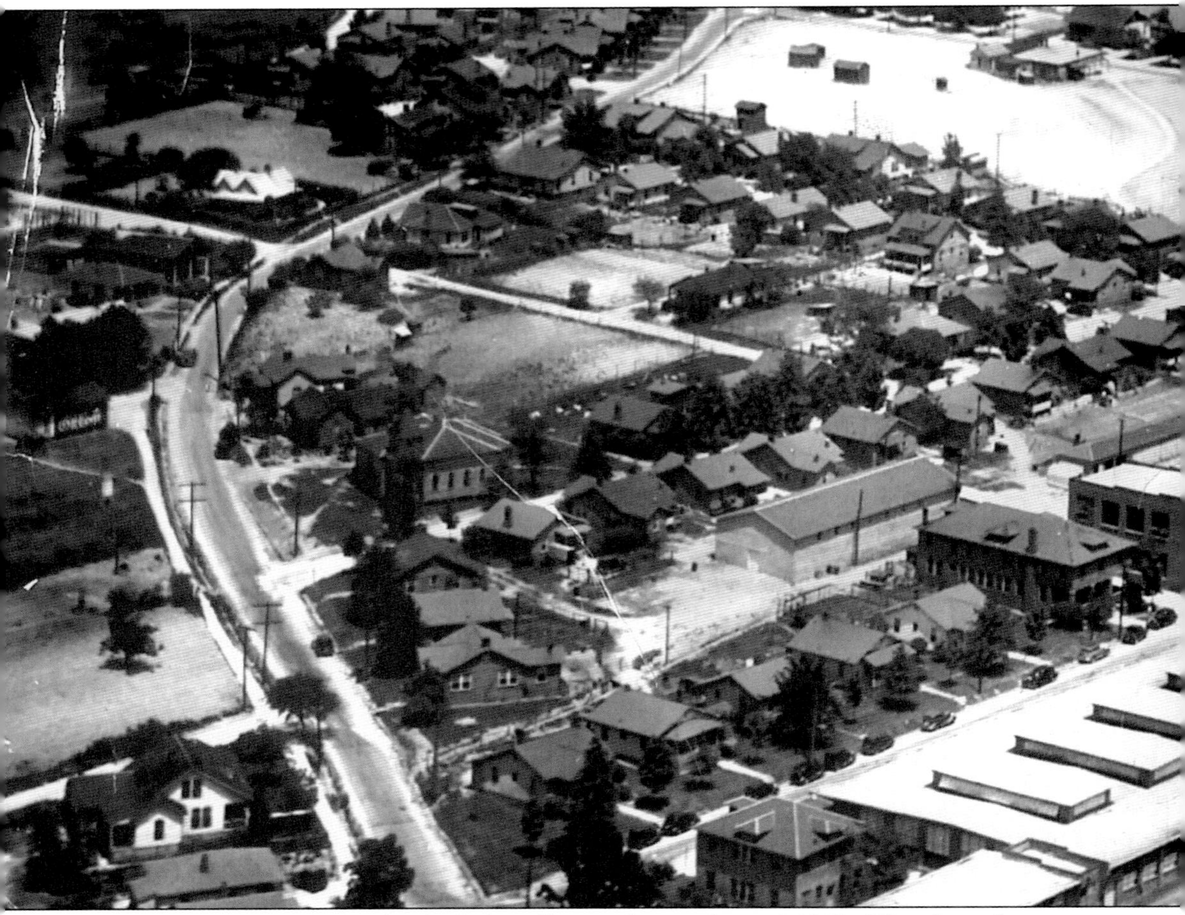

This aerial view of Cleveland Cloth Mill was taken in the mid-1940s. The photo demonstrates how a community grew around the textile mill. SHELBY was painted on the roof of the mill in

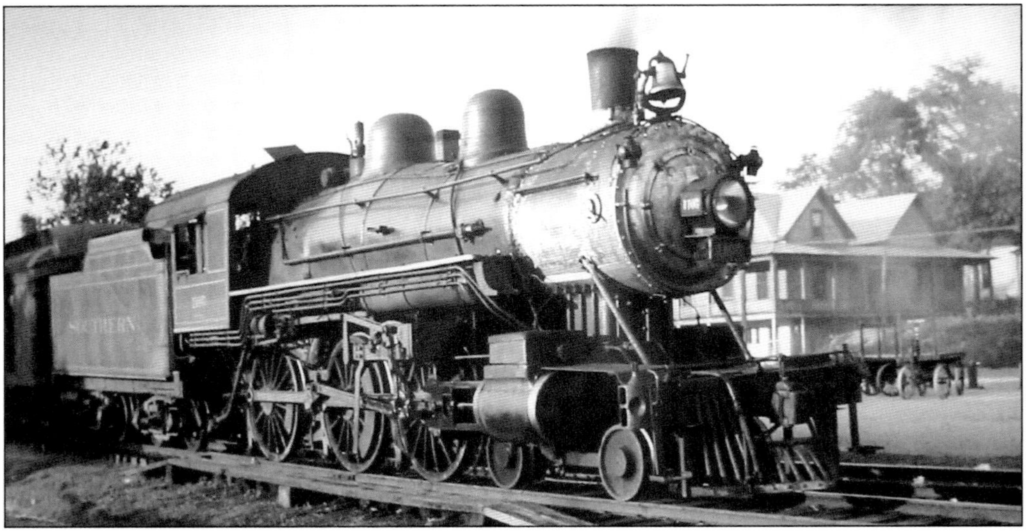

A Southern Railway steam locomotive pulls into the station on South Morgan Street. The Southern Hotel can be seen in the background of this 1941 photograph. (Tom Reese.)

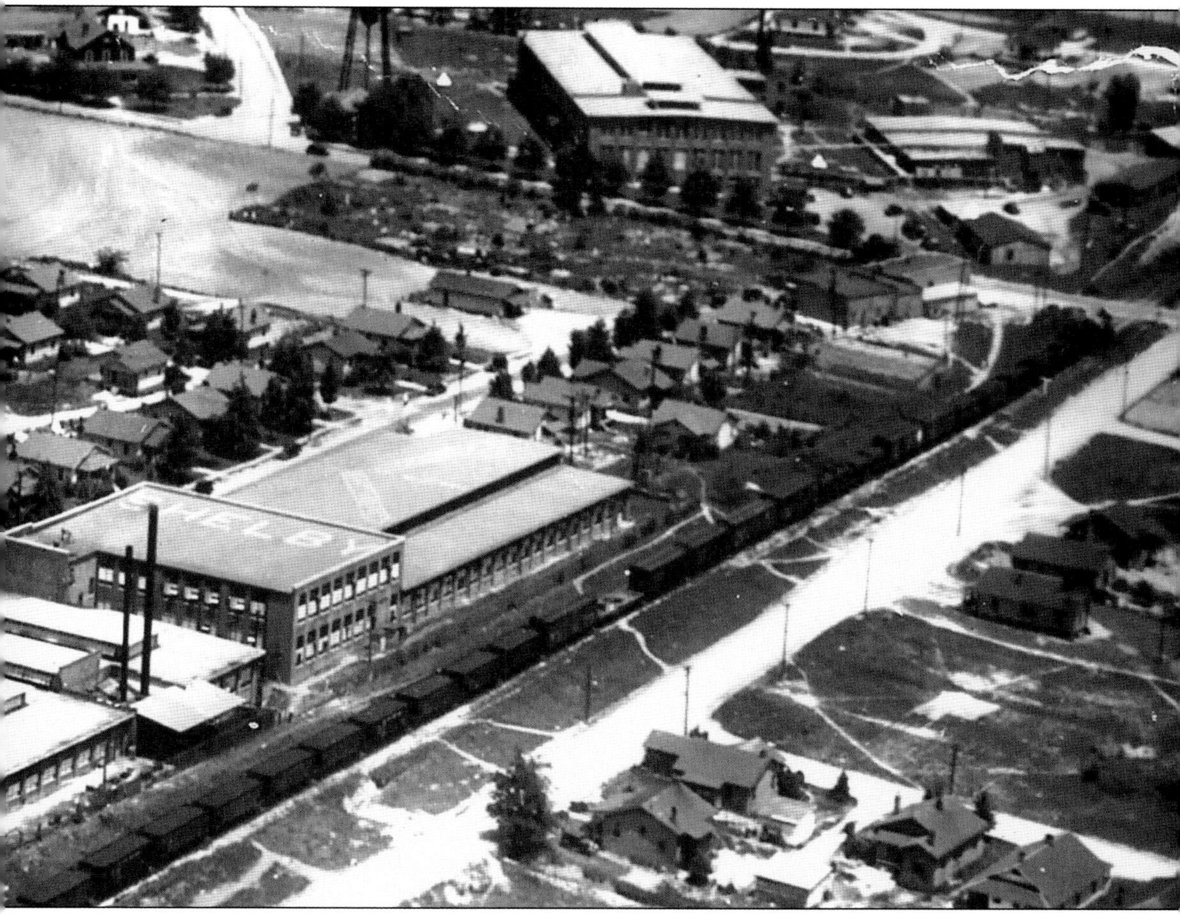

the 1930s as part of a national program providing identifying landmarks for airplanes. One of the Dover mills, the Ester Mill, can be seen at the top. (Dean Floyd.)

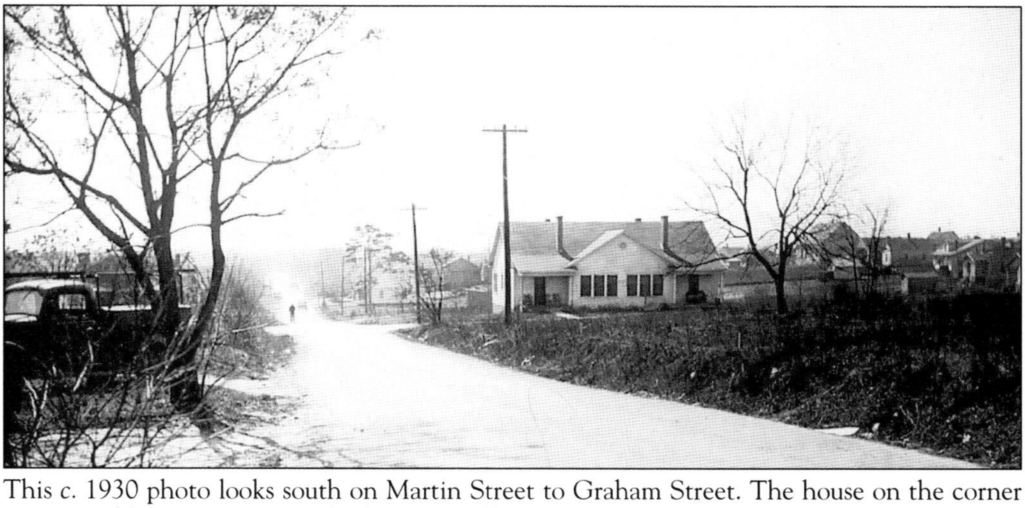

This *c.* 1930 photo looks south on Martin Street to Graham Street. The house on the corner was owned by I.G. Watson. The house is still occupied today. The houses visible on the right face Clegg Street. Much of the land was owned by H. Fields Young Sr. and had not yet been developed. (H. Fields Young III.)

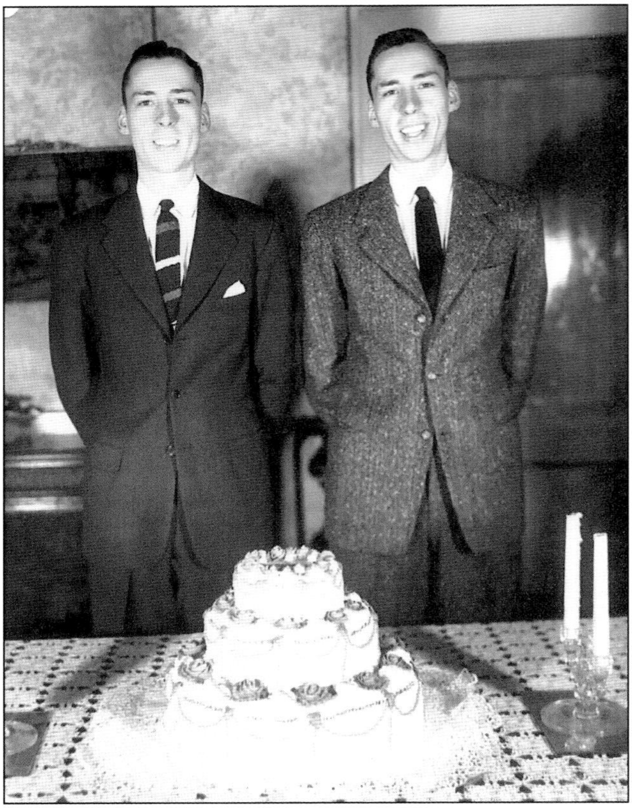

A late 1930s picture shows twins Lloyd and Floyd Bost. The 1937 graduates of Shelby High School went on to manage Bost Bakery with their brothers Bennett and Ned. The bakery was a leading Shelby business for several decades. (Uptown Shelby Association.)

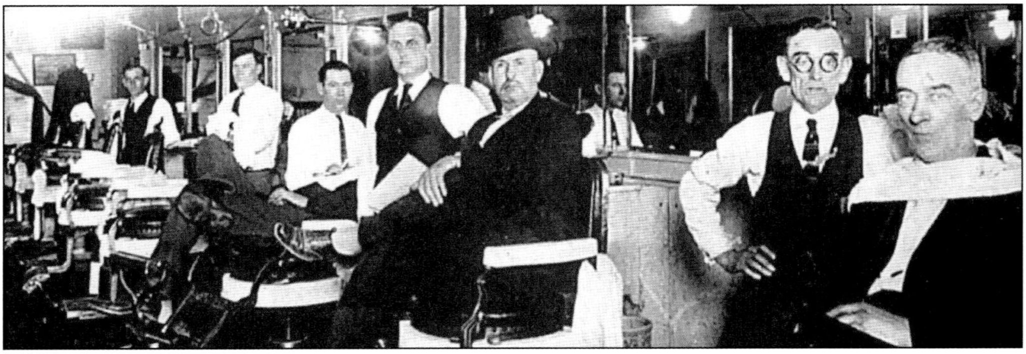

This 1930s tonsorial establishment was known as the J.P. Austell Barber Shop and was located across from the south side of the court square. The barbers standing, from left to right beside their chairs, are Mr. Willis, Ambrose McWhiter, Roscoe McWhiter, Doc Willis, and Jim Austell. Does your barber wear a tie and vest?

Two

SHELBY
MID-CENTURY

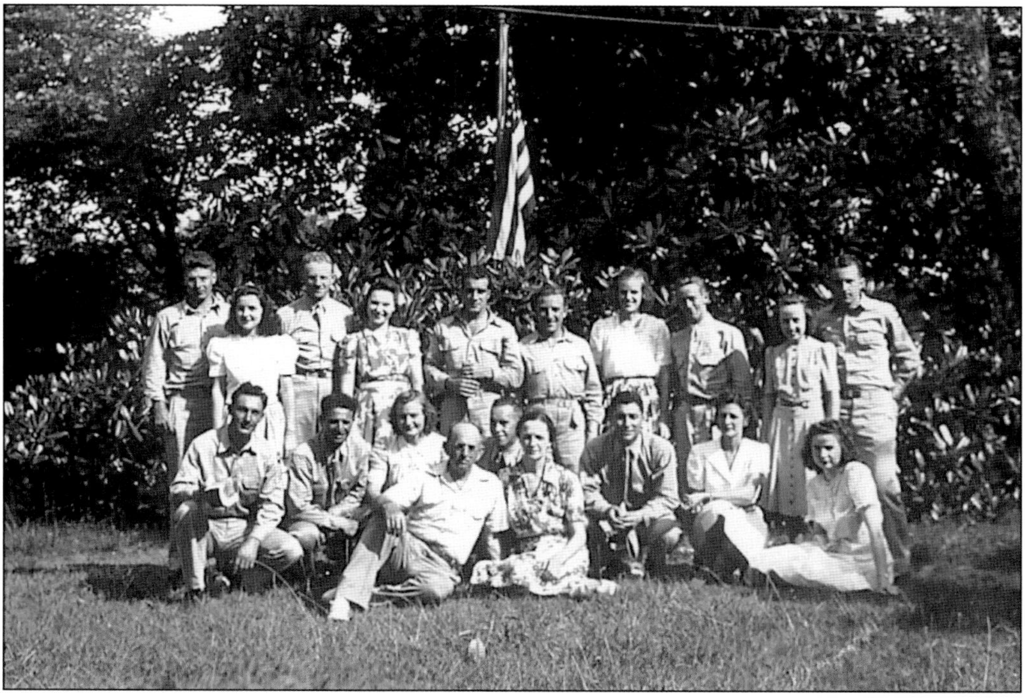

On a warm Sunday afternoon in 1942, Mr. and Mrs. H. Fields Young Sr. (seated in front row) entertained a group of local servicemen at their home. Throughout the summer of 1942, the Young's entertained area servicemen on Sunday afternoons. (H. Fields Young III.)

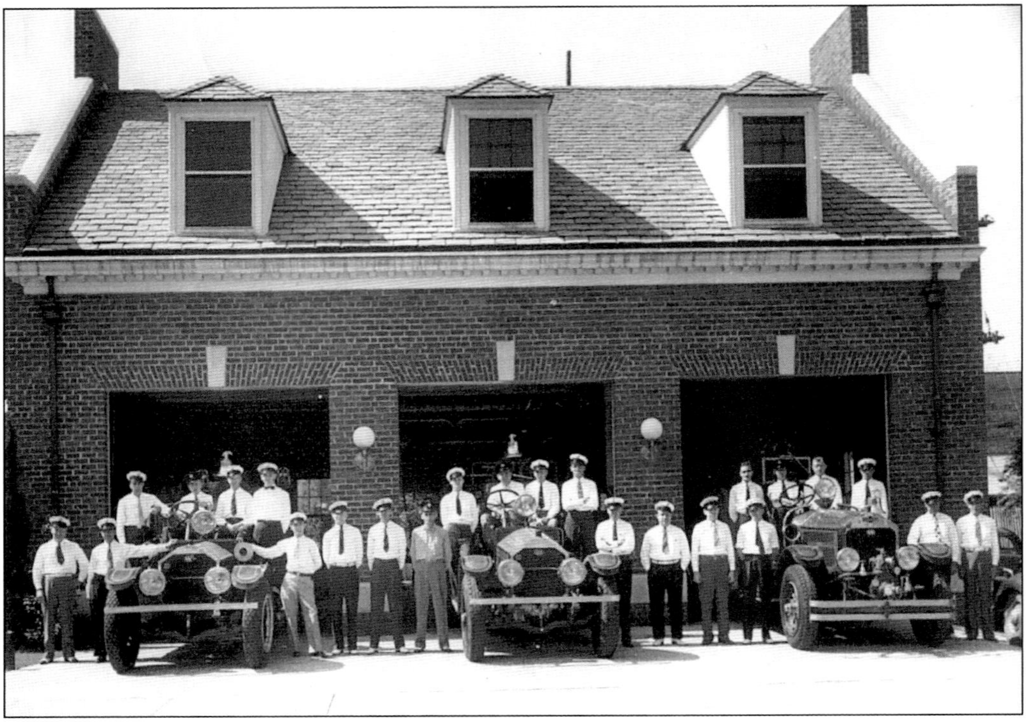

The Shelby Fire Department turned out for a photo in front of its new quarters on Graham Street. The first generation fire trucks would soon be replaced. (Dewey Cooke.)

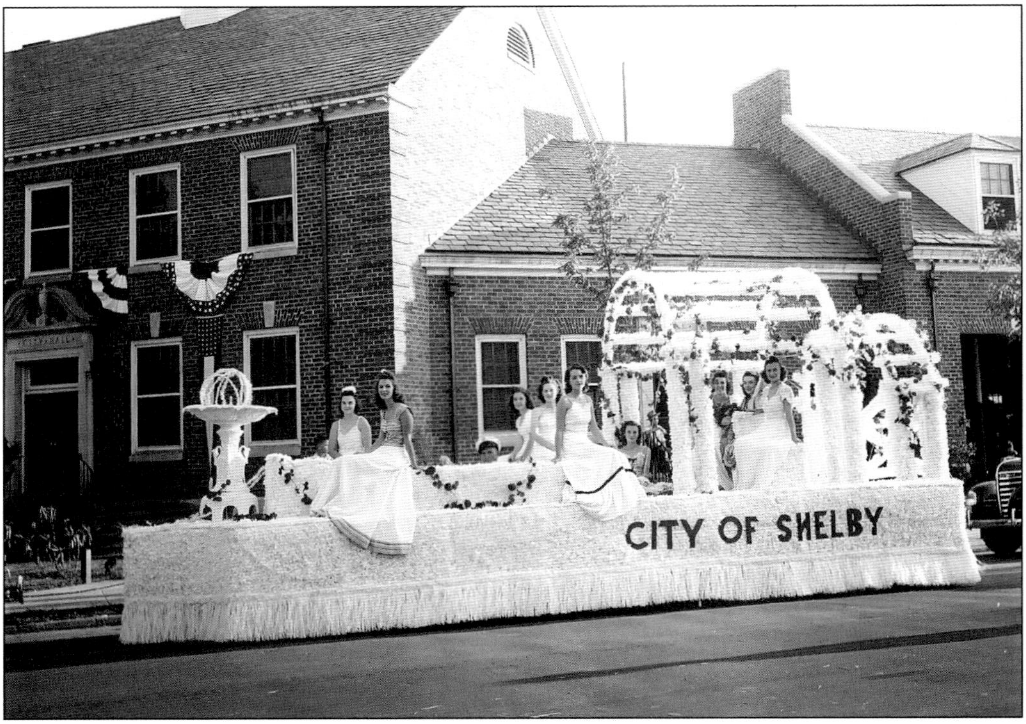

This photo from the Ellis Studios shows a parade float proceeding up Graham Street. The new city hall and fire station can be seen in the background. (Uptown Shelby Association.)

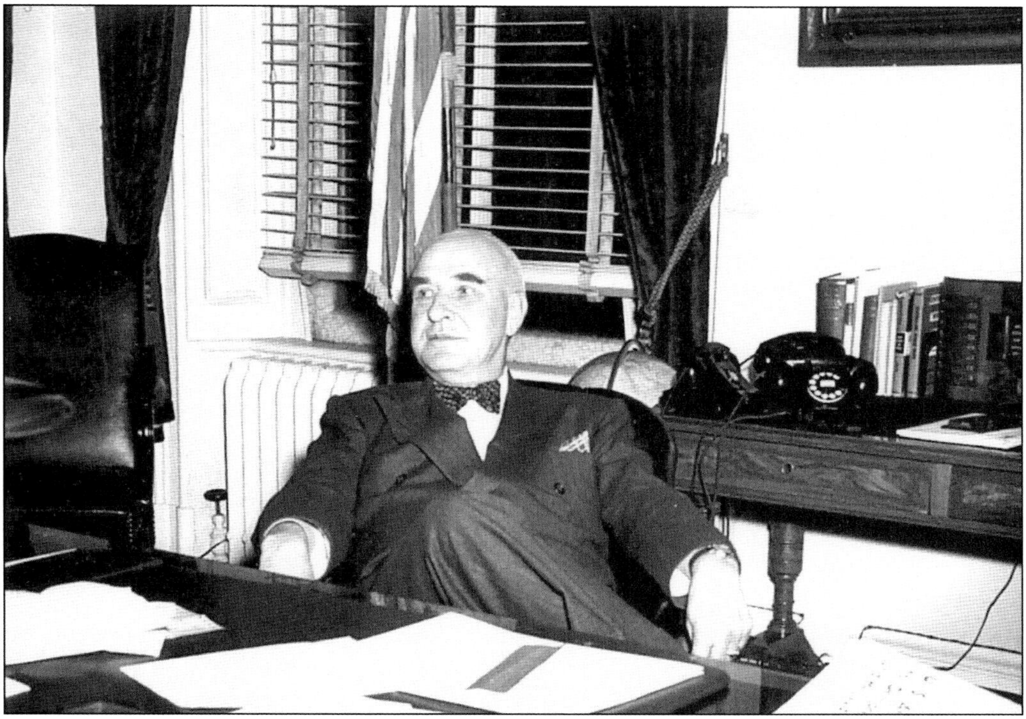

The former Governor Gardner stops his work to pose for this 1940s photo. (Madge Harris.)

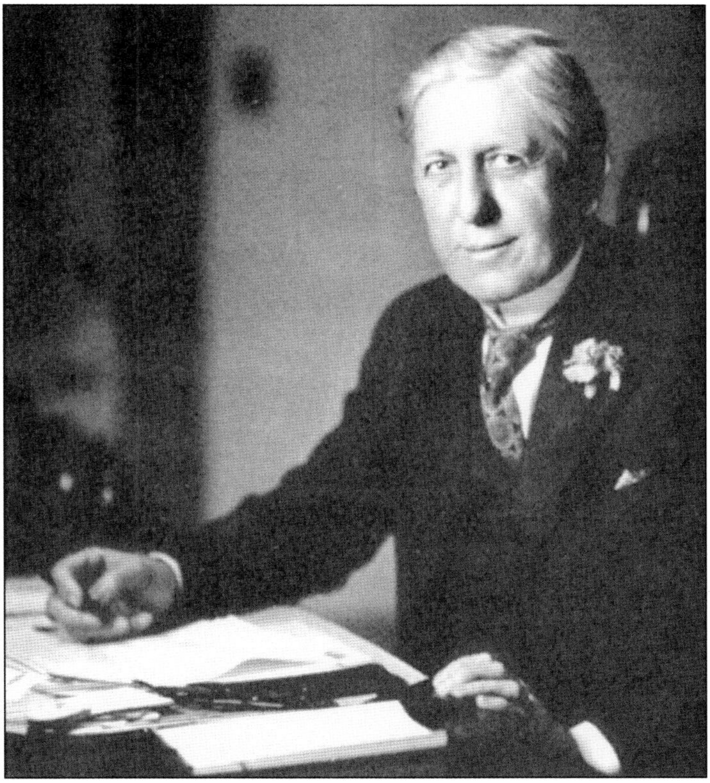

O. Max Gardner's brother-in-law, Clyde R. Hoey, served as North Carolina's governor from 1937 to 1941. The two governors were the cores of a political group known as the "Shelby Dynasty." Hoey served in the United States Senate from 1945 until his death in 1954. (*The Living Past of Cleveland County.*)

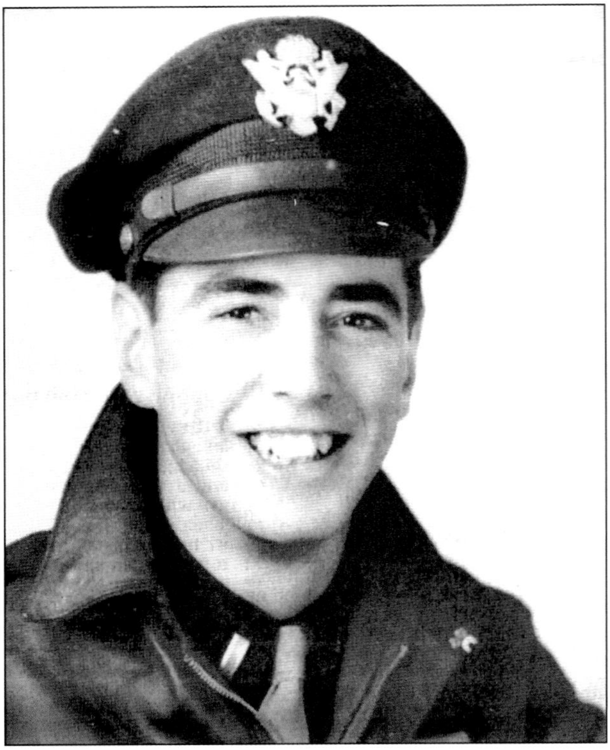

B-17 pilot Hugh Noell flew bombing missions until he was shot down on February 10, 1944. He made his first parachute jump on that day and spent the rest of the war in Stalag Luft 1. (*The Star.*)

Many Shelbians served in World War II. The young pilot in the center, who is being greeted in England after a bombing raid, is a Bryson City native who played basketball at Carson-Newman College. The pilot, Malcolm Brown, moved to Shelby in 1956 and led the Shelby City Schools as superintendent until his retirement. (*The Star.*)

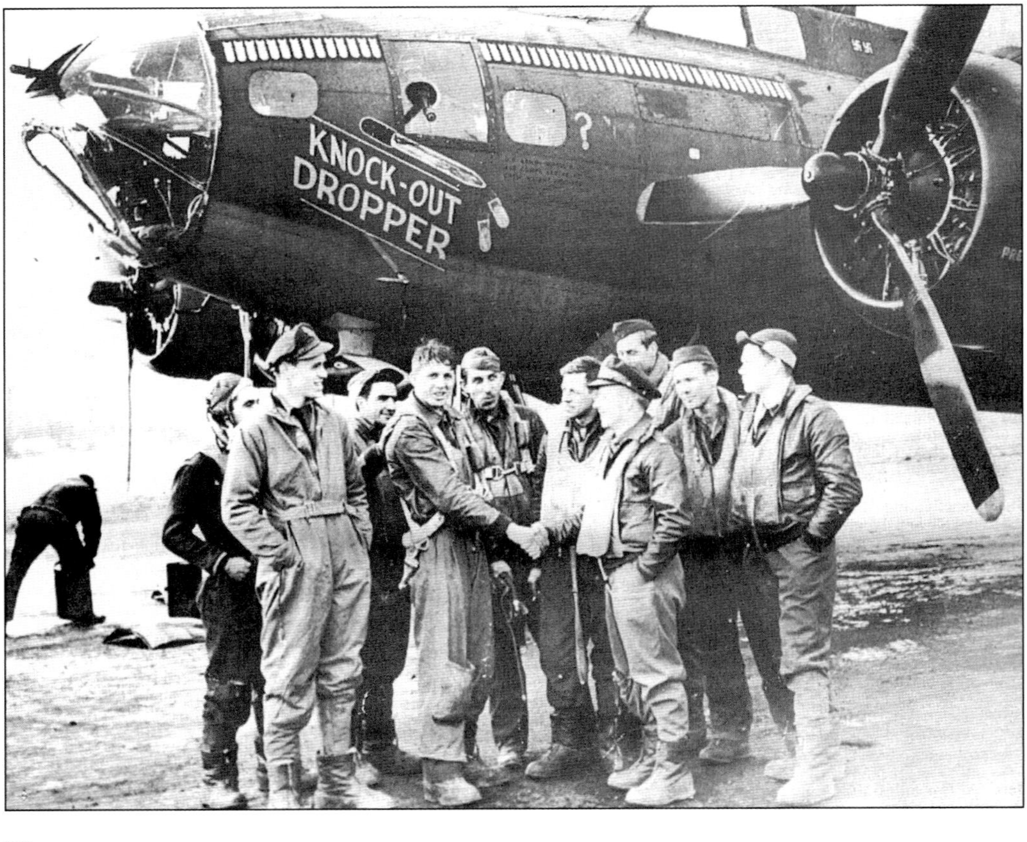

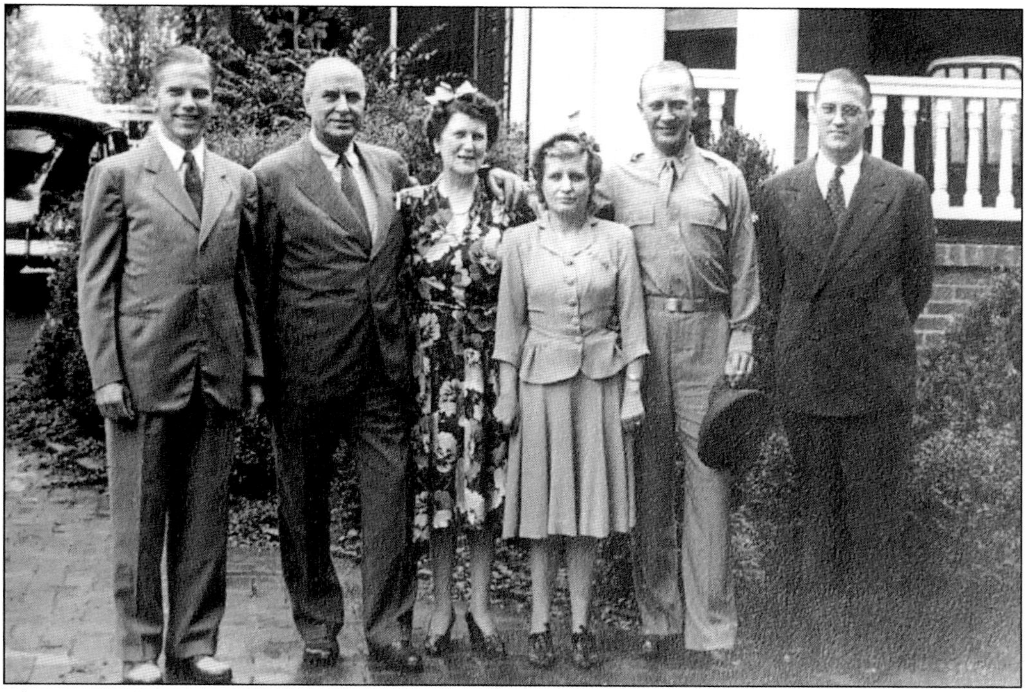

This 1943 photo taken at Webbly on South Washington Street shows, from left to right, O. Max Jr., Governor and Mrs. Gardner, Margaret Love Gardner Burgess, Ralph Gardner, and James W. "Decker" Gardner. (Uptown Shelby Association.)

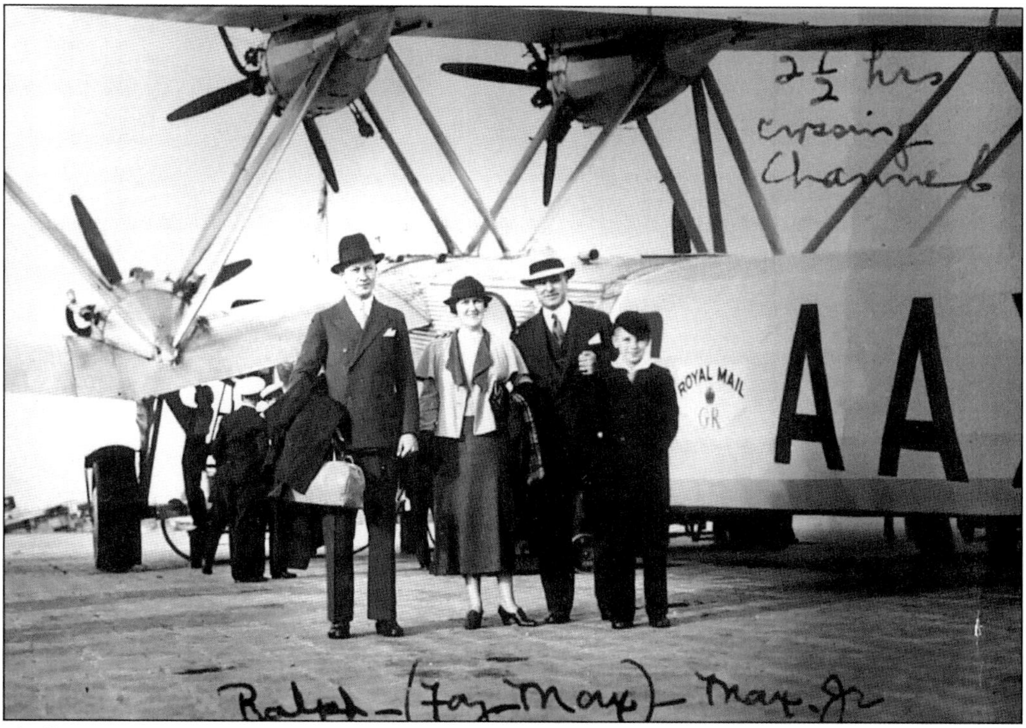

Shelby's first family in the 1940s was the former Governor O. Max Gardner and his wife, Faye Webb. Here they are pictured with their sons Ralph and Max Jr. (Uptown Shelby Association.)

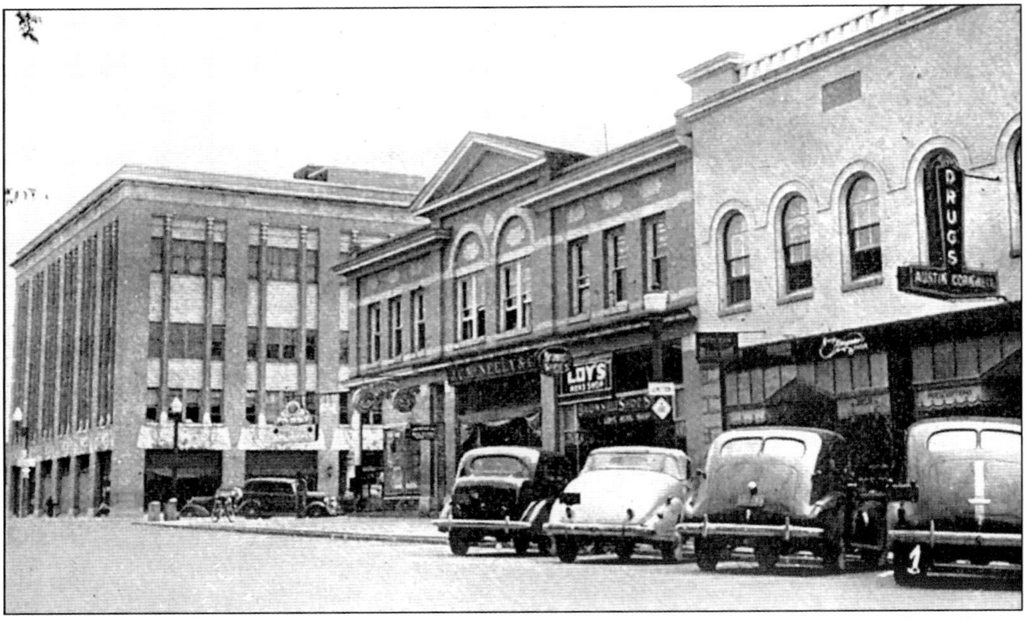

This *c.* 1940 view of Warren Street south of the court square shows an arrangement of merchants few can remember. Loy's Men Shop can be seen in the middle of the block. The corner location Loy's occupied for over 50 years until it closed in the 1990s was a bar in "wet" Shelby. A Pabst Beer sign extends from the corner of the Royster Building.

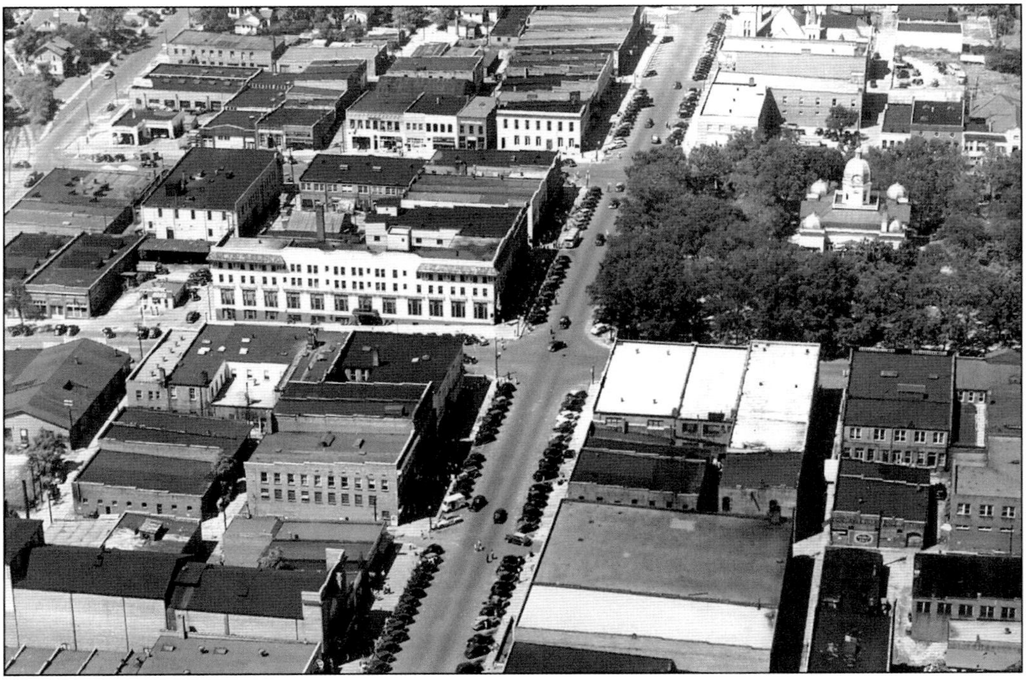

Shelby continued to grow in the 1940s. Uptown Shelby is pictured from the air looking north up Lafayette Street. To the bottom right, one can see the old Shelby Hotel. In the lower left, the long building with the tall facade was built by Zeb and Enos Beam in 1917 as the Princess Theater. The name was changed later to the Carolina Theater, which remained open until it was converted to a Woolworth's Store in 1960. (Robert Arey Sr.)

Ambassador and Mrs. O. Max Gardner posed for this February 3, 1947 photo on their way to a farewell party at the White House with President Truman. Gardner was unable to fulfill his appointment as Ambassador to England because he died from a heart attack in New York City on February 6, 1947, three days after this picture was taken. (*Governor O. Max Gardner.*)

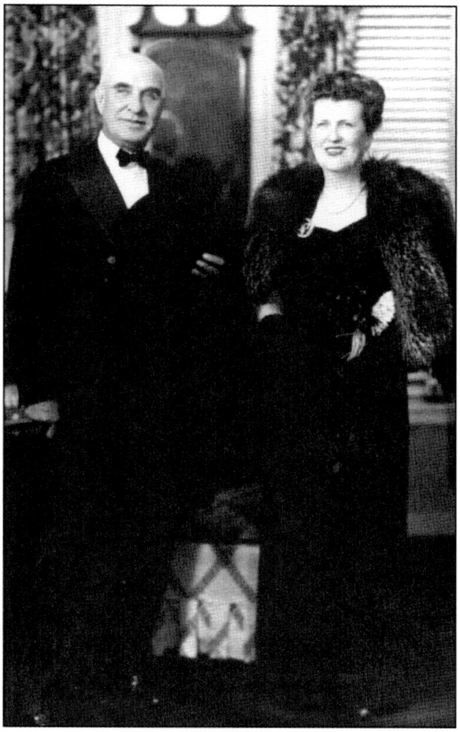

There was time for some fun on the home front early in World War II. This young people's group of the Freewill Methodist Church on Martin Street poses on Easter Sunday, April 5, 1942. From left to right are (front row) Luke Dover, Harold Carpenter, Beatrice McKee, Inez Sisk, Eiron McKnight West, Frances Jones Carpenter, and Christine Rainey; (middle row) Heaman Carpenter, Wallace Carpenter, Boyce Crawford, William Weldon McKnight, H.A. White, and Julian French; (back row) group leaders Hester Earwood Lowrance and Junior Parrish. Some of these young men were in uniform before World War II ended.(Wallace Carpenter.)

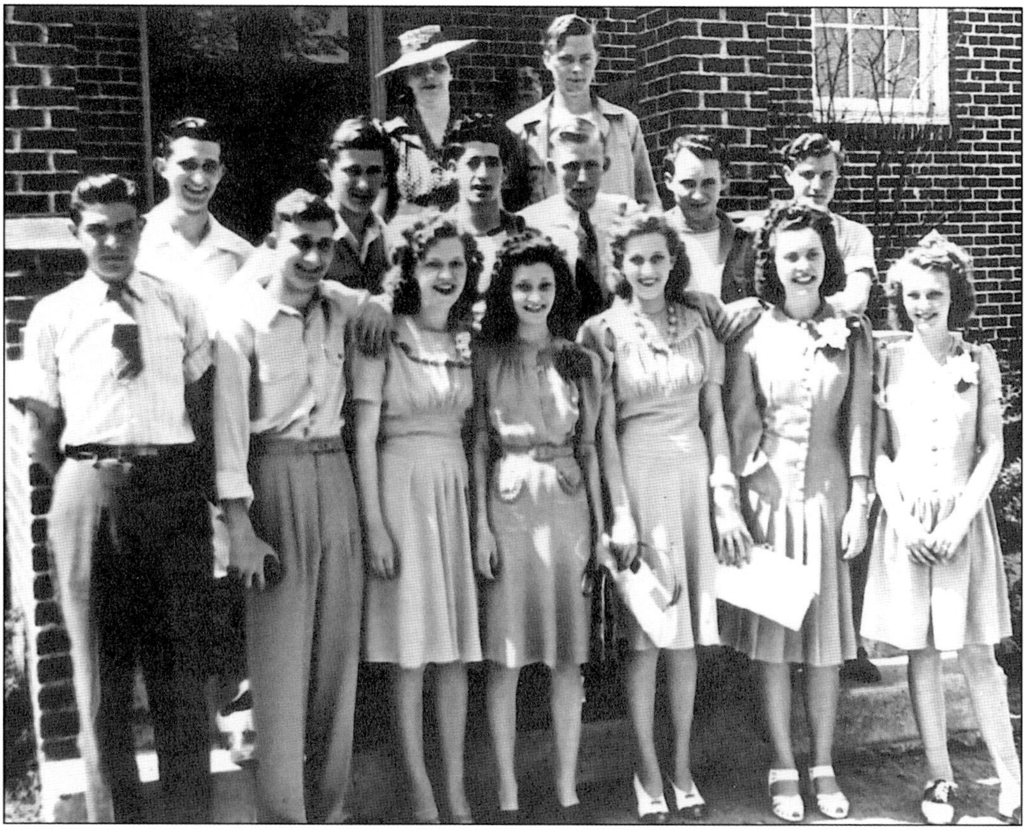

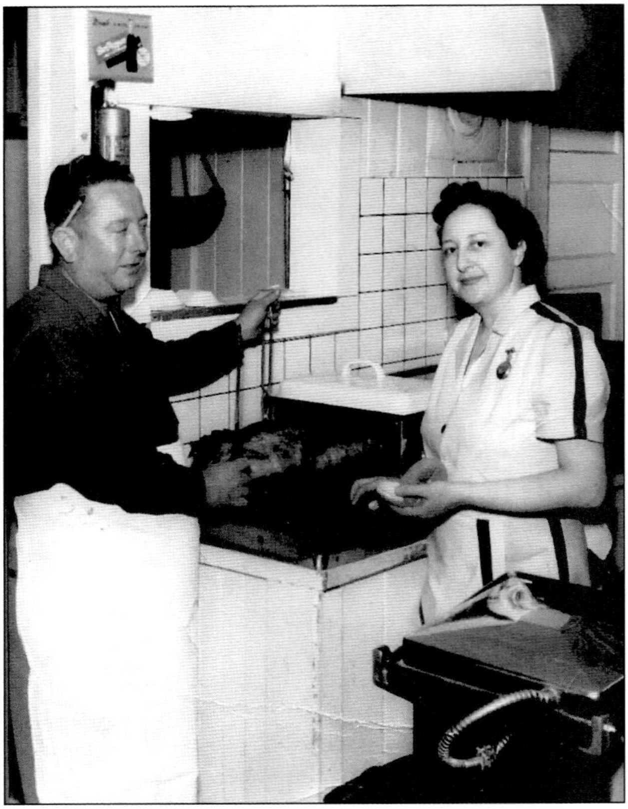

Since World War II, Shelby has become known for barbecue. It is said that the word is a noun in the South and a verb in the North. Just after World War II, Dedmon's Barbeque was opened on highway 18 just north of Shelby. Operators Red and Lyttle Bridges slice meat in this photo. (Debbie Bridges Webb.)

This group of service station dealers from Cleveland and Rutherford Counties poses in front of the Arey Amoco station at the corner of Washington and Graham Streets across from city hall. The three-story building to the left was the Shelby Hotel. (Robert Arey Sr.)

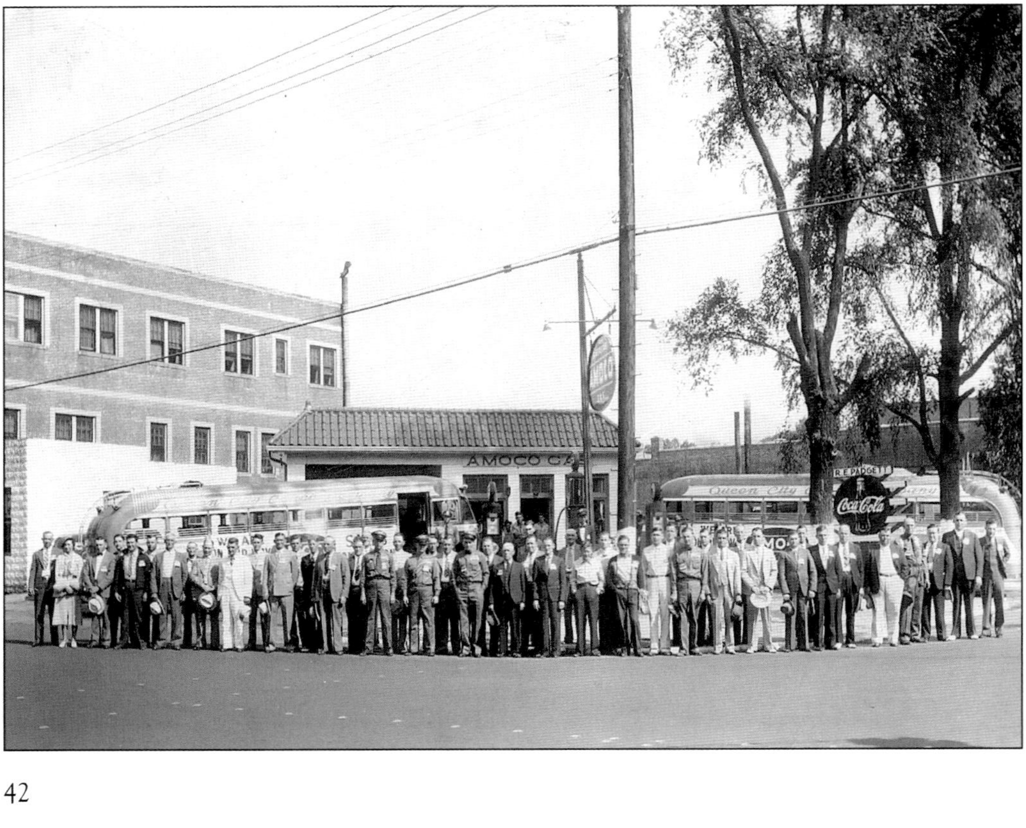

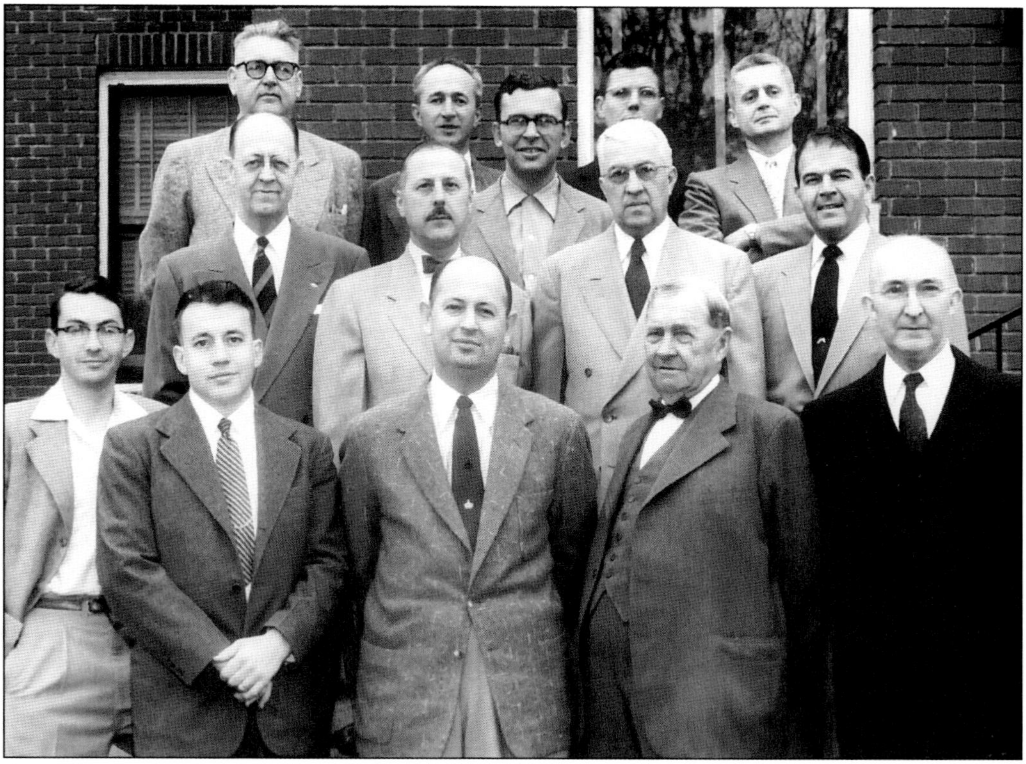

At mid-century, the fact that Shelby had only a few doctors made them well known to most. In this photo, pictured from left to right, are (front row) Doctors Hudson, Yeomans, Cloninger, Lattimore, and Harbison; (middle row) Kendall, Parker, King, and McMurray; (back row) Sherrill, Jervey, Crow, McMurray, and Jones. (Uptown Shelby Association.)

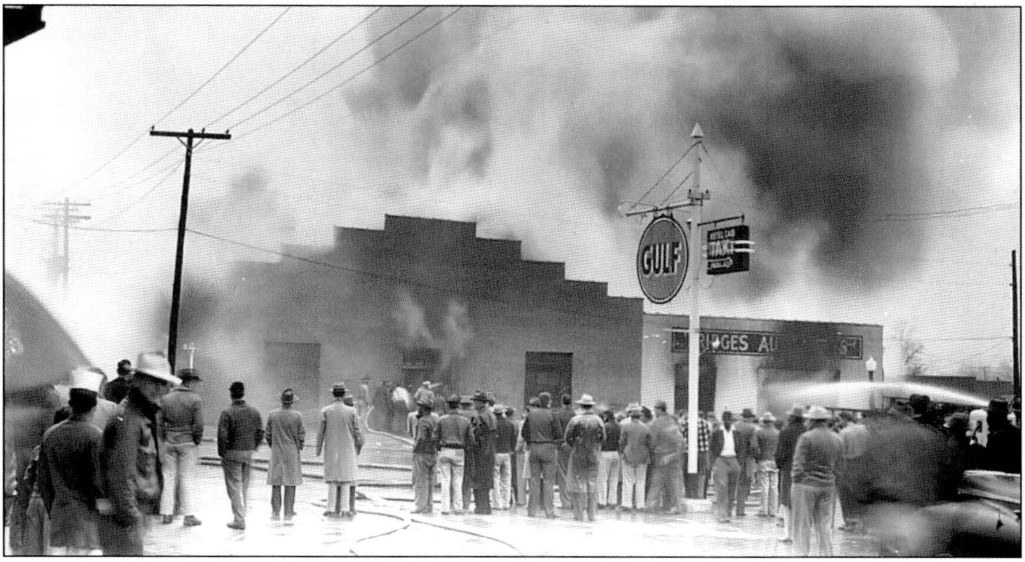

On March 5, 1950, Shelby experienced a major fire on West Warren Street. The block destroyed was occupied by Kendall Drug, Bridges Auto Parts, and Ellis Bicycle. Rebuilding produced a Sears Roebuck store where many people visited to experience air conditioning for the first time. (Uptown Shelby Association.)

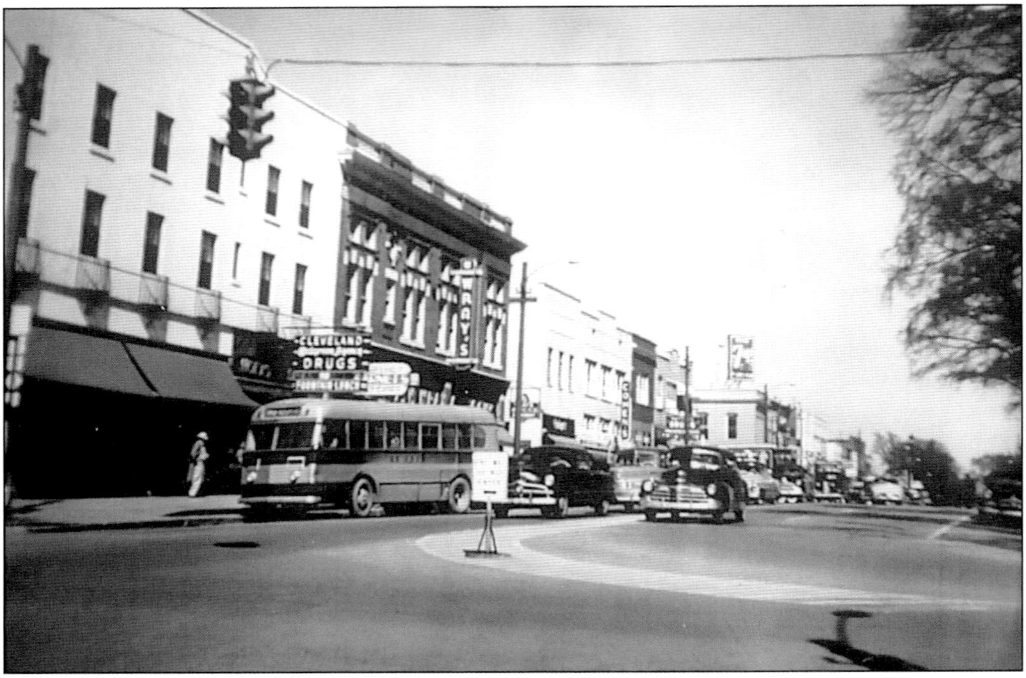

This early 1950s shot shows two things that are now history. First, traffic around the court square was one way. Second, Shelby had a local bus line that transported people to the uptown stores. (Uptown Shelby Association.)

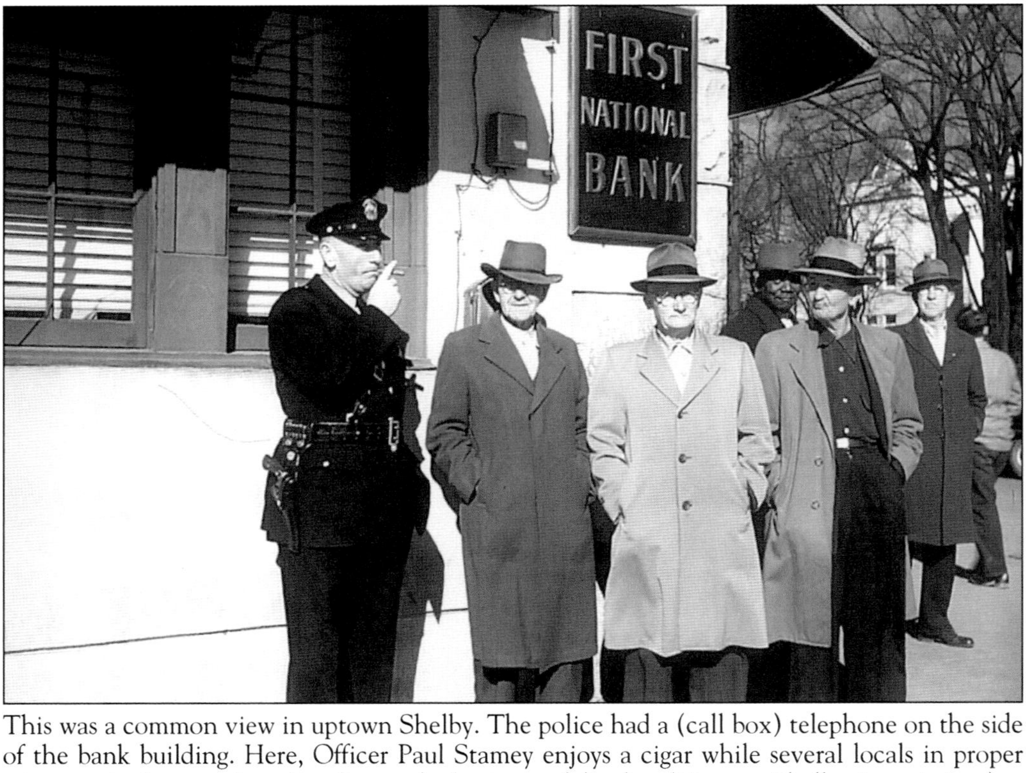

This was a common view in uptown Shelby. The police had a (call box) telephone on the side of the bank building. Here, Officer Paul Stamey enjoys a cigar while several locals in proper winter attire have gathered to discuss the business of the day. (Uptown Shelby Association.)

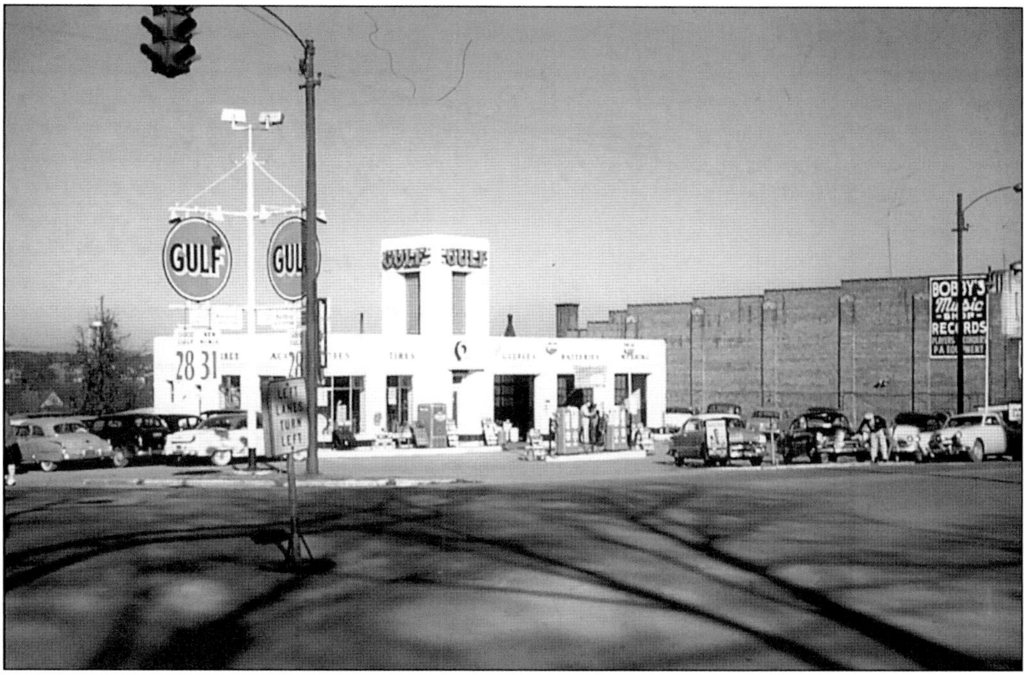

Royster Oil owned this Gulf station next to Rogers Theater on East Marion Street. The price of gas was a dollar less than prices today. The "left lane turns left" shows that traffic was one way around the court square. (Uptown Shelby Association.)

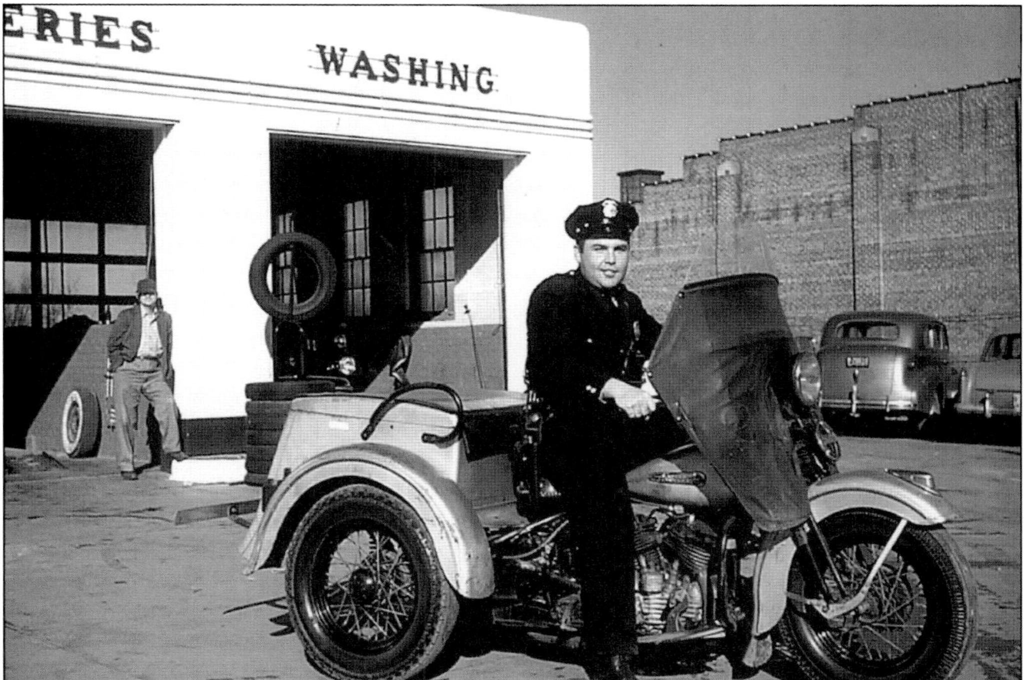

This view of the same Gulf station shows Officer Harold Smith on his three-wheeler. Smith spent his career with the Shelby Police Department and retired as a captain. (Uptown Shelby Association.)

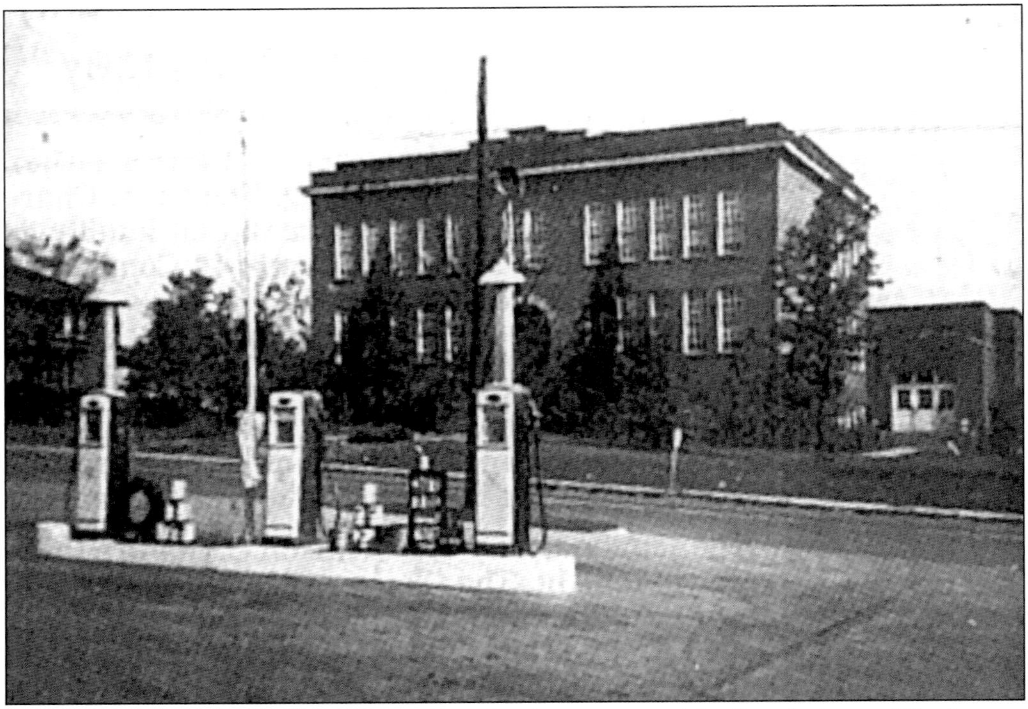

In the 1940s, most of Shelby's elementary schools were named for Revolutionary War heroes. Marion School was located on East Marion Street only two blocks from the court square. The school was removed at mid-century. Since then the site has been occupied by Dixie Home (later Winn-Dixie), Suttles Drug, and now Eckerd Drugs. (*The Star*.)

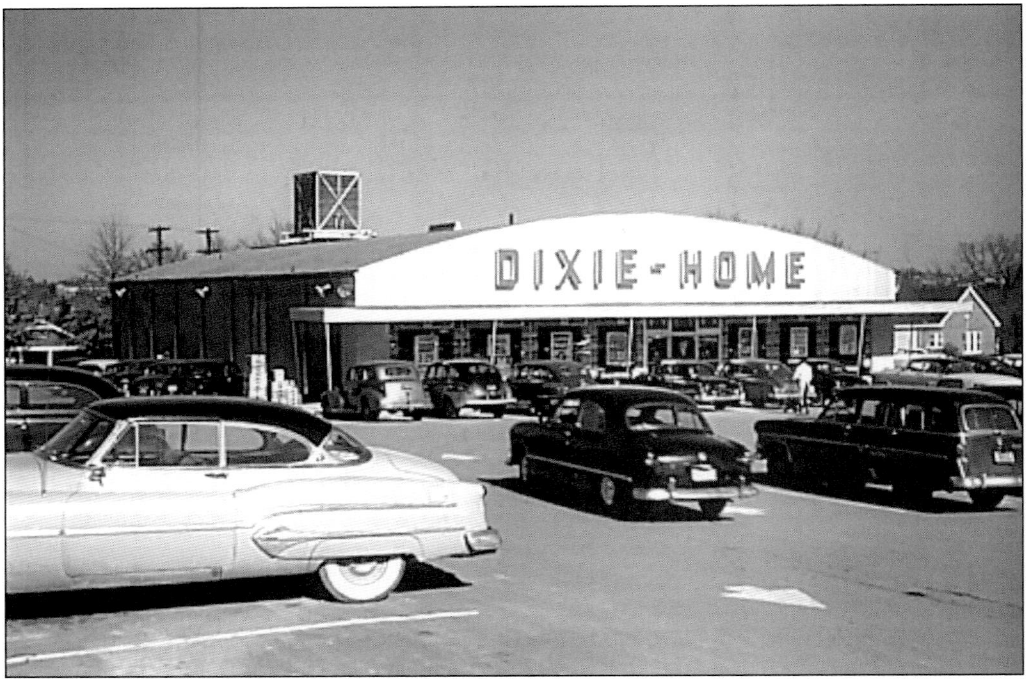

In the early 1950s, the old Marion School building was demolished to make room for a modern supermarket. Dixie Home would later become Winn-Dixie. (Uptown Shelby Association.)

Oscar Evans, Robert Morgan, Harrill Hamrick, and a young Jack Morgan take a moment from their work at Morgan and Co. by the railroad tracks on West Warren Street. (Jack Morgan family.)

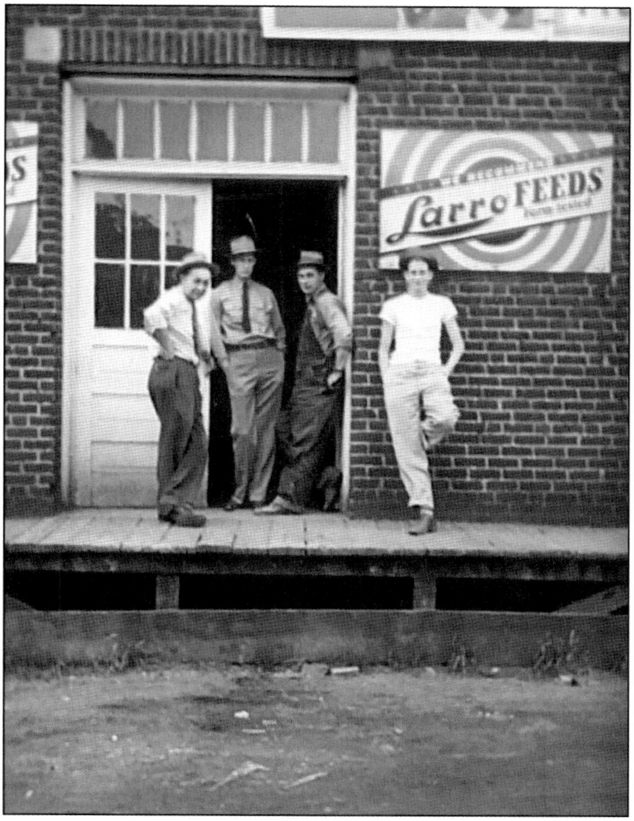

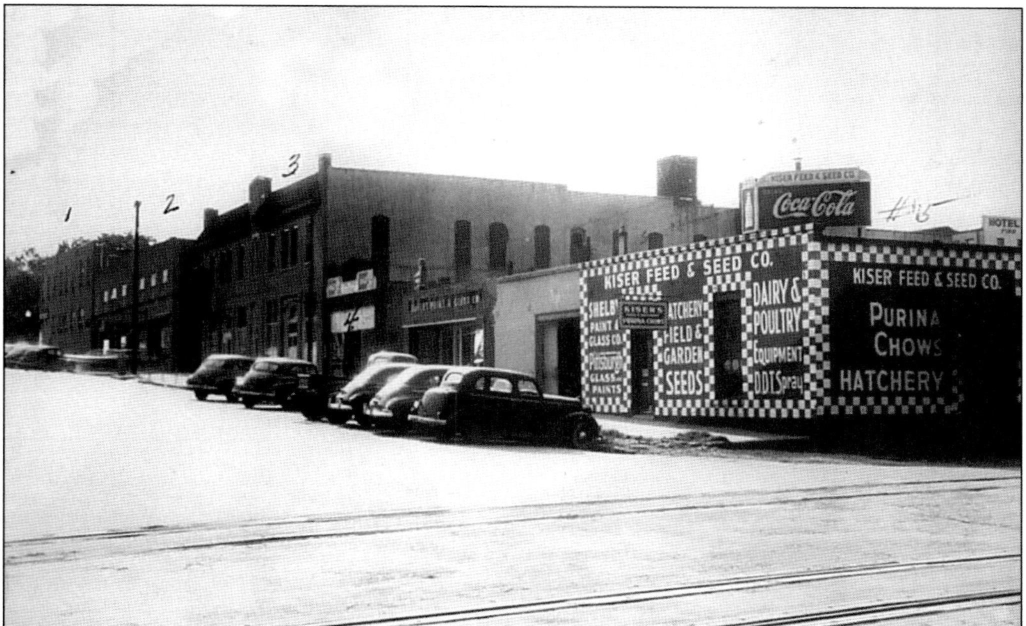

Around 1950, Kiser Feed and Seed Co. was located on West Marion Street by the Southern Railway. Vernon Kiser operated the business and served on the Shelby City School Board. (Uptown Shelby Association.)

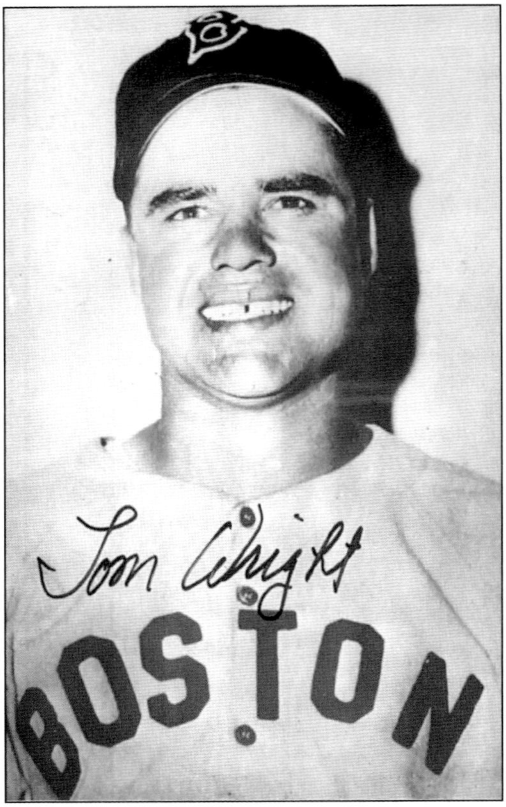

Tom Wright was an outfielder who played seven years in the American League. The first half of his career was spent with the Boston Red Sox where he was a teammate of Ted Williams. (Tom Wright.)

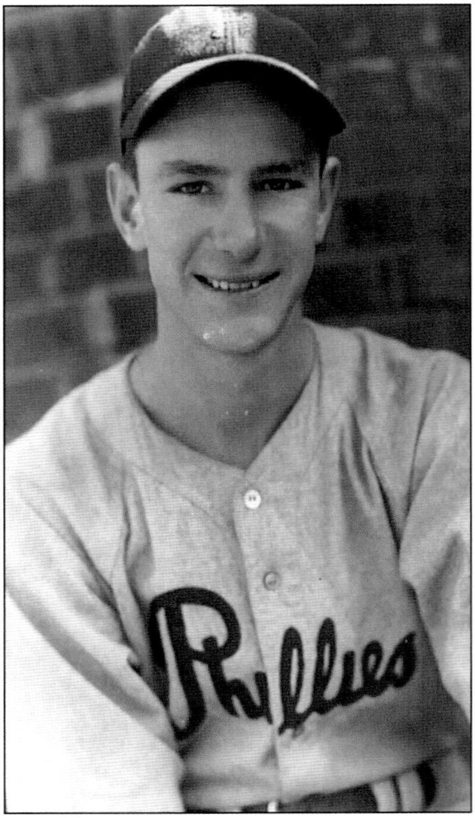

In an era when baseball was king, towns were proud of their major leaguers. Rogers Hornsby "Lefty" McKee pitched for the Philadelphia Phillies in 1943 and 1944 before entering military service. (Rogers Hornsby McKee.)

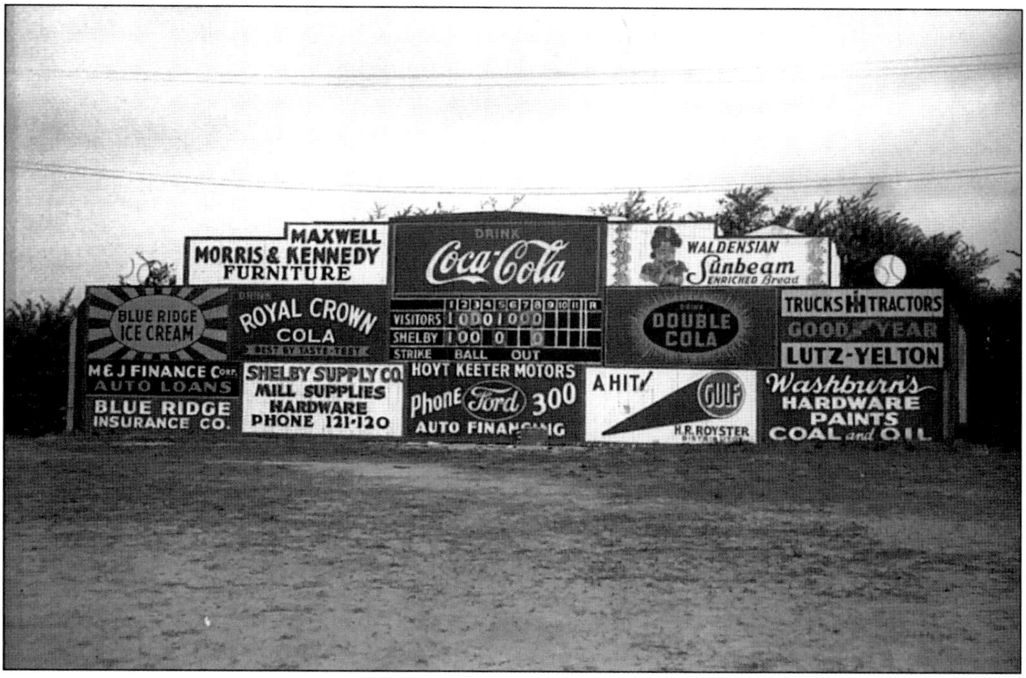

Right field at the old Shelby High field was short because of the railroad that ran beside the ballpark. In right center, a high scoreboard kept baseballs in the park. The distance to the left of the scoreboard was over 450 feet. A scoreboard boy sat on a box and put numbers up at the end of each half inning. The advertisements represented several leading businesses. Note the three-digit telephone numbers in the advertisements. (Lloyd Hamrick Collection.)

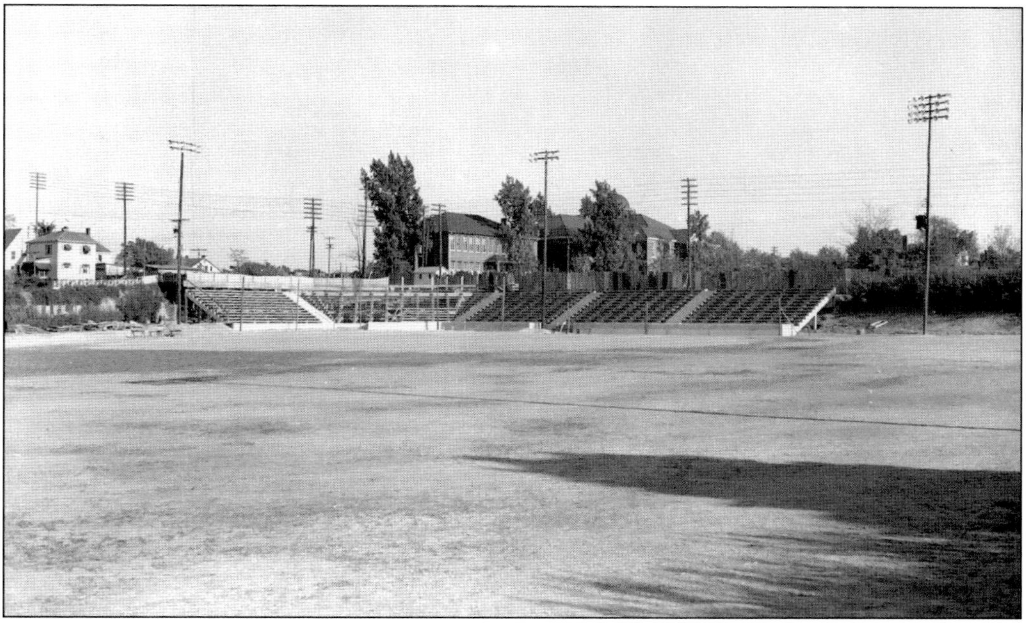

In the 1940s, 1950s, and 1960s, the baseball center of Shelby was the Shelby High Park on West Sumter Street. This view from center field shows the stands before the roof was added. In the background is the school that served Shelby as a graded school, a high school, and finally as a junior high school. (Lloyd Hamrick Collection.)

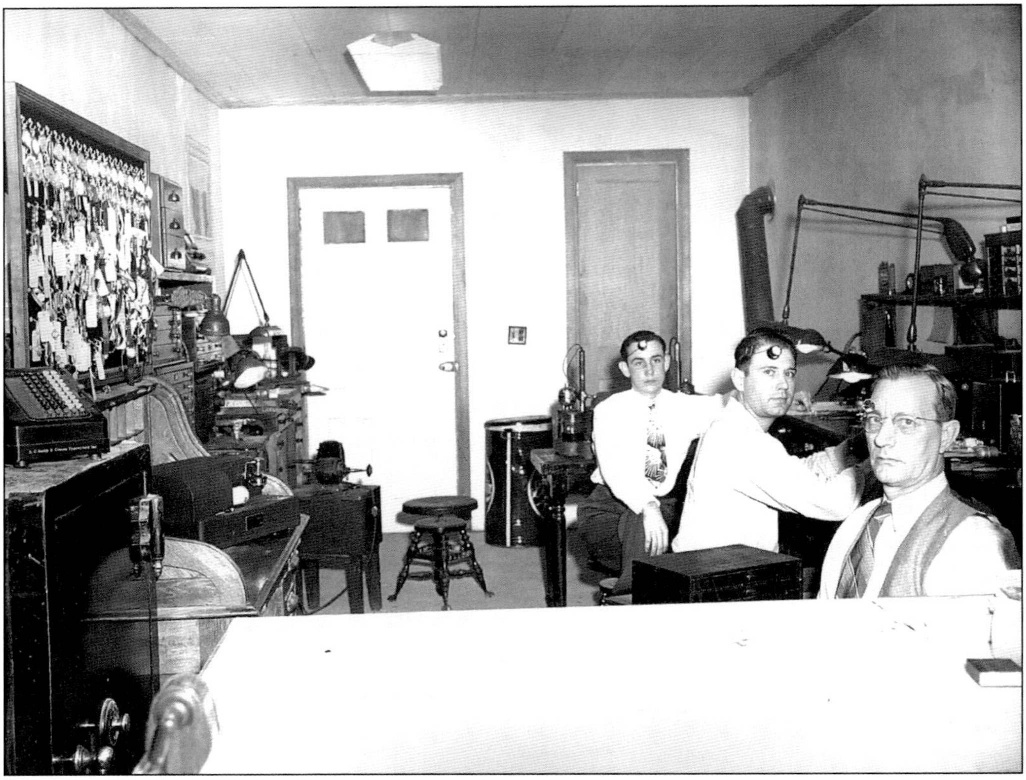

Lawrence Davis, his son Delane Davis, and Ned Costner are pictured in the Davis Jewelry Co. repair shop. The business was located on East Graham Street beside the Shelby Hotel. The business continues today one block west on Graham Street. (Delane Davis.)

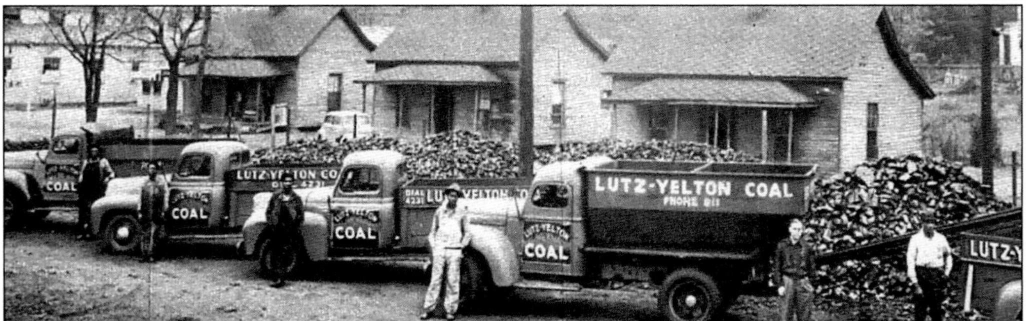

Coal as a fuel for heating was common around 1950. Since coal arrived by train, the Lutz Yelton Coal Co. was located beside the Southern Railway on South Morgan Street. The houses were located across South Morgan (now Market Street) from the coal yard. (*The Star*.)

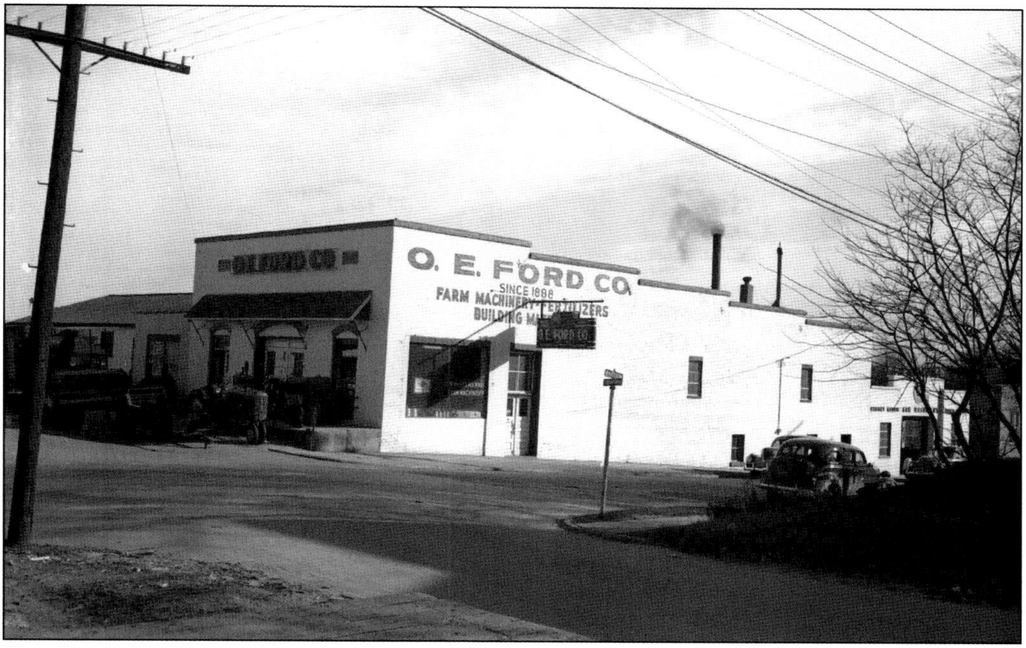

For decades, O.E. Ford Co. sold farm machinery and building supplies. The business was located at the intersection of North Washington Street and the Seaboard Railway. (Lloyd Hamrick Collection.)

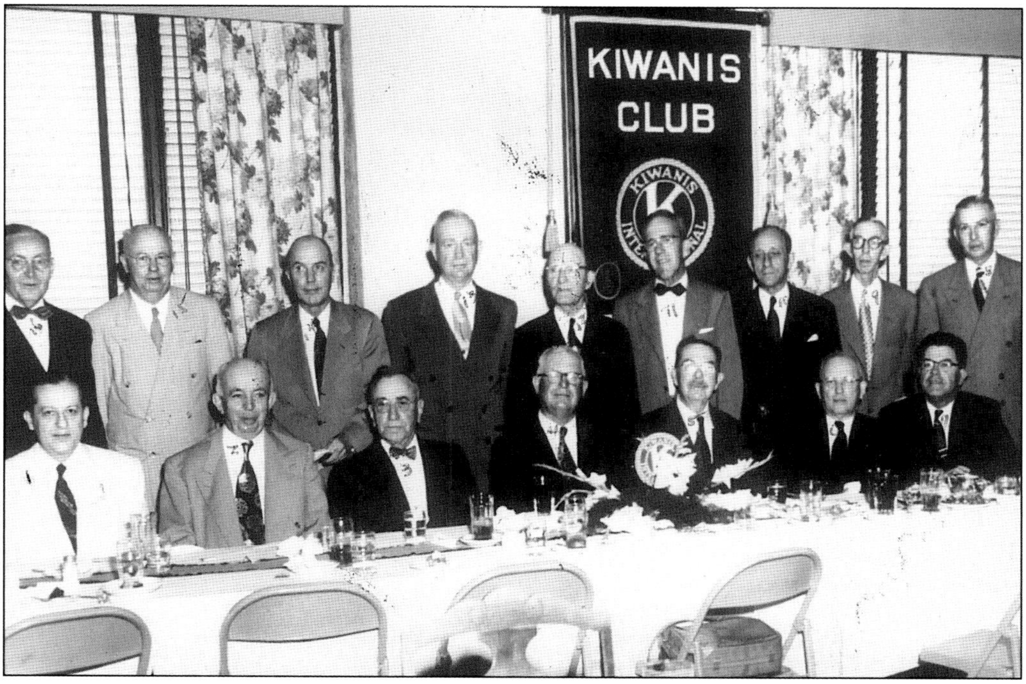

The Hotel Charles was the regular meeting place for the Kiwanis Club. Posed for the picture, from left to right, are (front row) Frank Hoey, D.W. Royster Sr., R.T. LeGrand Sr., Sam Lattimore, Capt. J. Frank Roberts, Charles A. Burris, and Mal A. Spangler; (back row) an unidentified person, D.Z. Newton, Oliver S. Anthony Sr., Horace Grigg, Rush Hamrick Sr., Earle Honeycutt, Dr. J.S. Dorton, John McKnight, and Ben Smith. (Bill Lattimore.)

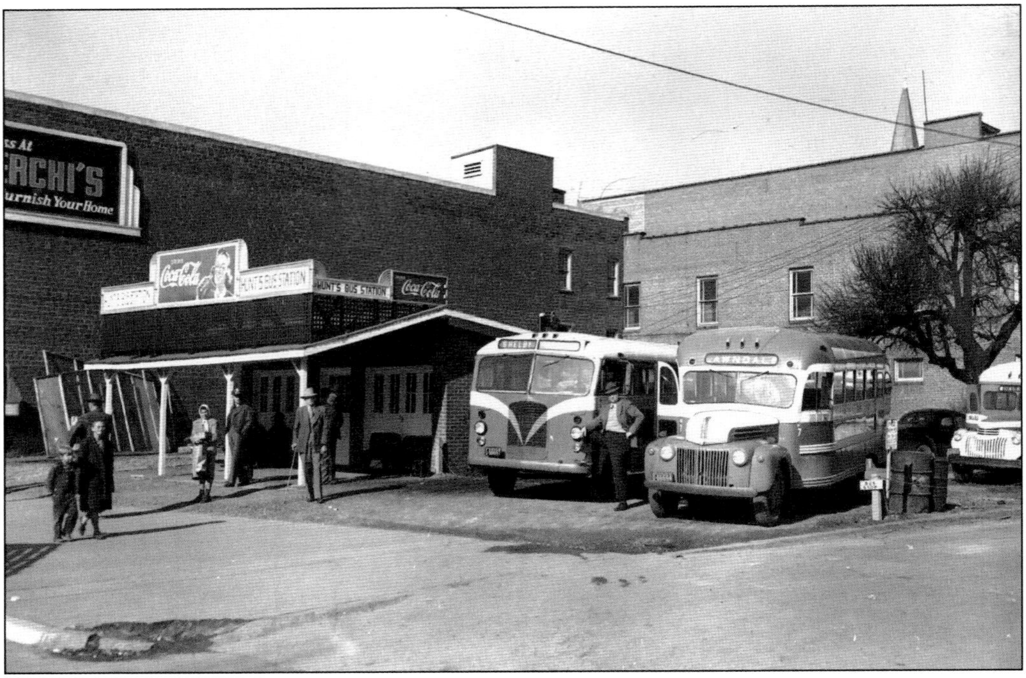

In the late 1940s, the Hunt Bus Station operated from the lot on Marion Street beside Sterchi's Furniture. Buses transported people from around the county to Shelby. The three buses parked in the photo list destinations as Shelby, Lawndale, and Casar. (Lloyd Hamrick Collection.)

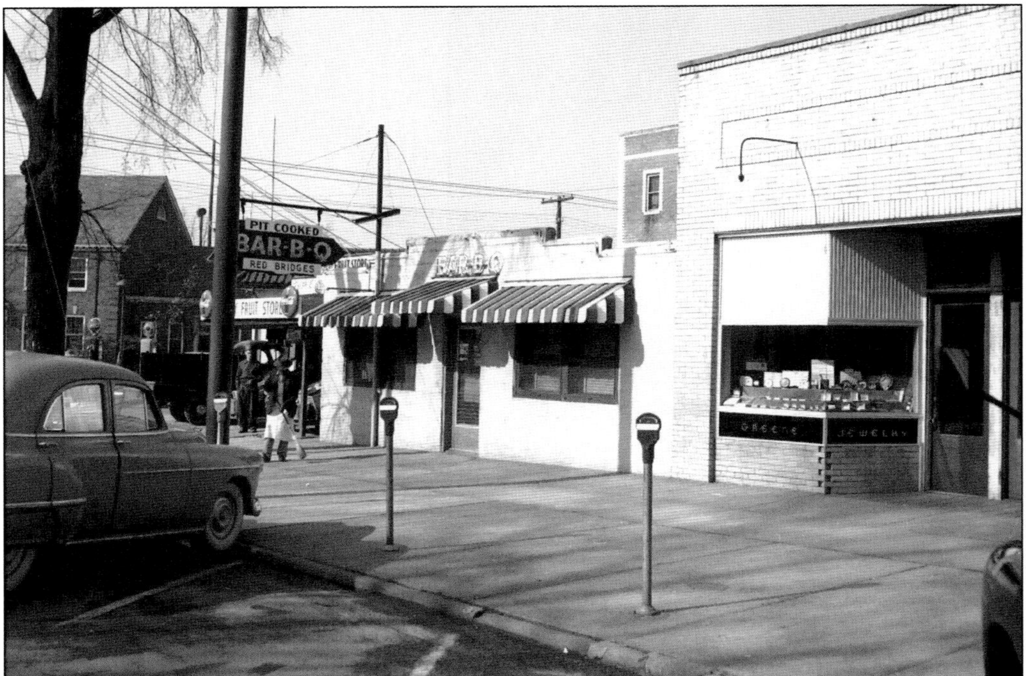

Before Red Bridges built his restaurant off U.S. 74 east of Shelby, he operated a barbecue restaurant on South Washington Street. City Hall is can be seen in the background. Sweeping the sidewalk is longtime employee Robert McConnell. (Lloyd Hamrick Collection.)

In 1950, the Masonic Building housed the Dixie Home Supermarket. Crawley Chevrolet is in the background. Note the highway sign showing state Highway 26 following Washington Street south. Later NC 26 become 226 and now bypasses uptown Shelby. (Lloyd Hamrick Collection.)

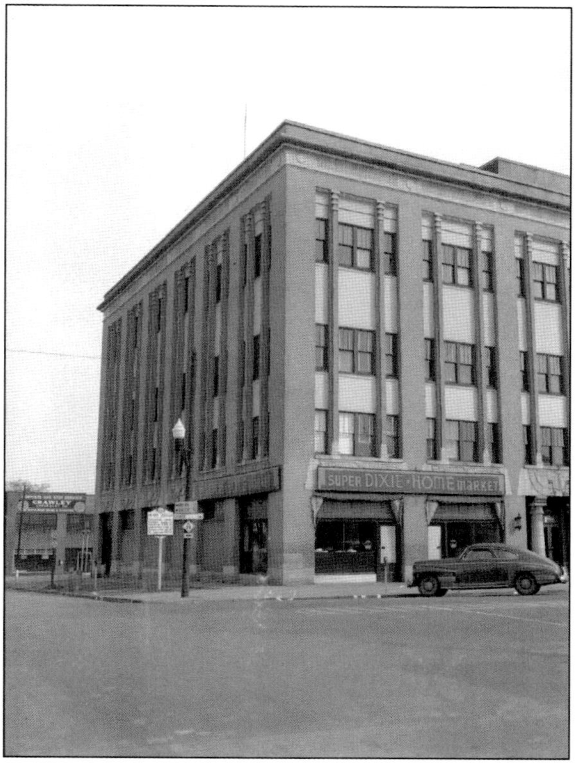

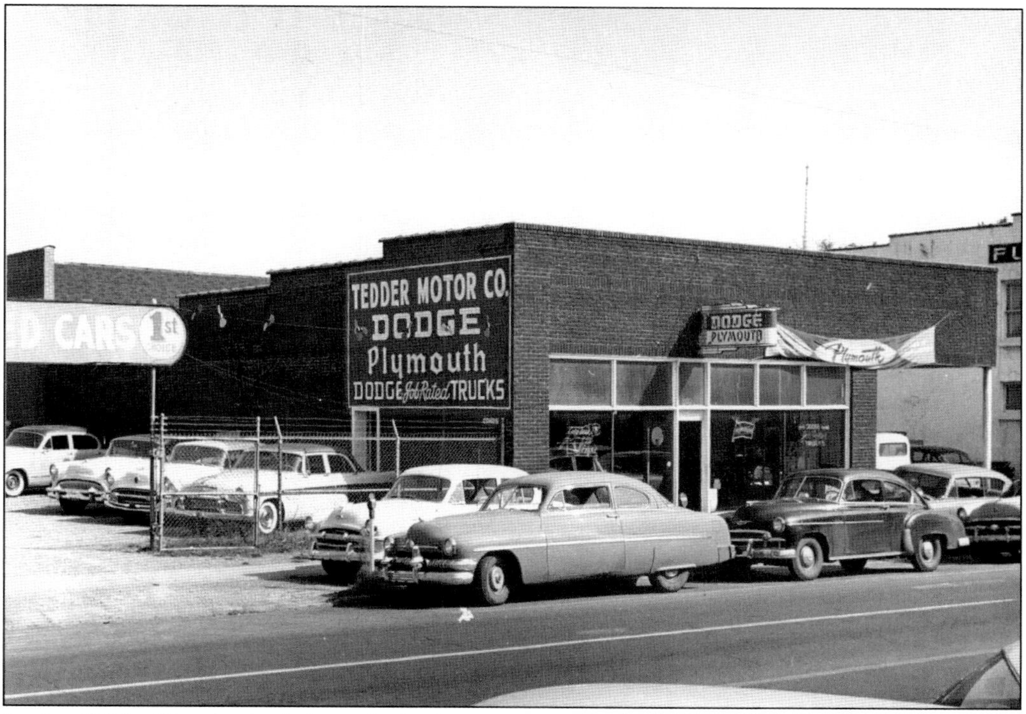

In the 1950s Chrysler had three dealerships in uptown Shelby. Each sold Plymouths and one other Chrysler product. Tedder Motors on South Washington Street sold Plymouth and Dodge. (Tommy Tedder.)

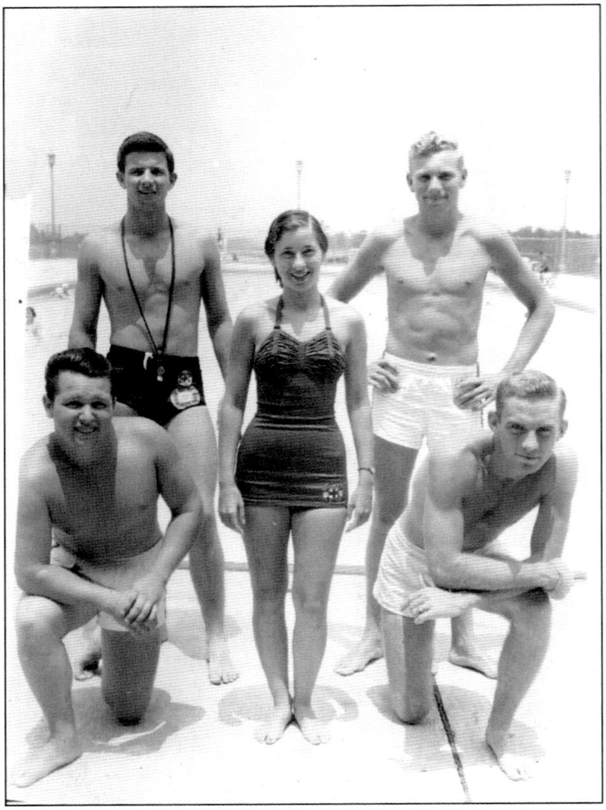

The City Park pool became a popular recreation site for Shelby's teenagers and youth in the 1950s. Five lifeguards pose in this 1951 picture. Kneeling, from left to right, are Jerry Neal and Robert Litton. Standing are Bob Brooks, Mary Anna Peck (Dunn), and Ben Davis. (Shelby Parks and Recreation.)

The City Park had attractions beyond the swimming pool in 1952. The Rotary Special pulls in to the station with a load of happy children and a few brave adults. After 30 years of service, the train was retired. The train has recently undergone an extensive renovation and is again delighting children of all ages. (City of Shelby Parks and Recreation.)

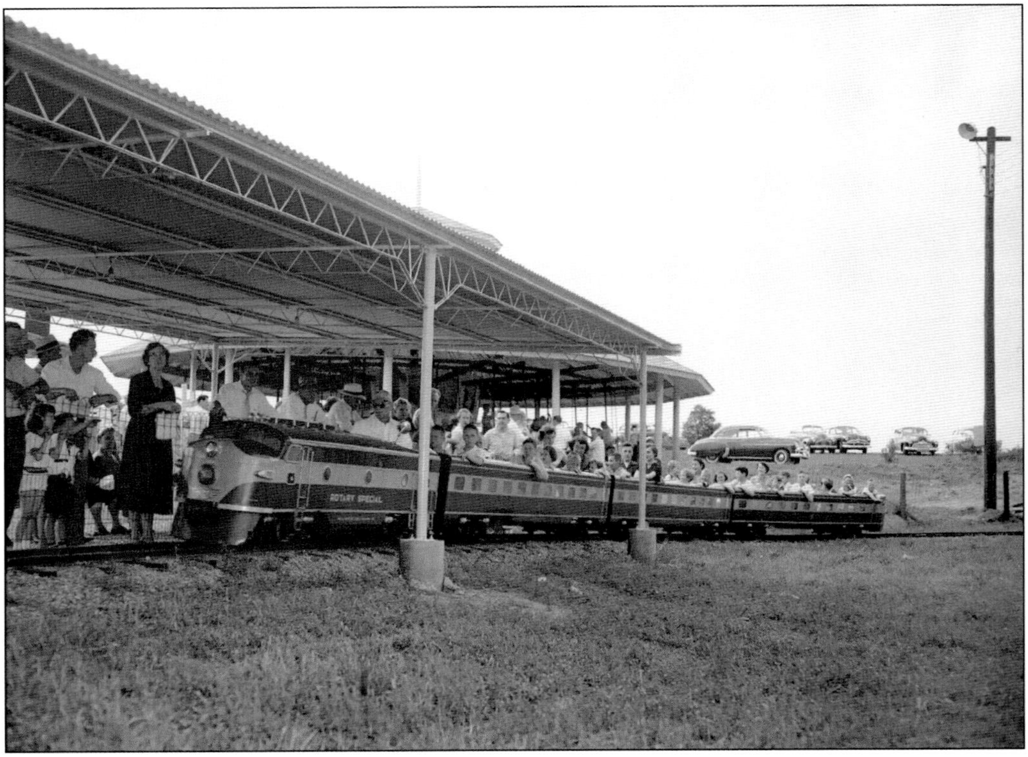

Former First National Bank President Ed Hamilton played football on the Georgia Tech freshman team. "Irish Eddie" once threw four touchdowns before almost 40,000 fans at Grant Field. Hamilton gave up football for academics and went on to a successful career in banking, *c.* 1952. (*The Star.*)

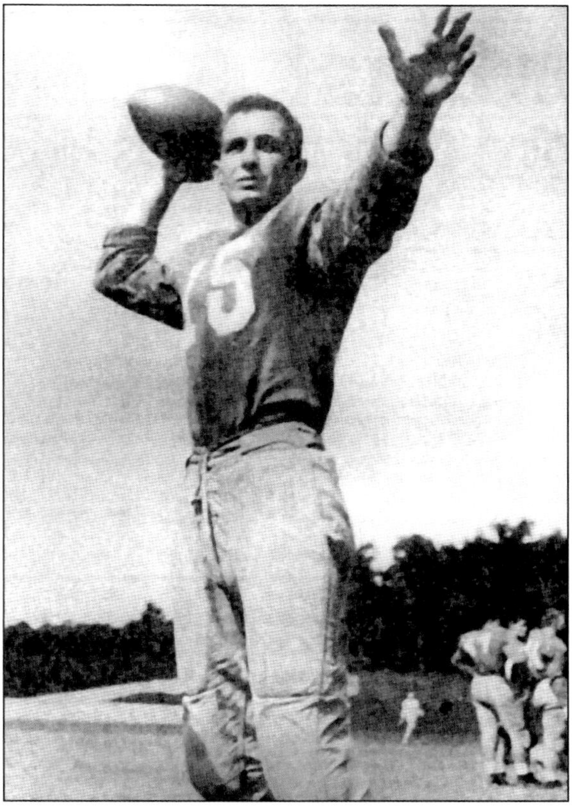

This Graham Elementary School football team of 1951 shows us the state of youth programs at that time. Notice that the uniforms are beginning to have some uniformity. Volunteer coaches came after school to drill young boys on less than perfect fields. (Shelby Parks and Recreation.)

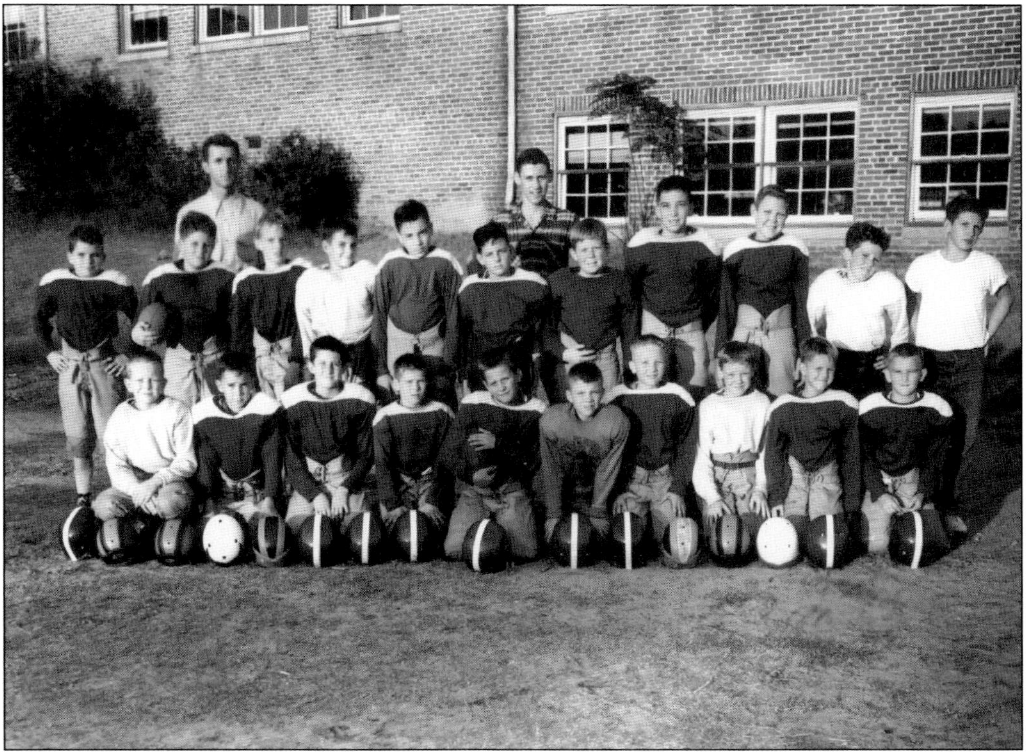

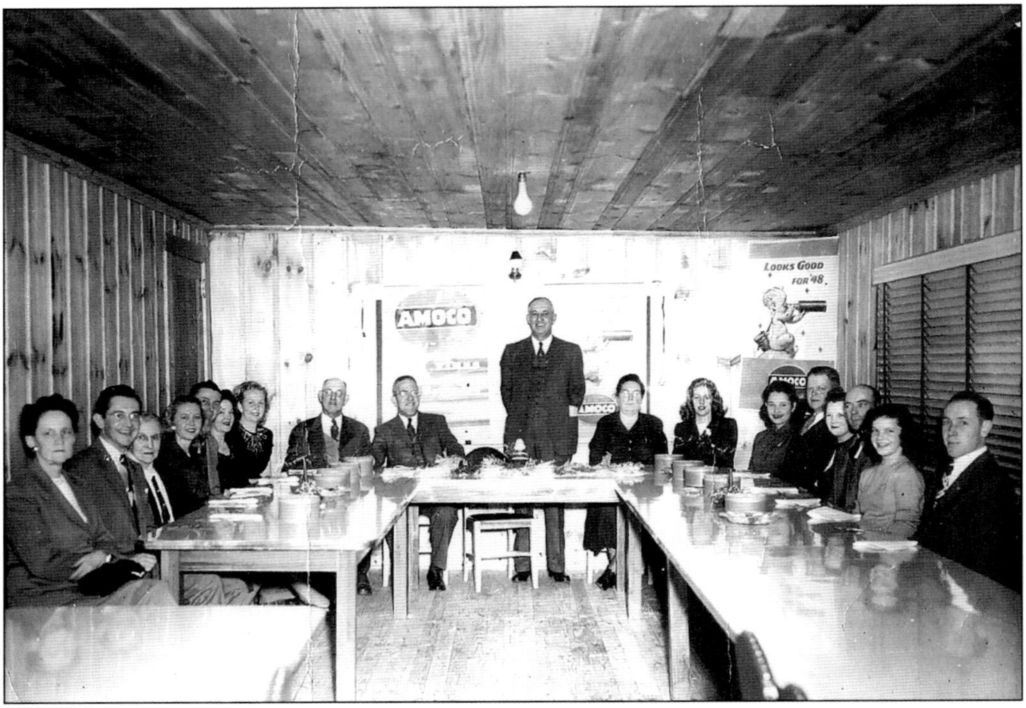

The Arey Oil Co. Christmas party of 1947 was attended by the following people, pictured from left to right: Catherine Arey, Robert J. Arey Sr., Virginia Washburn, Clayton Absher, an unidentified person, Mrs. Clayton Absher, Andrew Dellinger, Earl Hunnicutt, W.G. Arey Sr., Mrs. Andrew Dellinger, Sara Ellen Honeycutt Hamrick, Inez Conner, Hub Ellis, Vivian Ellis, Hoyt Adams, an unidentified person, and Dick Conner. (Robert Arey Sr.)

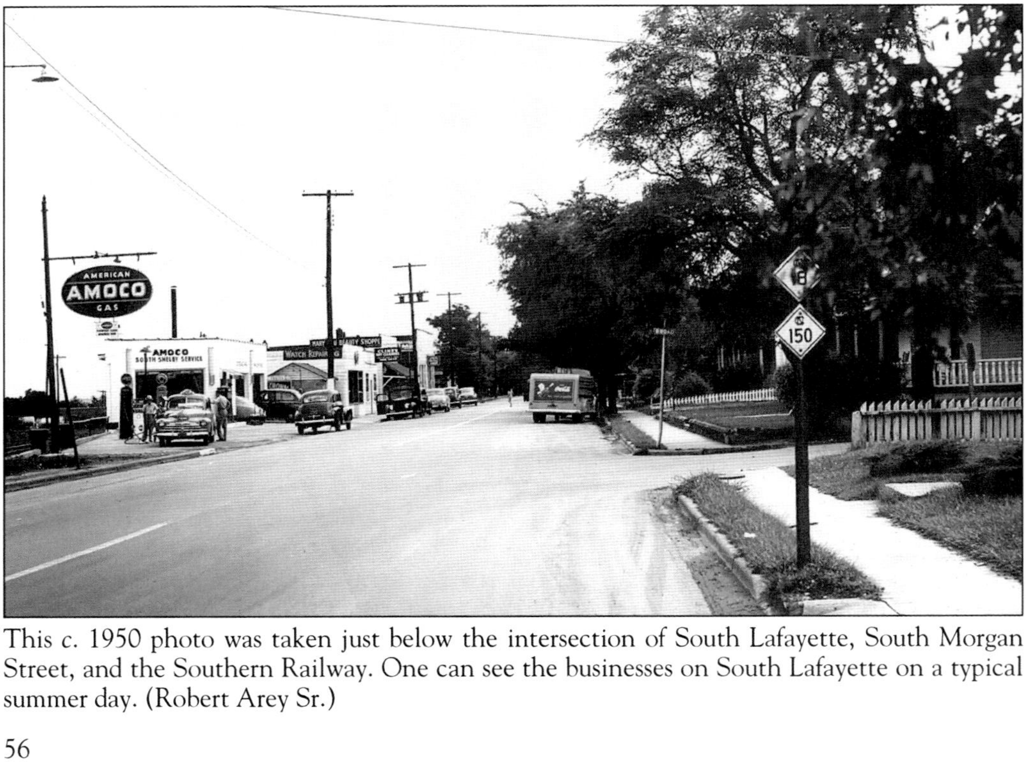

This *c.* 1950 photo was taken just below the intersection of South Lafayette, South Morgan Street, and the Southern Railway. One can see the businesses on South Lafayette on a typical summer day. (Robert Arey Sr.)

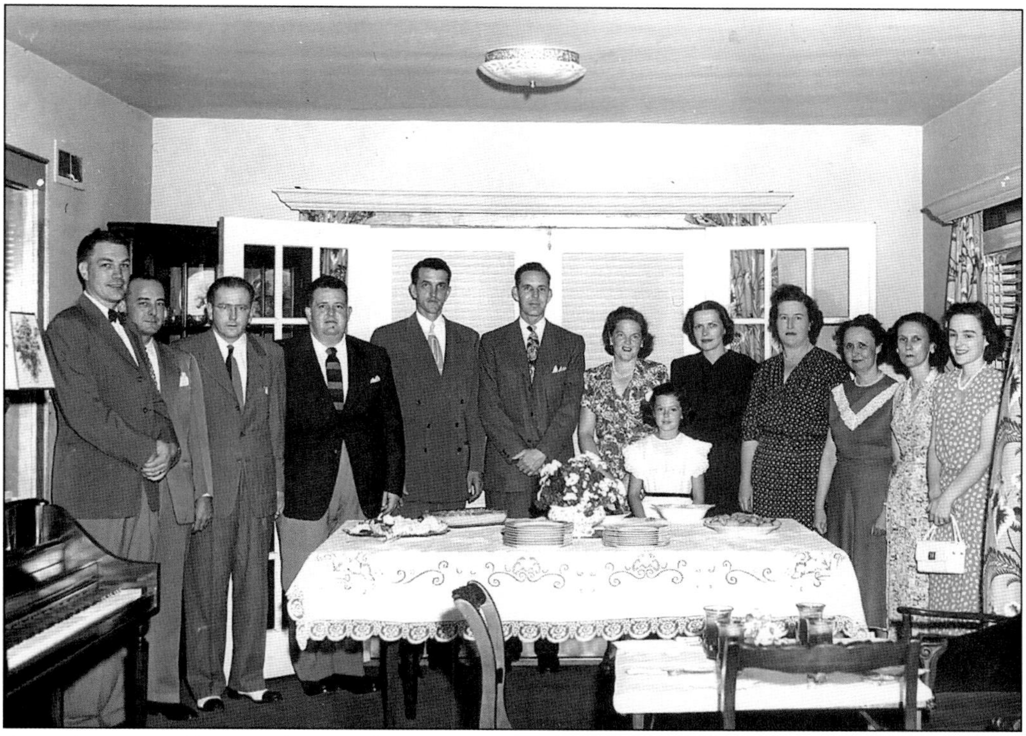

At mid-century, "having the preacher over" was common. Members of First Baptist Church are dining at the home of Fields and Ruth Young on West Graham Street with the pastor and the revival speaker. Pictured from left to right are Rev. Harlan Harris, an unidentified person, Jody Welch, Carl Hand, H. Fields Young Jr., Rev. Robert Stanley, Ruth Young, Sally Young Barker, Mrs. Stanley, Louise Hand, Janie Wray, an unidentified person, and Madelyn Harris. (H. Fields Young III.)

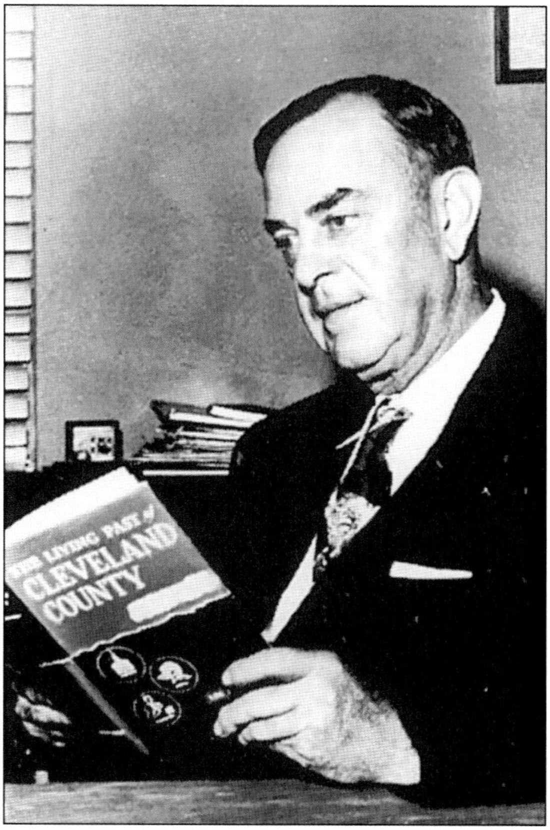

One of Shelby's leading figures until his death in 1958 was Lee B. Weathers. Weathers owned the *Shelby Daily Star* for well over 40 years. He was also an associate of Shelby's leading political figures and served several terms in the state senate.

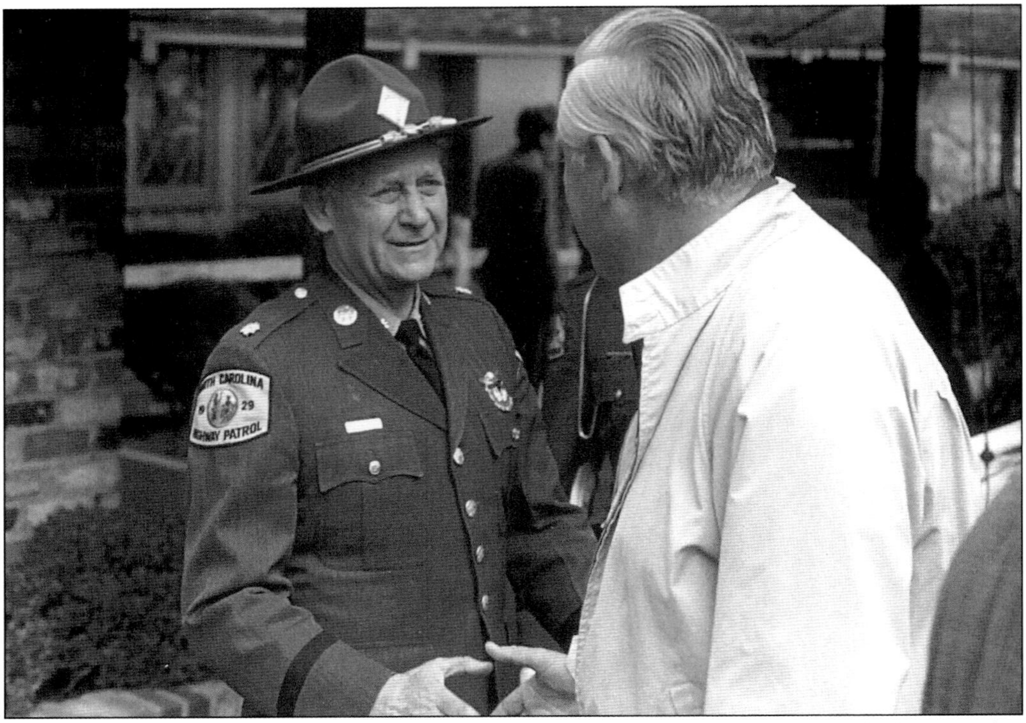

A familiar face in the law enforcement during the 1950s was Sgt. J.B. Kuykendall who spent his career with the North Carolina Highway Patrol. (Peggy Kuykendall Conlan.)

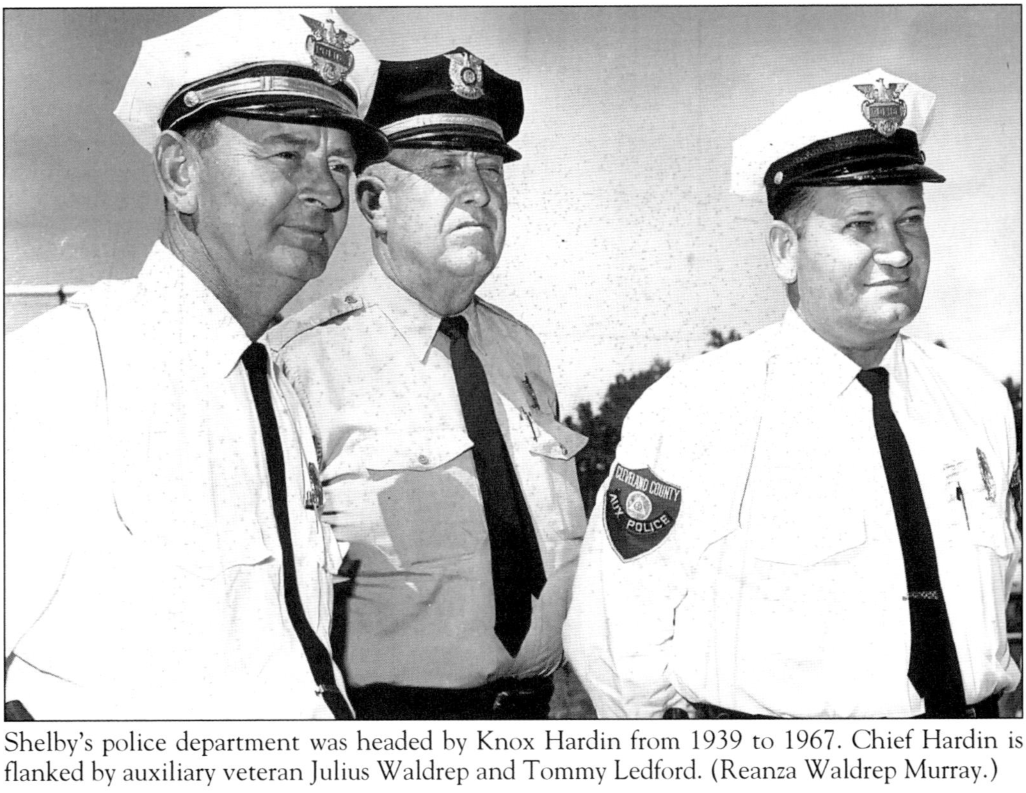

Shelby's police department was headed by Knox Hardin from 1939 to 1967. Chief Hardin is flanked by auxiliary veteran Julius Waldrep and Tommy Ledford. (Reanza Waldrep Murray.)

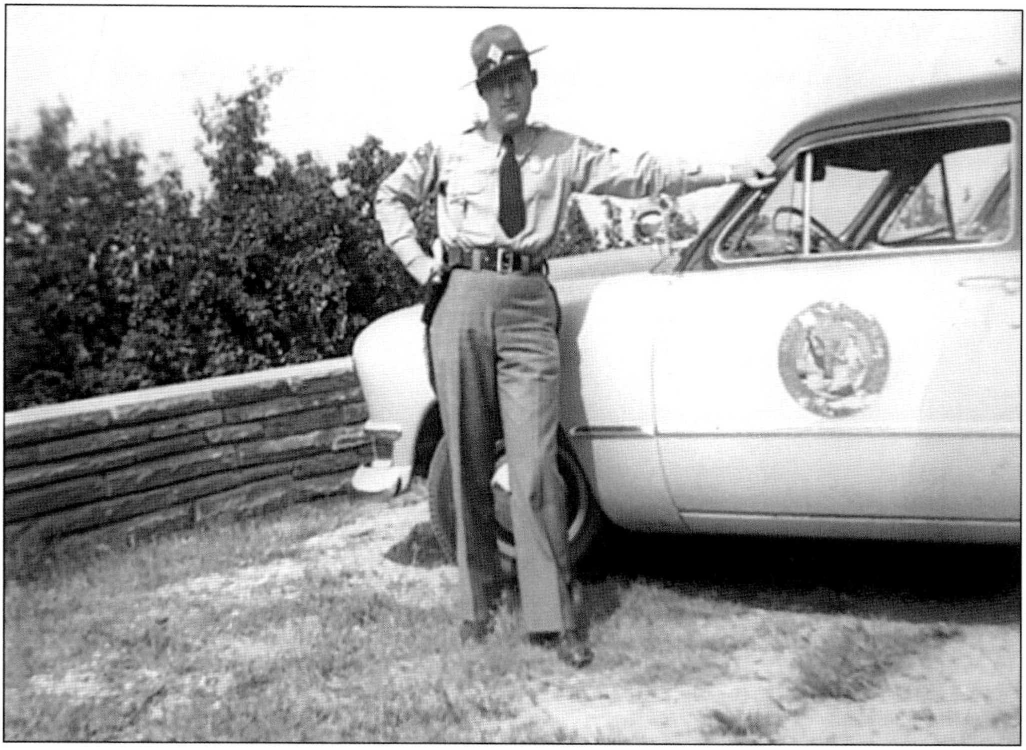

North Carolina highway patrolman E.T. VanHoy was stationed in Cleveland County for half of his 38-year career. Retired, Sergeant VanHoy entertains as the magician Hoy Toy. (E.T. VanHoy Family.)

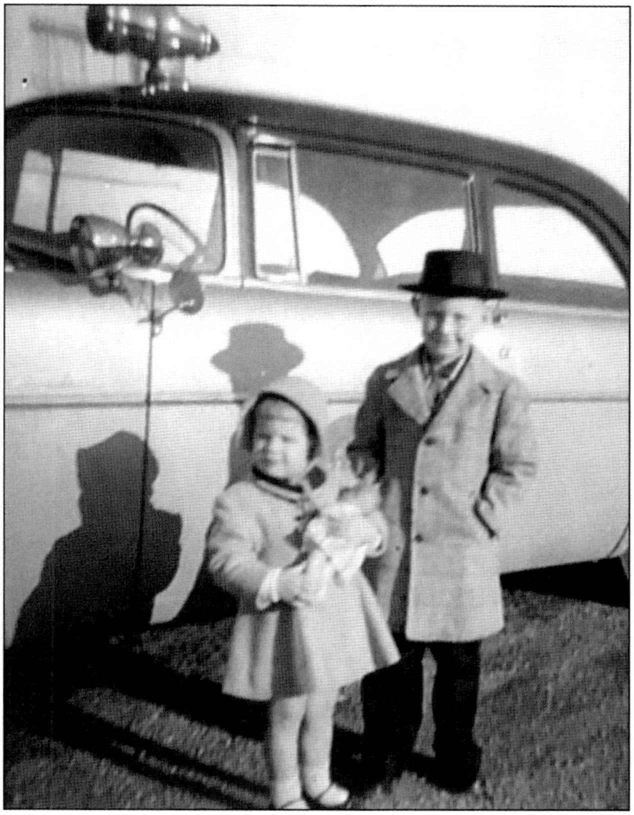

VanHoy's children, Charlie and Jane, are seen in this *c.* 1958 picture. Charlie followed his father into law enforcement. In 1995, Charlie returned home to become Shelby's chief of police. (E.T. VanHoy Family.)

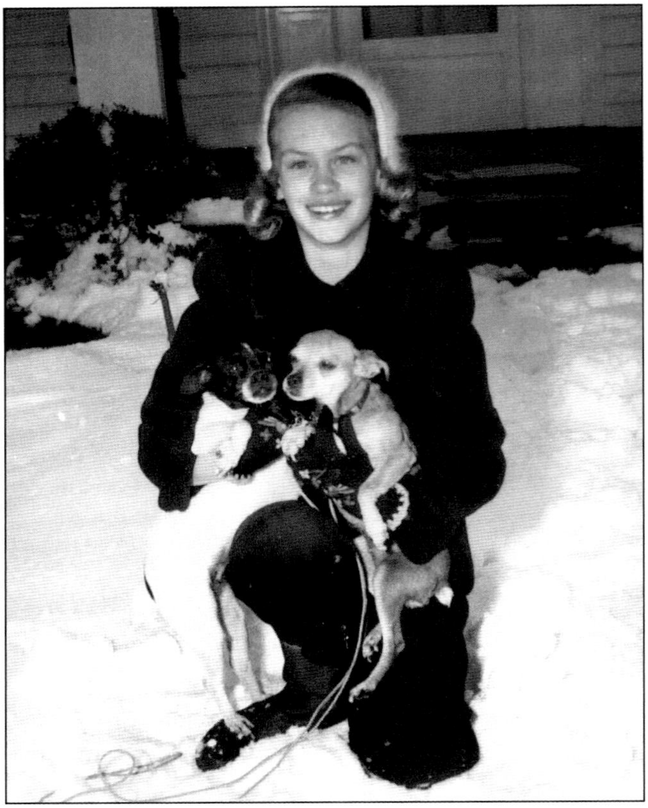

In 1954, Charles and Mary Adelaide Austell built a new home on West Marion Street. Their daughter Adelaide is pictured with two puppies on a snowy winter day. Adelaide became Cleveland County's first female attorney and today is CEO of First National Bank. (Adelaide Austell Craver.)

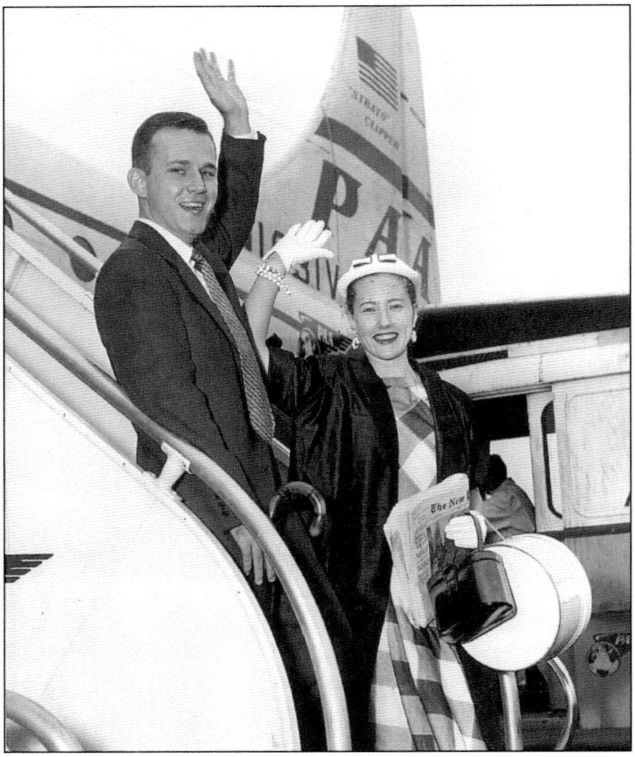

Newlyweds Harvey and Kathleen Dover Hamrick board a Pan Am flight in New York bound for Bermuda in June of 1954. (Harvey Hamrick Jr.)

Small businesses operated throughout Shelby. Waldrep's Florist was operated by Julius and Ponder Reba Waldrep. Julius is pictured here completing a six-foot cross—a mark of the quality design work they were known for producing. (Reanza Waldrep Murray.)

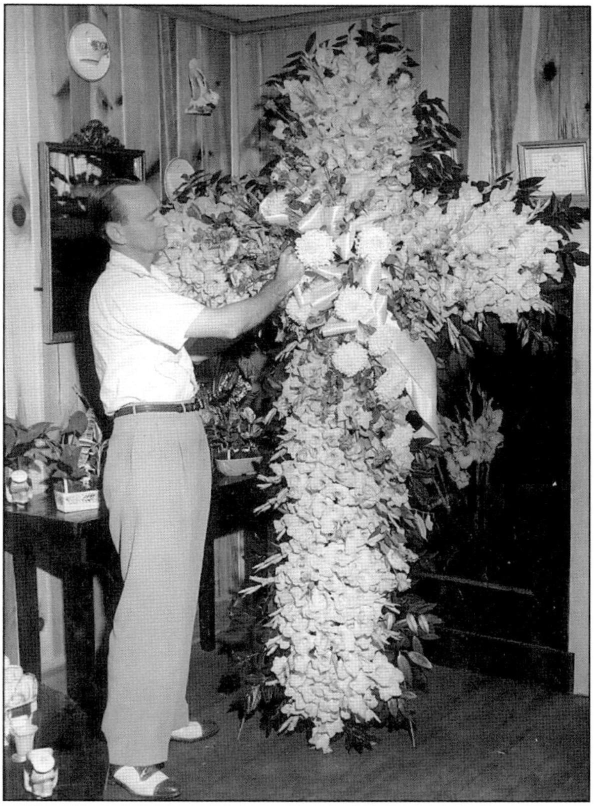

Ernest Spangler built a concrete business at the railroad on West Graham and South Morgan Streets. This 1950s shot shows his two sons, Pat and Bud, who continued the business. (Eloise Spangler.)

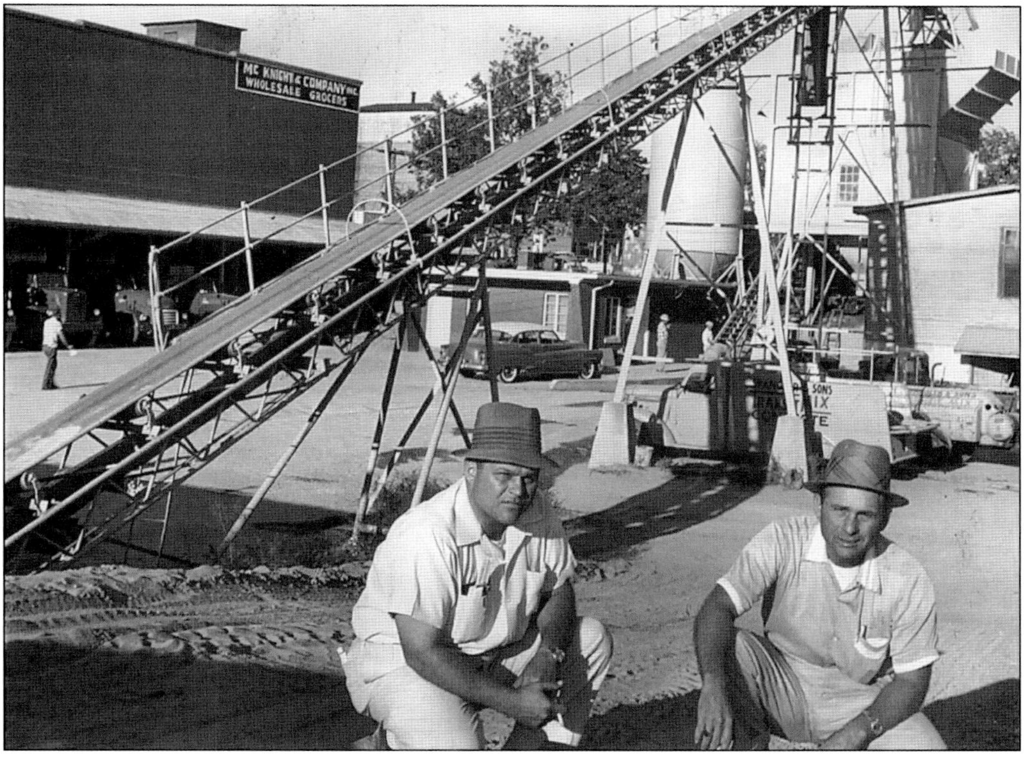

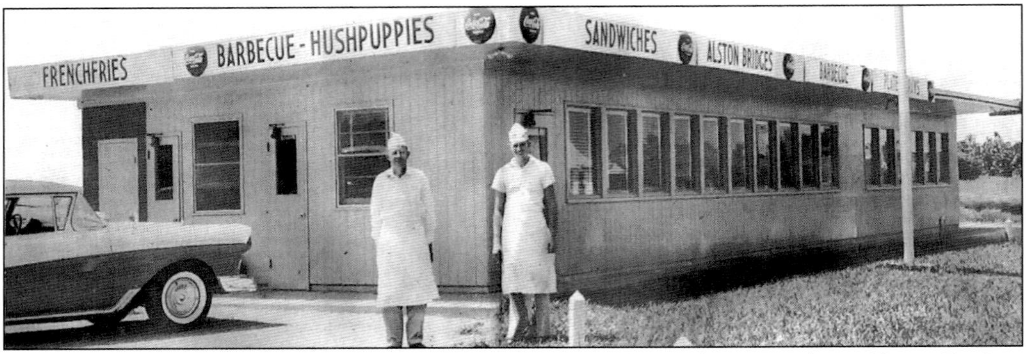

Shelby gained another popular barbecue restaurant in the mid-1950s when Alston Bridges returned to Shelby and opened a store on Grover Street. Here, Alston and his son Kent pose with the restaurant behind them. (Alston Bridges Family.)

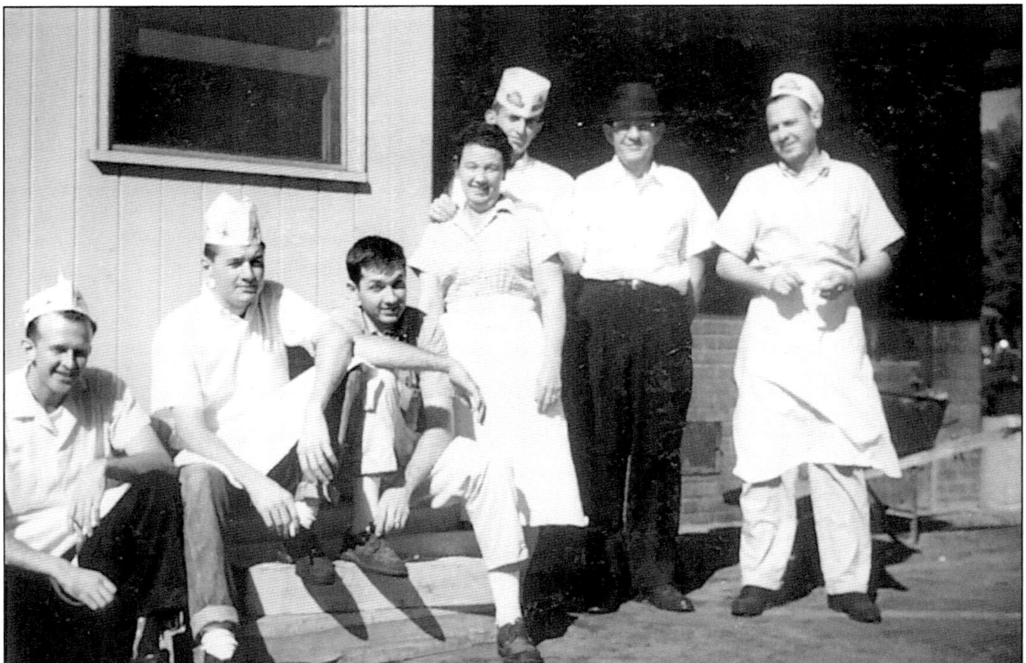

The cooking crew pauses for a photo behind Alston Bridges Barbecue. From left to right are Howard Granger, Don Bridges, Milton Bridges, Mabel Bridges, Kent Bridges, Alston Bridges, and Bob Bridges. (Alston Bridges Family.)

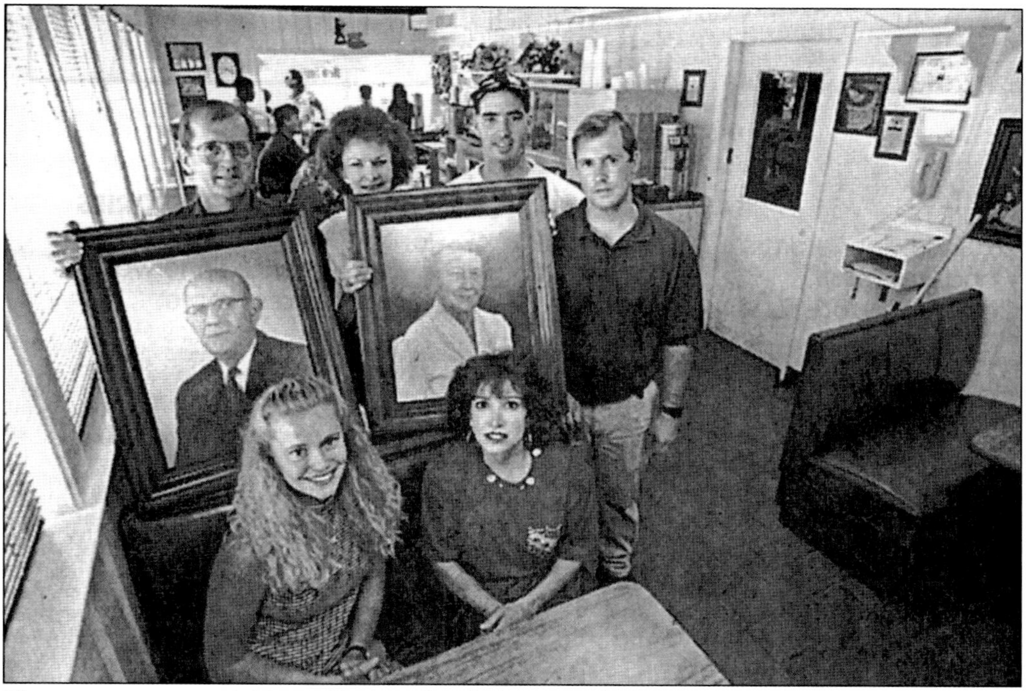

Three generations of Alston Bridges family have worked in the family business on Grover Street. In the portraits are founders Alston and Mabel Bridges. Kent and Linda pose with their children Jay, Reid, Michelle, and Laura. (Alston Bridges Family.)

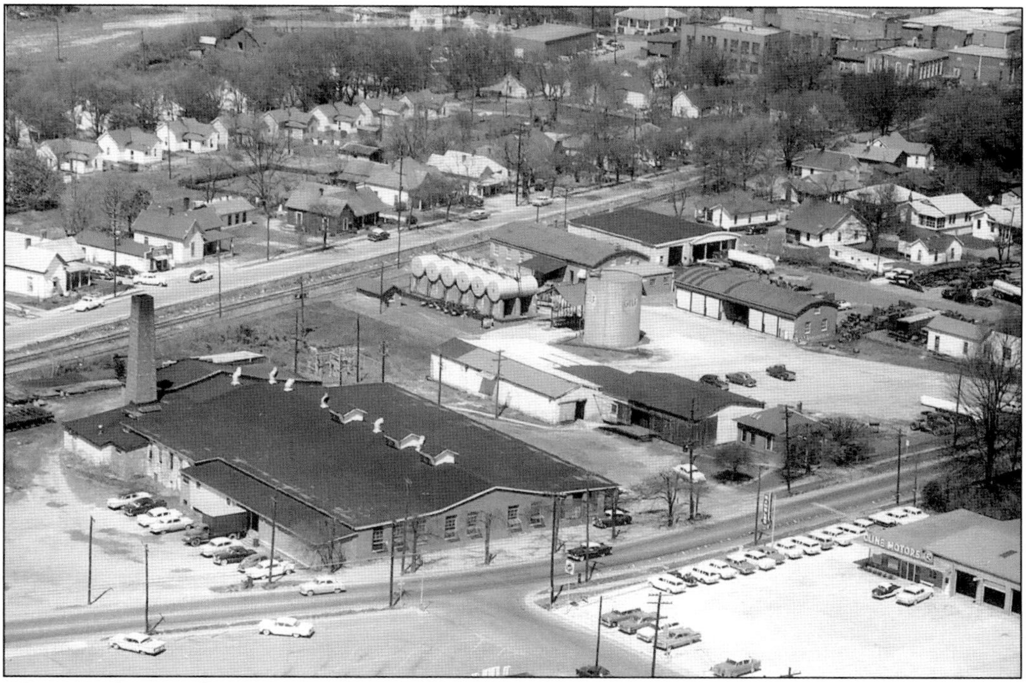

This aerial view shows the Neisler Belmont Mill located next to Royster Oil Co. on South Lafayette Street. In the background is the Shelby Cotton Mill on South Morgan Street and a portion of the mill village. (C.E. Neisler Family.)

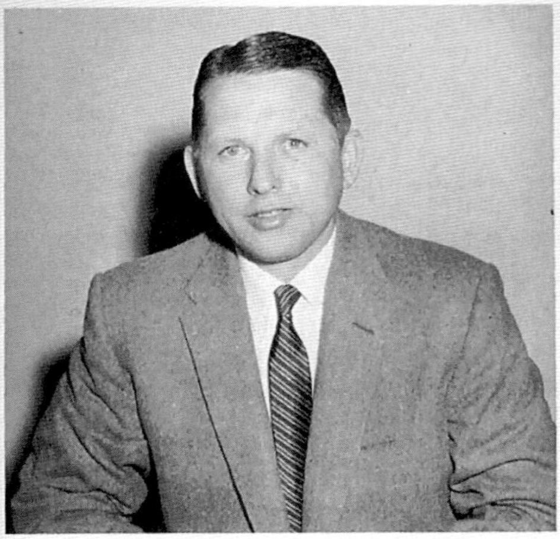

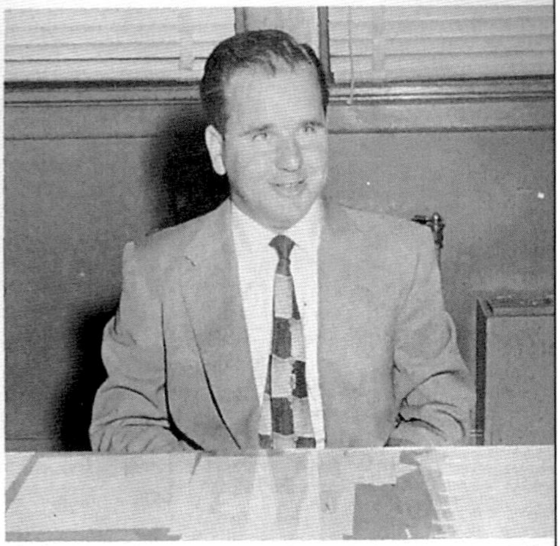

Mr. Malcolm Brown
Superintendent

Mr. Wayne Caudill
Principal

School Board: Mr. Cecil Gilliatt, Mr. Vernon Kiser, Mr. Paris Yelton, Mr. Hazel Howard, Mr. B. P. Sherer.

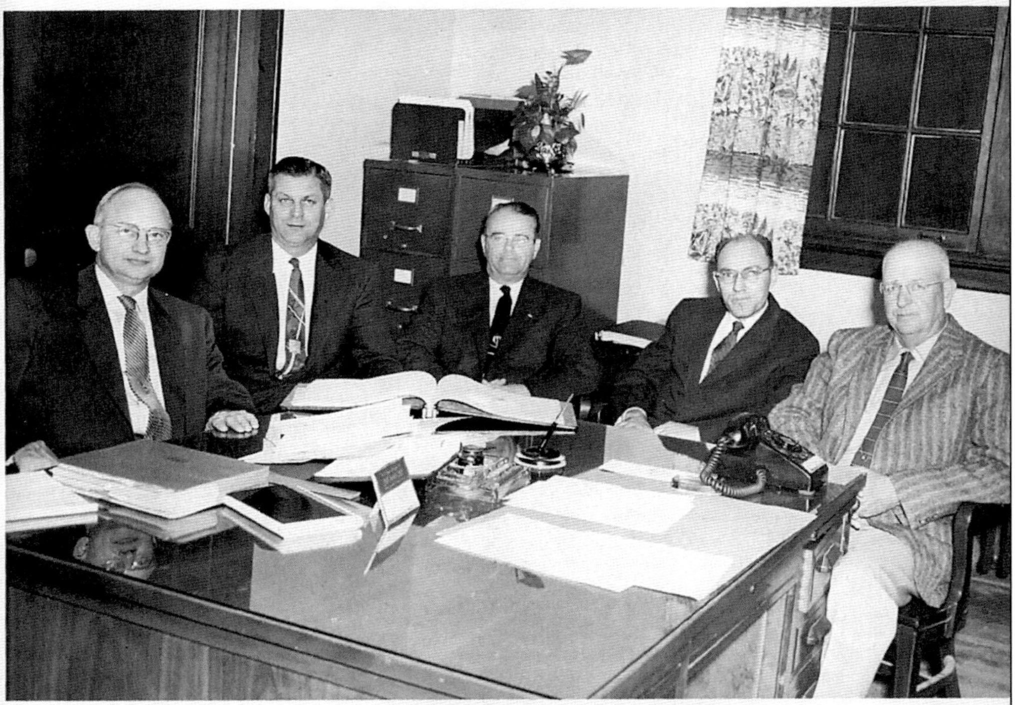

Shelby prided itself in having an excellent school system in the 1950s. Part of this excellence resulted from good leadership. Each school board member in this 1957 picture was a civic and business leader. Malcolm Brown and Wayne Caudill built a solid reputation based on their work and dedication to excellence in education. (Shelby High School.)

A generation of Shelby High students remembers this teacher, coach, and friend with love and respect. They called him Mr. Allen in class and Coach on the field, but he was always known as "Pearly." Coach Gerald Allen grew up in Shelby and graduated from UNC-Chapel Hill. He spent his career teaching and molding students and athletes. In 22 years as head football coach, he never had a losing season. (Shelby High School.)

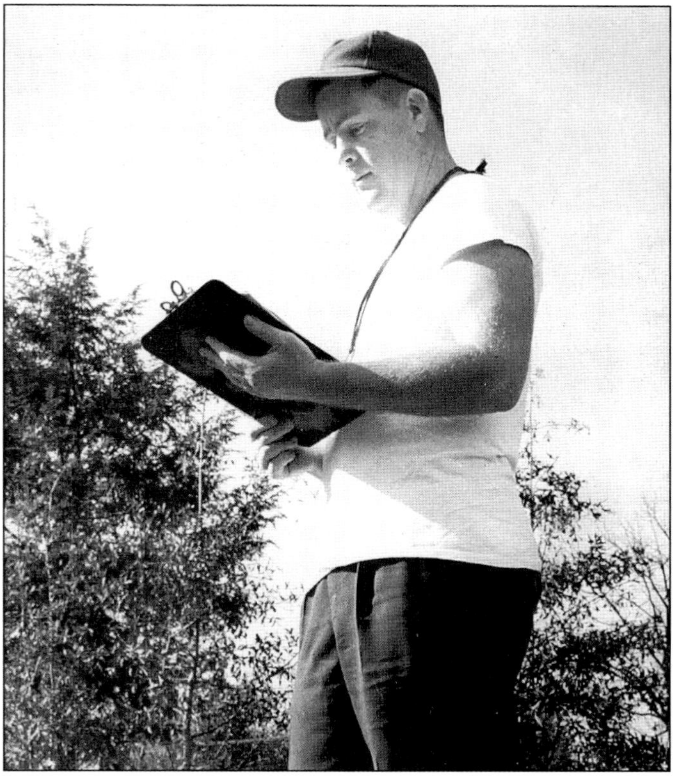

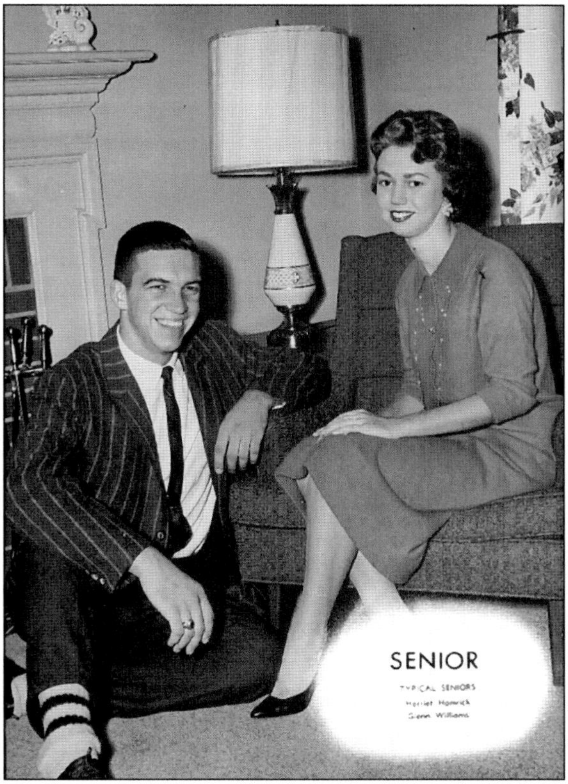

High school annuals regularly pictured senior superlatives. Categories covered things such as best dressed, most intelligent, best looking, and wittiest. The Shelby High class of 1959 chose Harriet Hamrick and Glenn Williams as "typical seniors." Glenn played football for Pearly Allen. These typical seniors married and live in Boiling Springs today. (Shelby High School.)

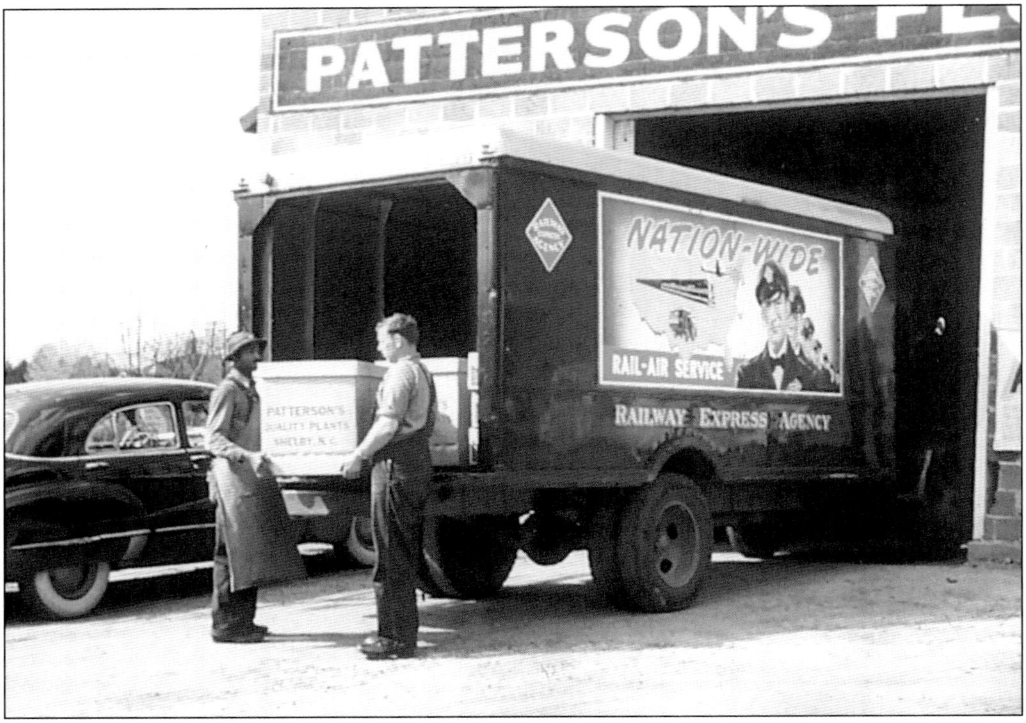

For over 60 years Patterson's Flowers was one of the largest commercial flower growers in the nation. They shipped live plants throughout the Southeast.

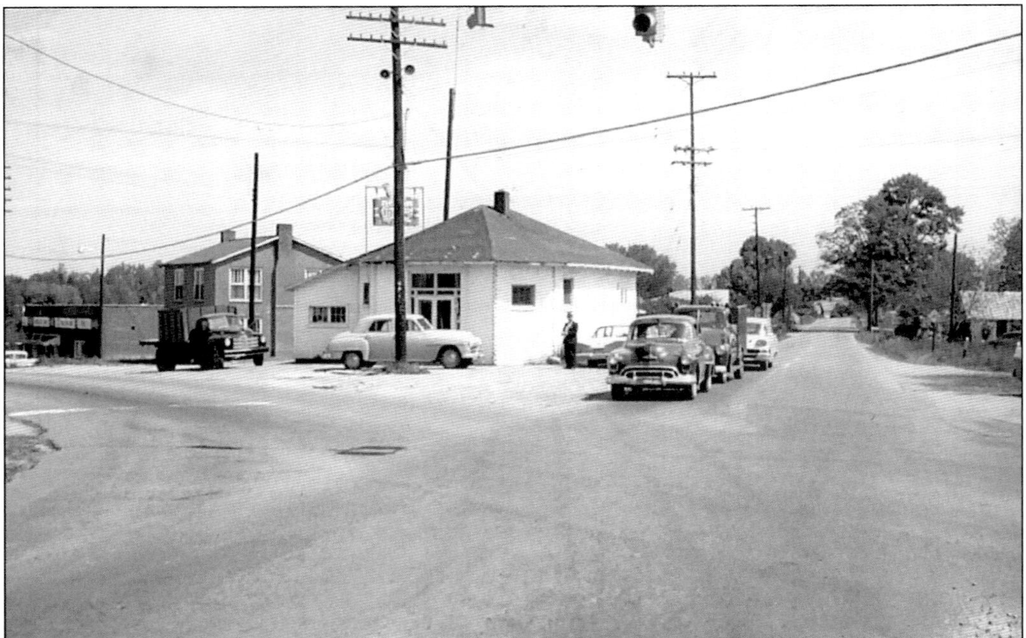

Dr. L. Gene Yarboro has practiced veterinary medicine for 51 years in Shelby with the assistance of his wife Margaret. This 1950s photo shows the first location for Cleveland Veterinary Hospital at the intersection of North Post Road and East Marion Street. (Gene and Margaret Yarboro.)

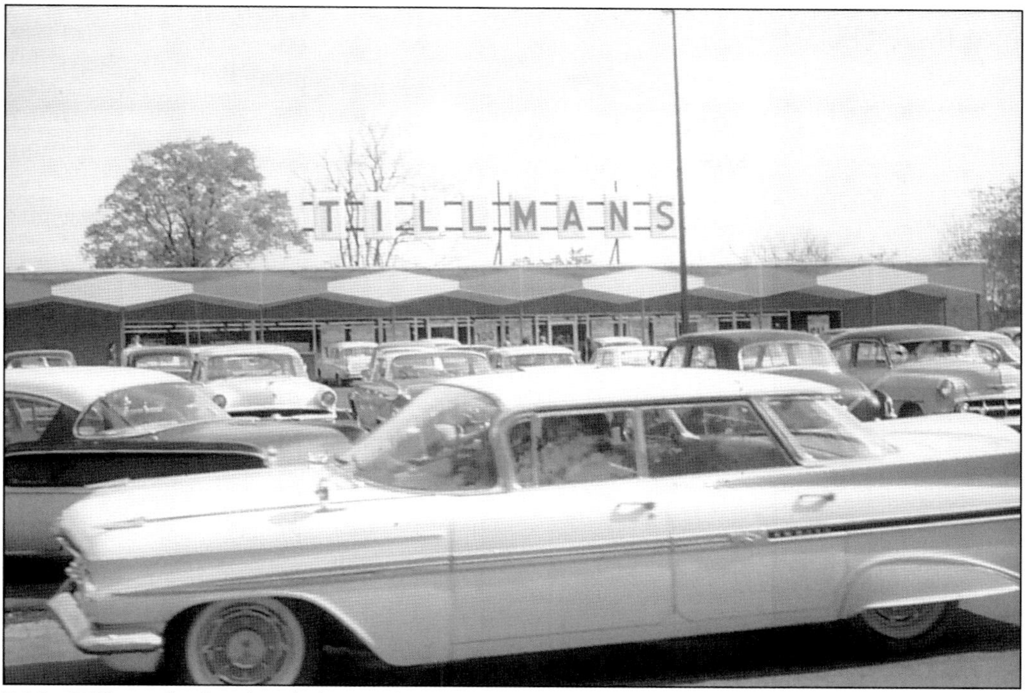

Eddie Tillman built a local chain of supermarkets with six stores, four in Shelby. In time, he sold the business to the Harris Teeter chain. This *c.* 1960 store was on Suttle Street near the intersection with East Marion Street. (Gene and Margaret Yarboro.)

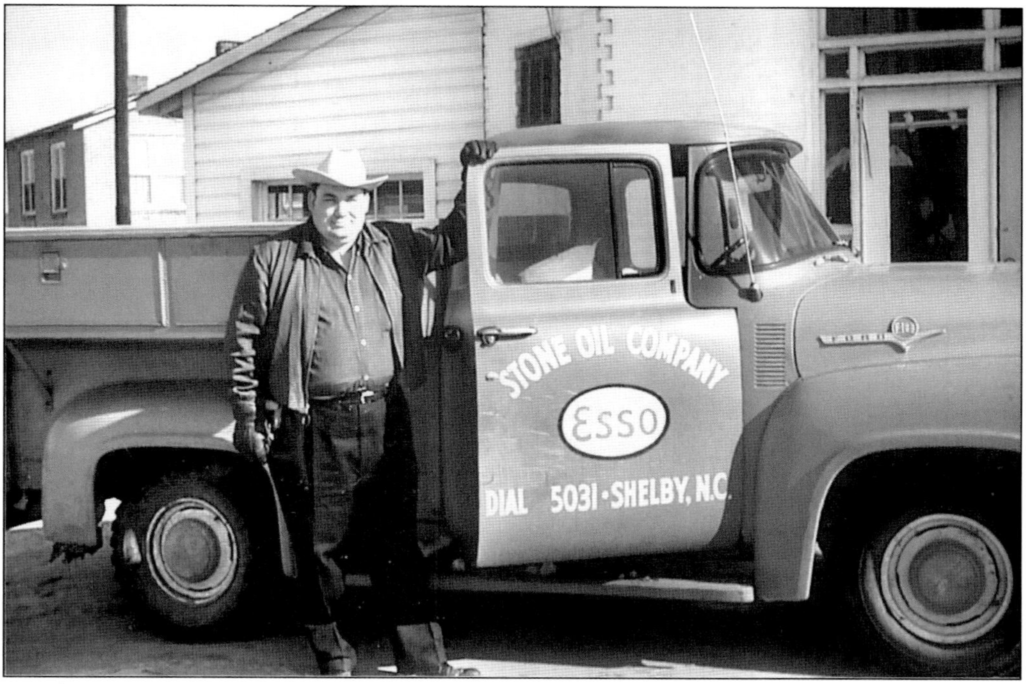

Another local business was Stone Oil Co., which served as the distributor for Esso gasoline. Bobby Stone is pictured beside his truck in the mid-1950s in front of Cleveland Veterinary Hospital. (Gene and Margaret Yarboro.)

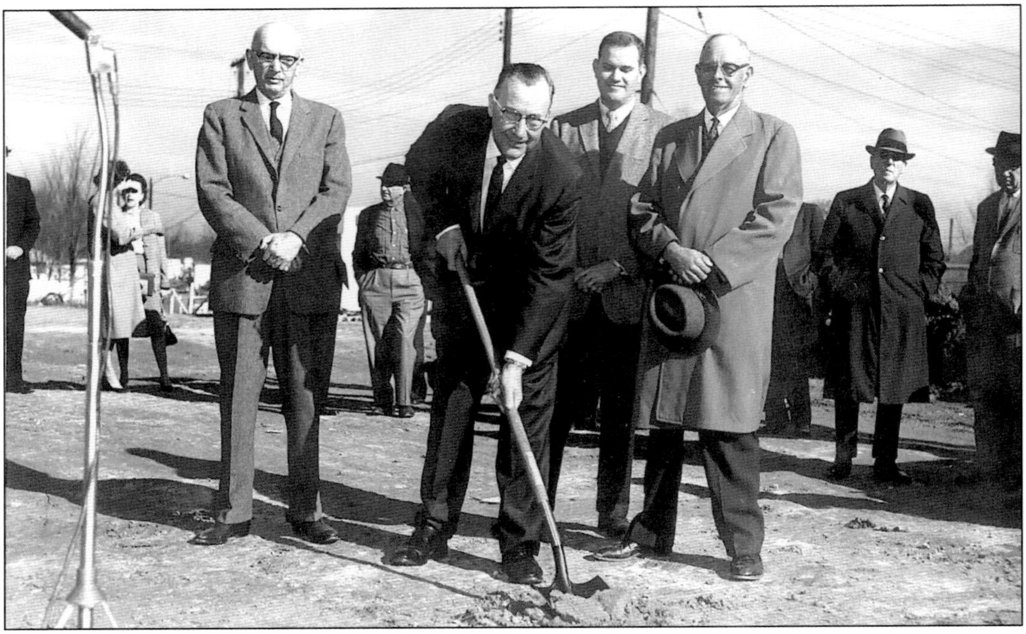

One of Shelby's two banks in 1961 was Union Trust Co. The old Webb Theater at the corner of East Marion and North Washington Streets was torn down to make room for Union Trust's new headquarters. Pictured at the groundbreaking, from left to right, are J.L. Lutz (bank president), Clyde Stutts, Edwin Ford, an unidentified person, Rev. Zeno Wall, and Floyd Farris. (Edwin and Esther Anne Ford.)

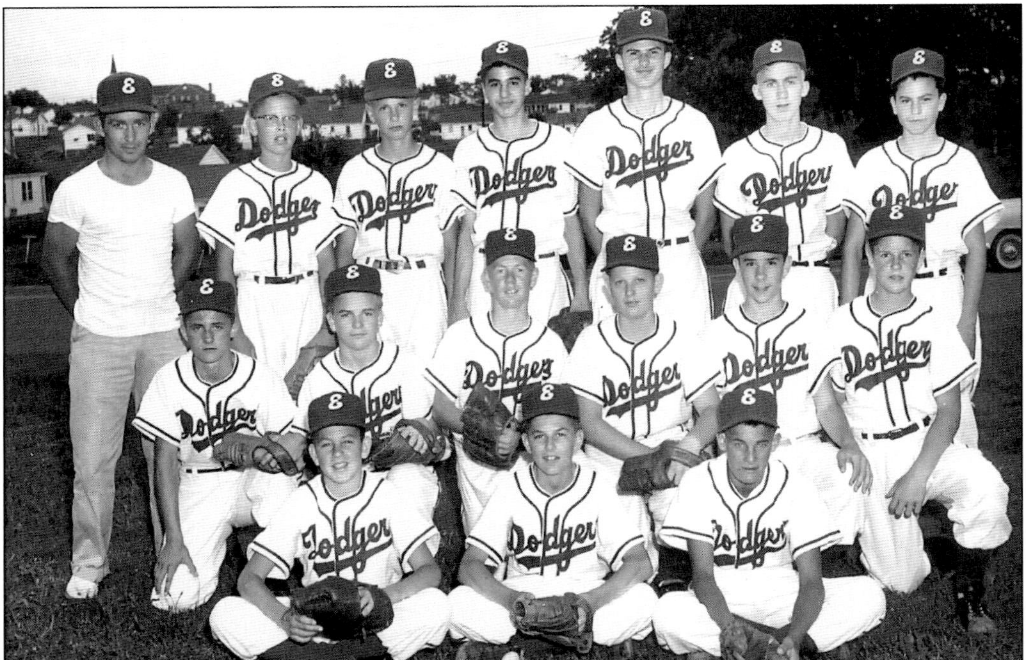

Businesses and civic groups sponsored teams and provided uniforms. This mid-1950s team included Charles Tucker, Don Loftis, John Kouri, Art Moss, and Robert Camp. (Uptown Shelby Association.)

One of Western North Carolina's favorite sons is the famous Billy Graham. Billy and his wife Ruth pose on one of their visits to Cleveland County with Bridges Barbecue owner Red Bridges. (Debbie Bridges Webb.)

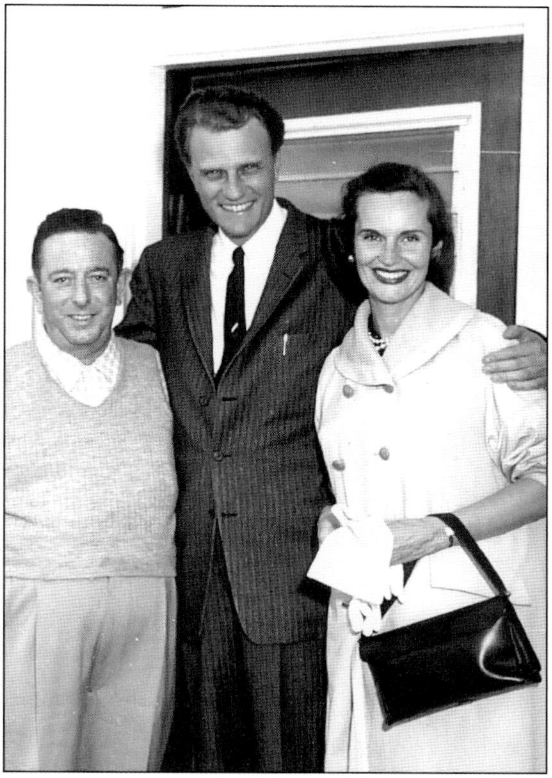

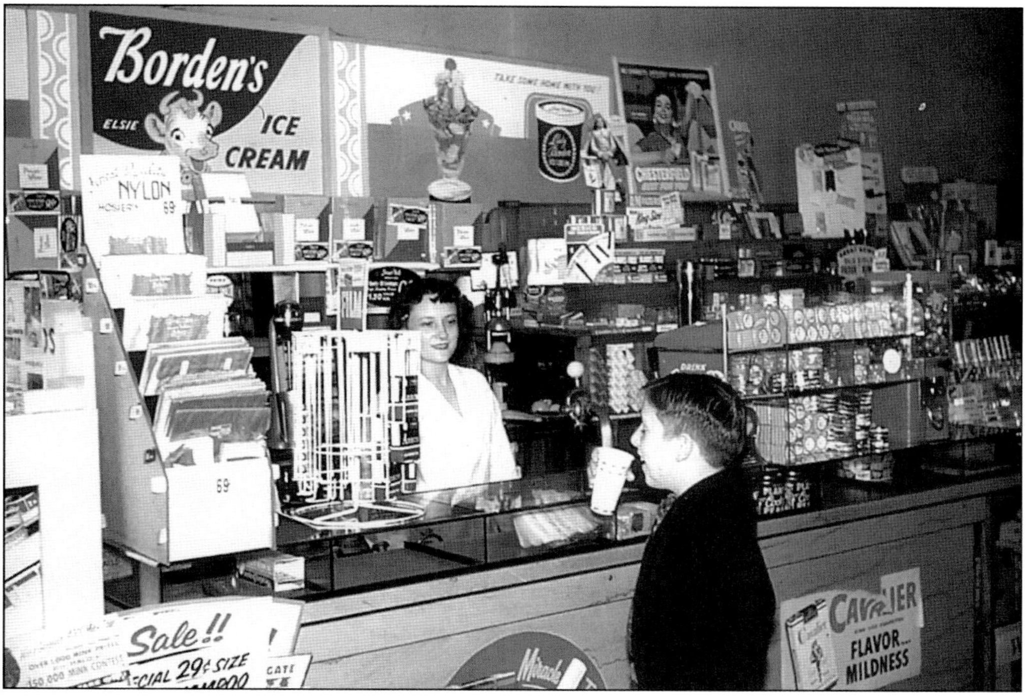

In the 1950s, Shelby had five uptown drug stores. All were locally owned. The Shelby Drug Store was on the first floor in the old Doctors Building on South Washington Street. It was typical for them to have a soda fountain and serve ice cream. (Uptown Shelby Association.)

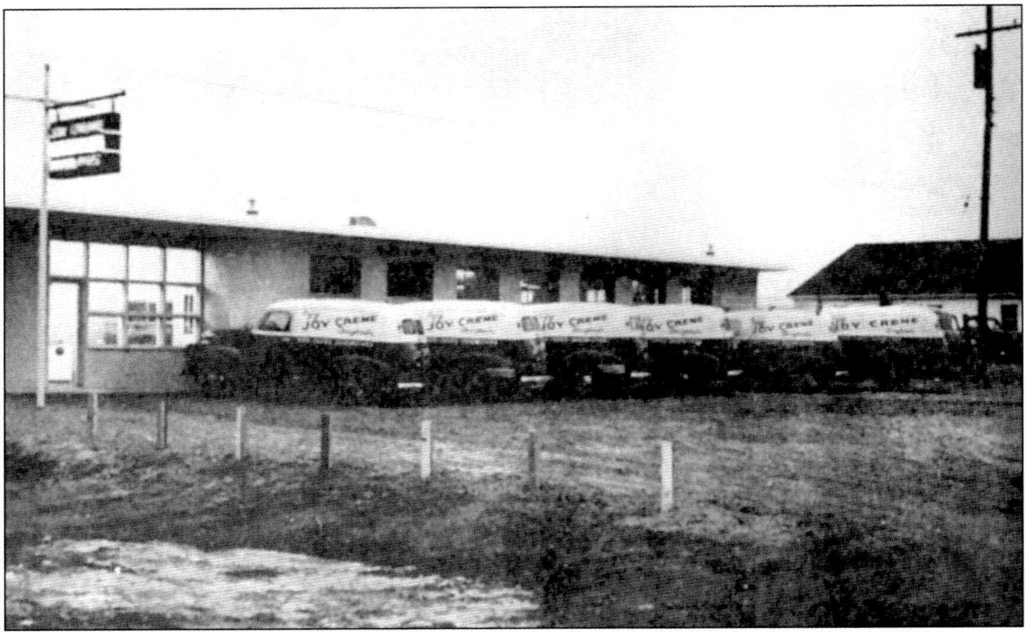

Before Krispy Kreme took the market, Shelby had its own successful doughnut bakery. The Joy Crème Doughnut Co. was established by brothers Ralph and Charles Walters in 1950. With a fleet of 15 delivery vans, the company produced and distributed doughnuts and fried pies throughout the western Carolinas for over 25 years. (Susan Walters Martin.)

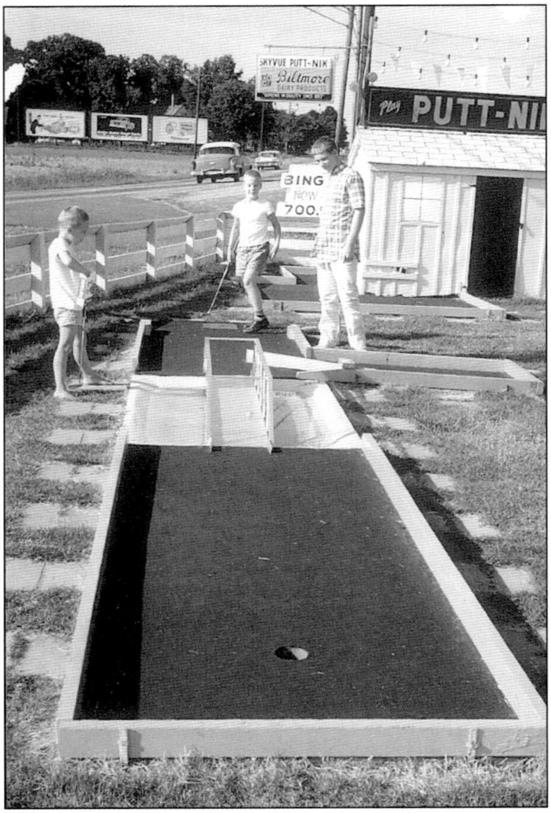

The Putt Nik miniature golf course was a part of the attractions at Sky-Vue Drive-In in South Shelby. Jimmy Yarboro putts as brothers Tommy and Robert look on. (Gene and Margaret Yarboro.)

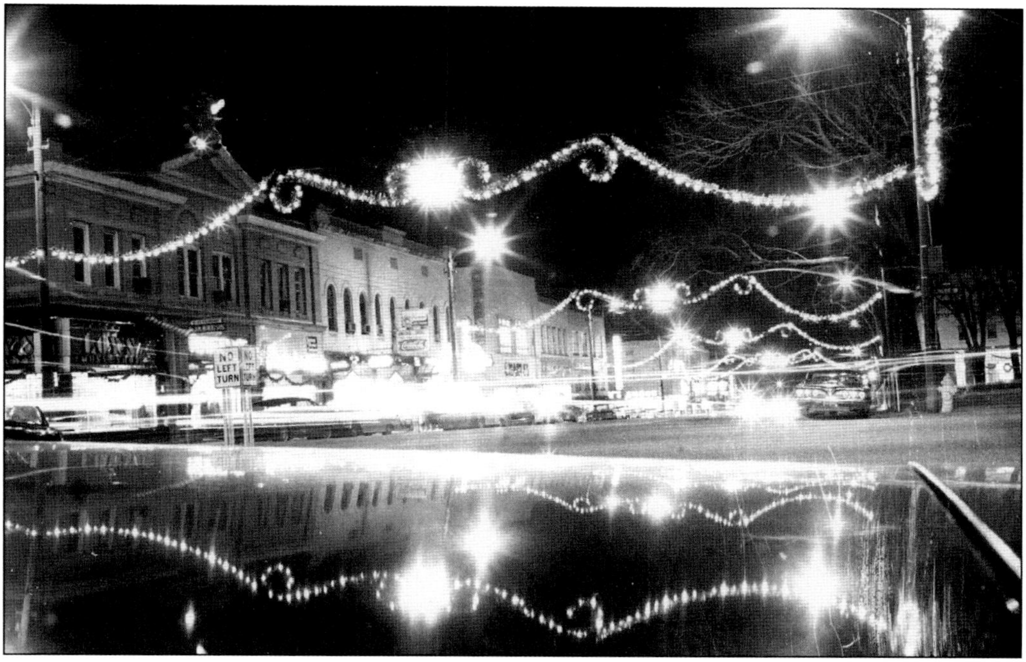

For years, uptown Shelby had these Christmas lights around the court square. In the days before shopping malls, people flocked to the uptown stores in this decorative atmosphere. (City of Shelby.)

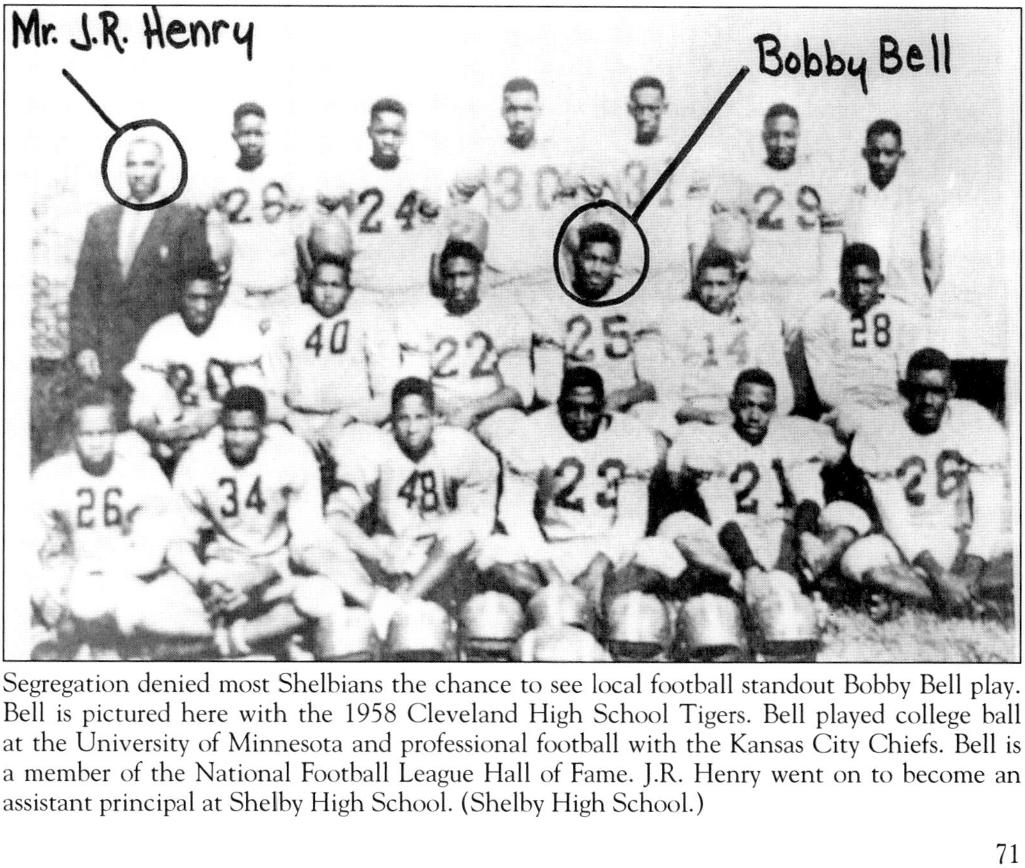

Segregation denied most Shelbians the chance to see local football standout Bobby Bell play. Bell is pictured here with the 1958 Cleveland High School Tigers. Bell played college ball at the University of Minnesota and professional football with the Kansas City Chiefs. Bell is a member of the National Football League Hall of Fame. J.R. Henry went on to become an assistant principal at Shelby High School. (Shelby High School.)

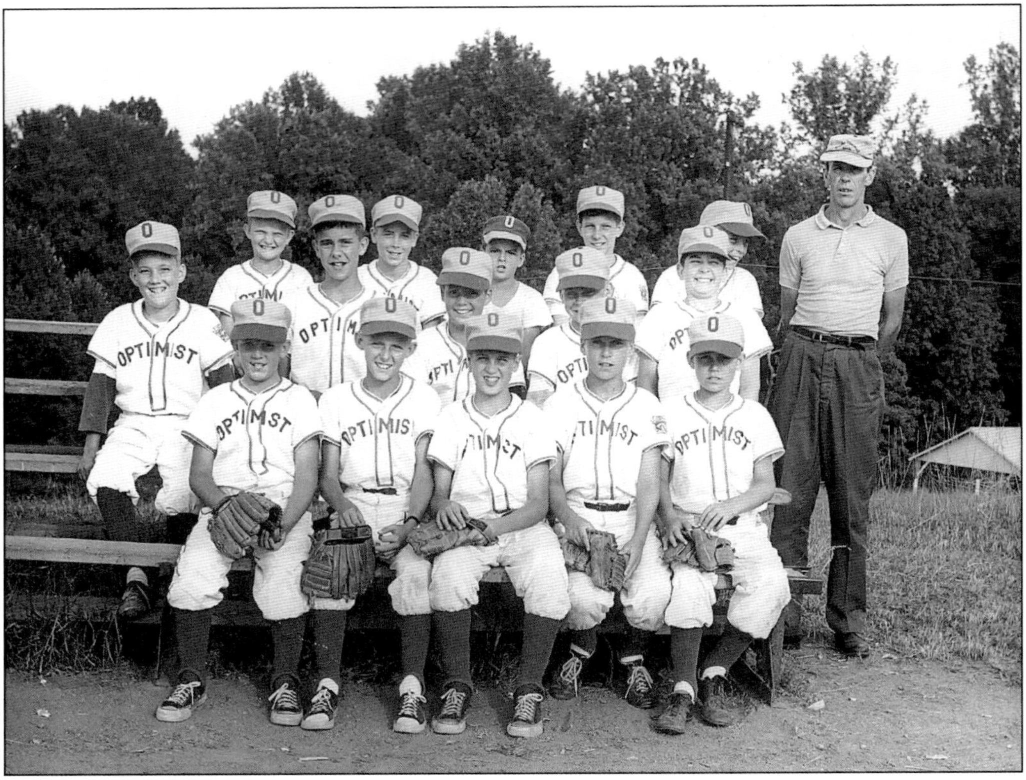

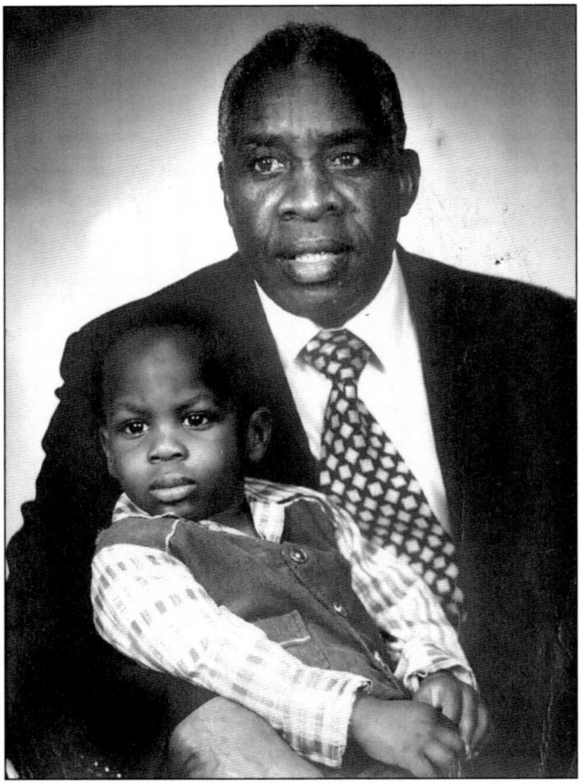

The 1965 Shelby Optimist Little League baseball team poses for this pre-game photo. From left to right are (front row) David Lynn, Eddie Sisk, Charles Matheson, Ed Gantt, and Larry Lane; (middle row) Donnie Bridges, Randy Creswell, Mike Holman, Mike Jackson, and Mike Hilton; (back row) Gary Patterson, Steve Boatwright, Mark Hamrick, Mike Huntsinger, Richard Ivey, and Coach Bill Lynn. (David Lynn.)

Rev. Sam Raper has served as leader in Shelby for decades. Reverend Raper has served as minister of Mount Calvary Baptist Church in Shelby for over 35 years. He also served on the Shelby City Council from 1967 to 2001. The Reverend is pictured here with his grandson, Kynny Raper-Polk. (Uptown Shelby Association.)

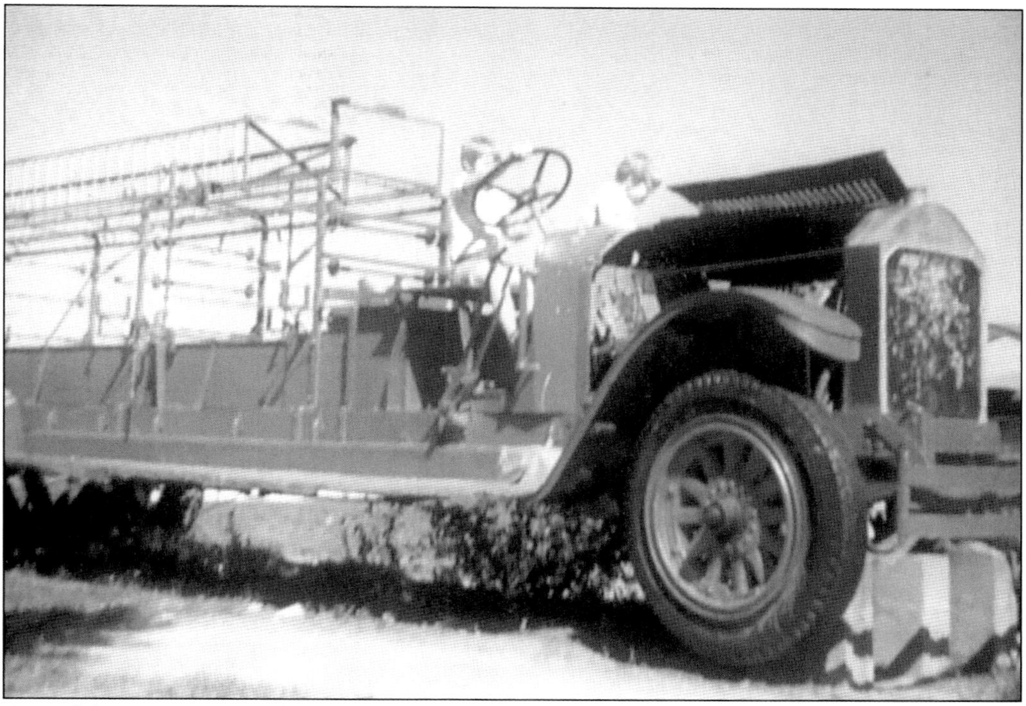

One of the attractions at the City Park in the 1960s and 1970s was the fire truck. Children of all ages climbed and played on the old engine. The fire truck was one of the original vehicles used by the City Fire Department 30 years earlier. (Paul Durst.)

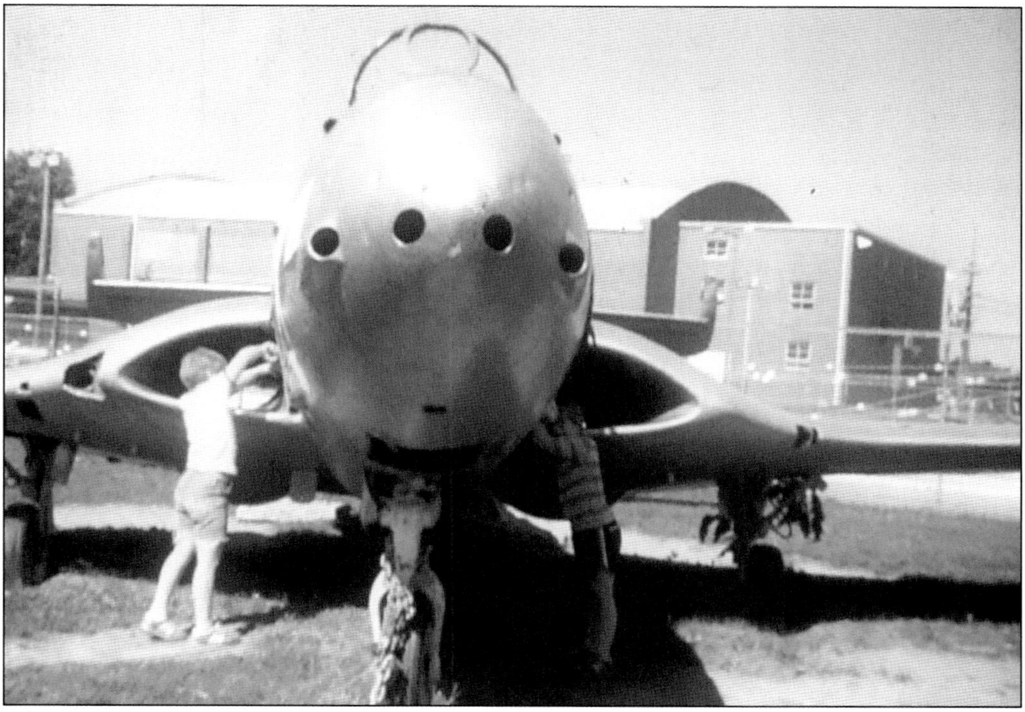

Alongside the fire truck was this Navy jet. The two attractions had few moving parts yet helped create countless imaginary adventures. (Paul Durst.)

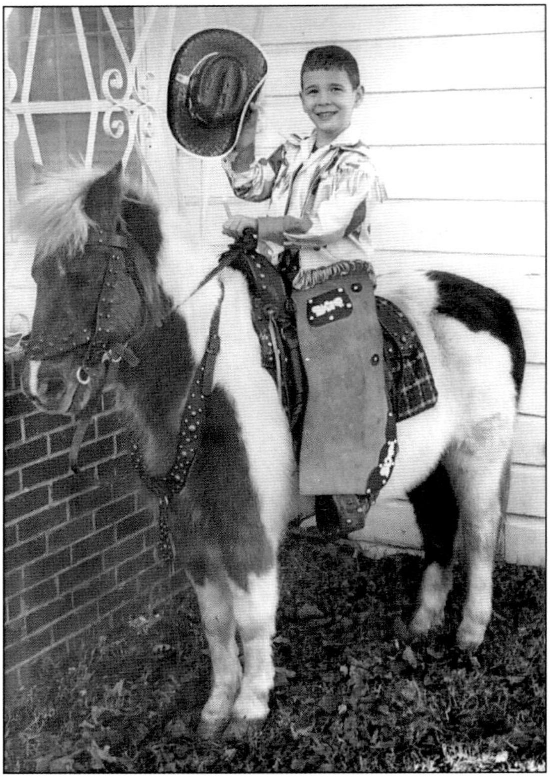

A common visitor to the area was a traveling photographer with a camera and pony. Hundreds of local children sat on the pony, willingly or unwillingly, so that their parents could purchase a memory. Here a young Rusty Patterson poses atop "Tumbleweed."

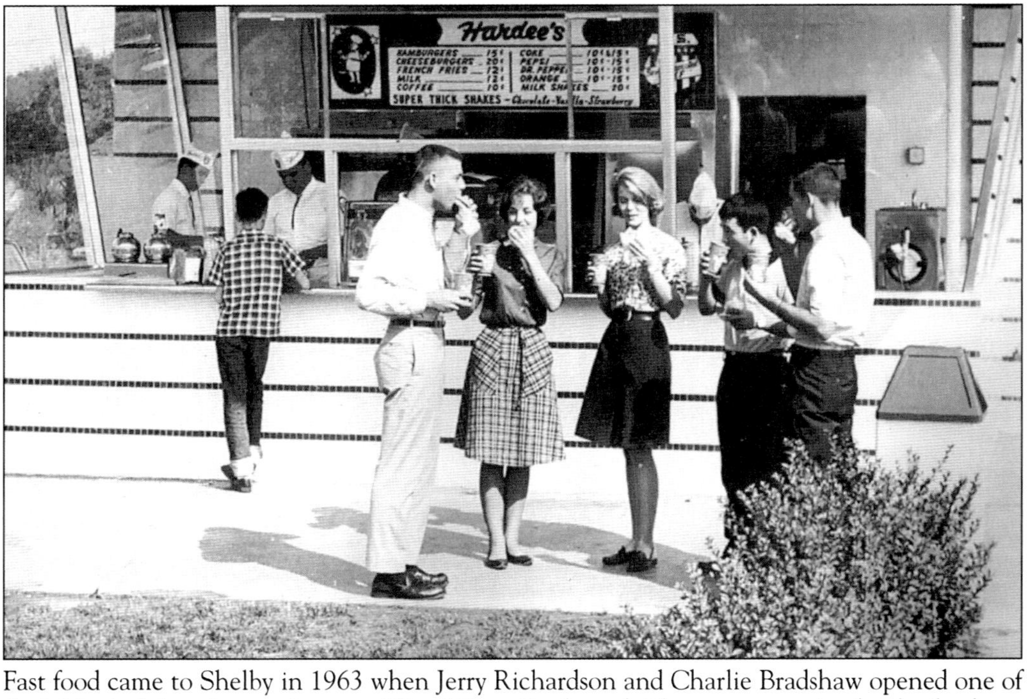

Fast food came to Shelby in 1963 when Jerry Richardson and Charlie Bradshaw opened one of their Hardee's hamburger shops on West Dixon Boulevard. The menu was simple, the food was inexpensive, and there was only window service. The clerk in the window to the left is Barry Hambright. (Shelby High School.)

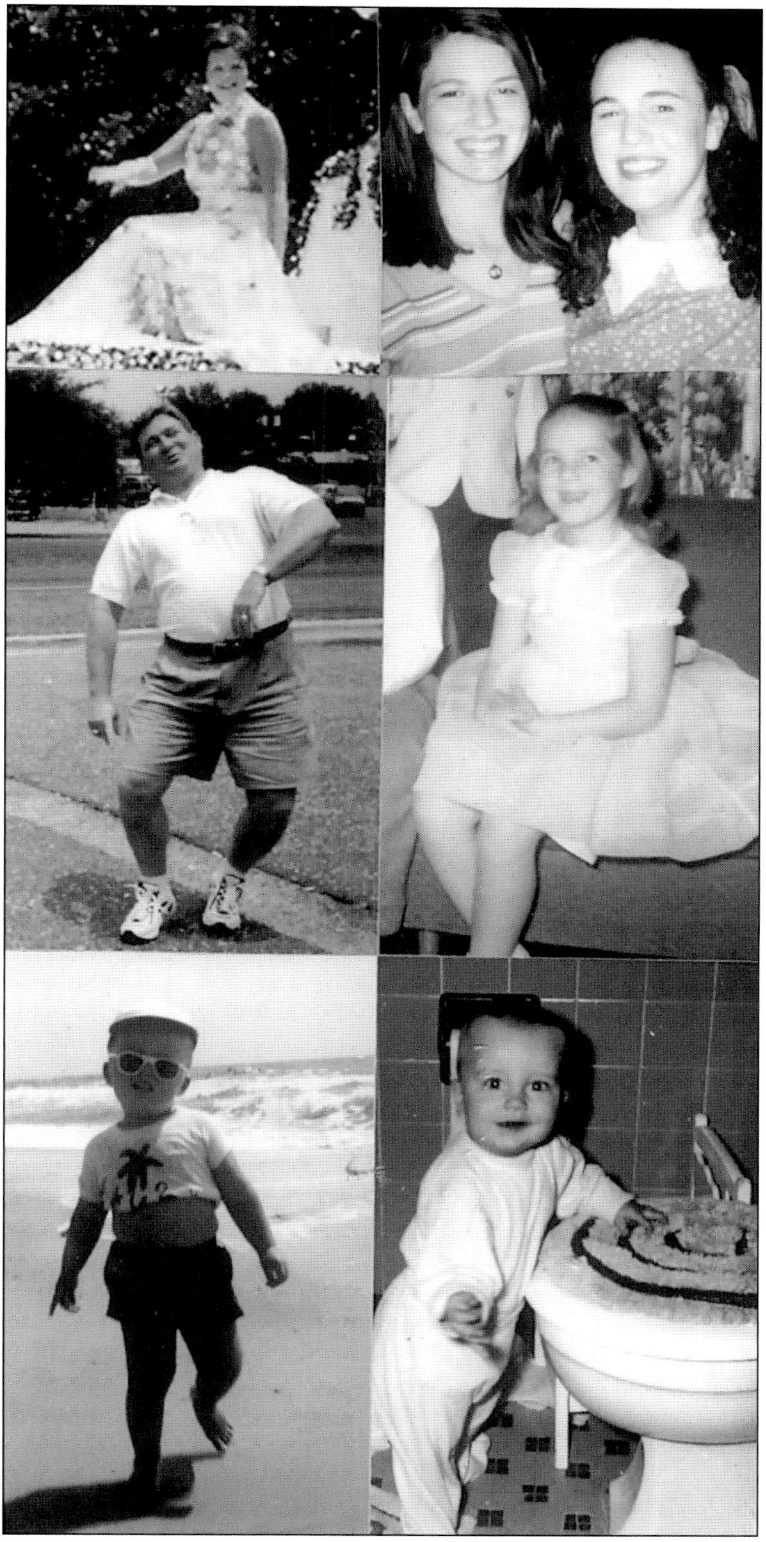

Family and Friends.

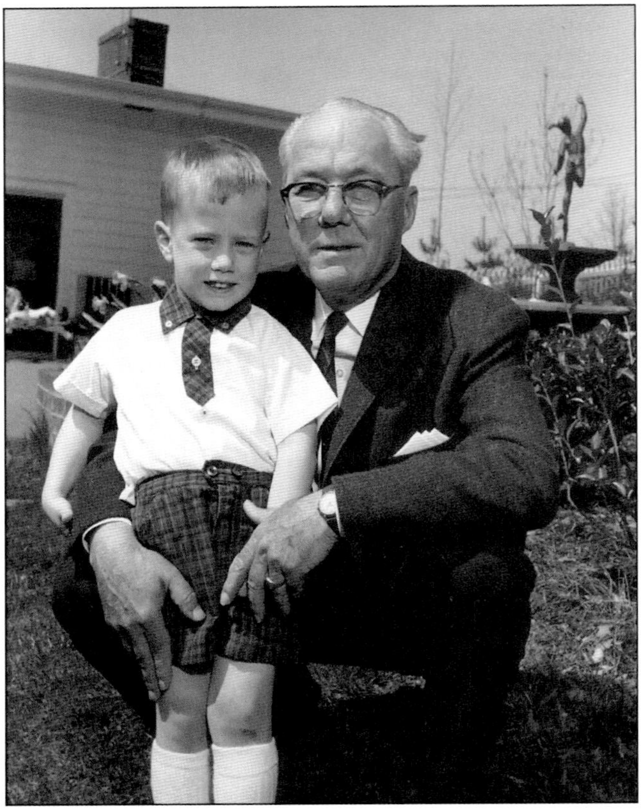

Charles I. Dover proudly poses with his grandson and namesake, young Charles Hamrick, in this 1963 photo. (Harvey Hamrick Jr.)

This 1970s picture shows a young Jim Hunt on a campaign swing through Shelby. Hunt would serve four terms as governor of North Carolina. Local democratic supporters R. Patrick Spangler and Ezra Bridges join with the future governor. (Eloise Spangler.)

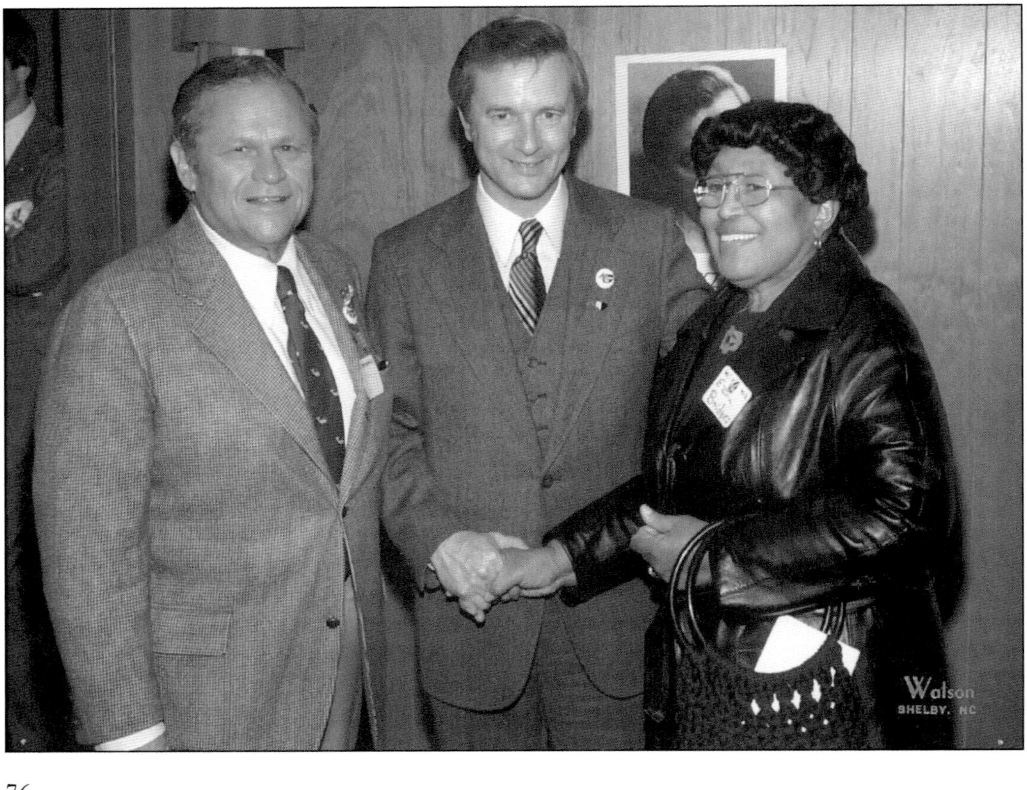

Three

Kings Mountain

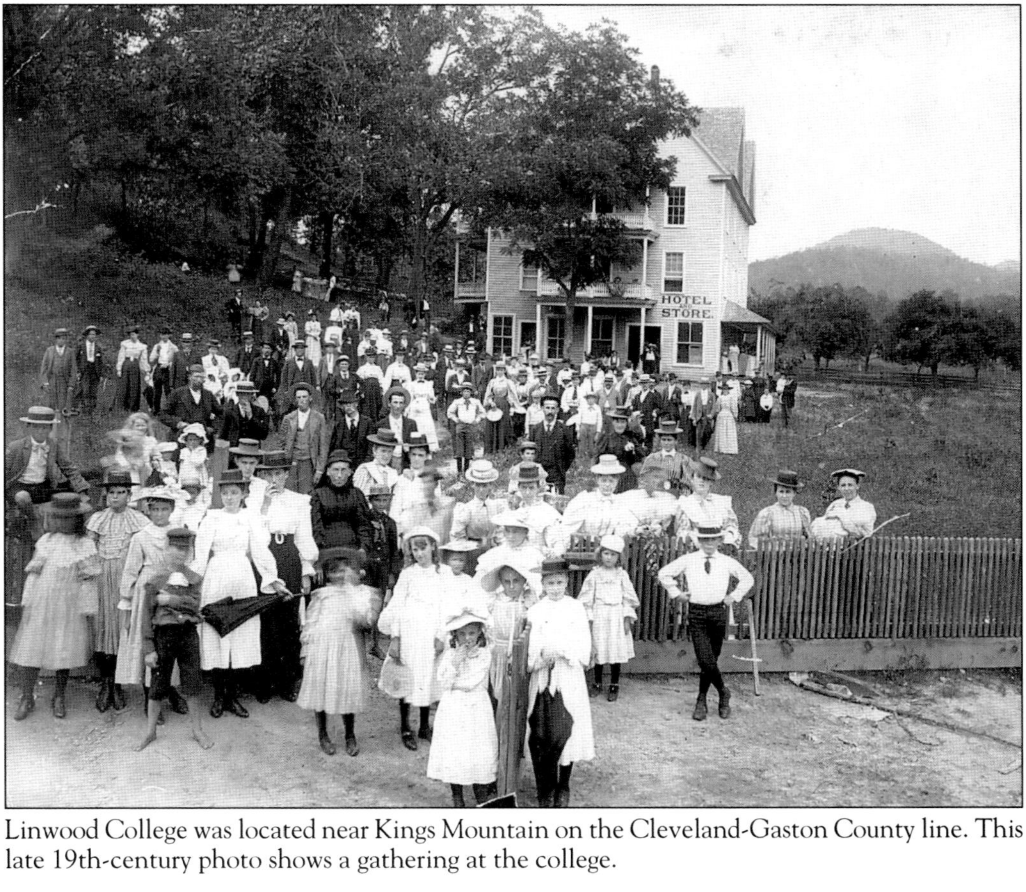

Linwood College was located near Kings Mountain on the Cleveland-Gaston County line. This late 19th-century photo shows a gathering at the college.

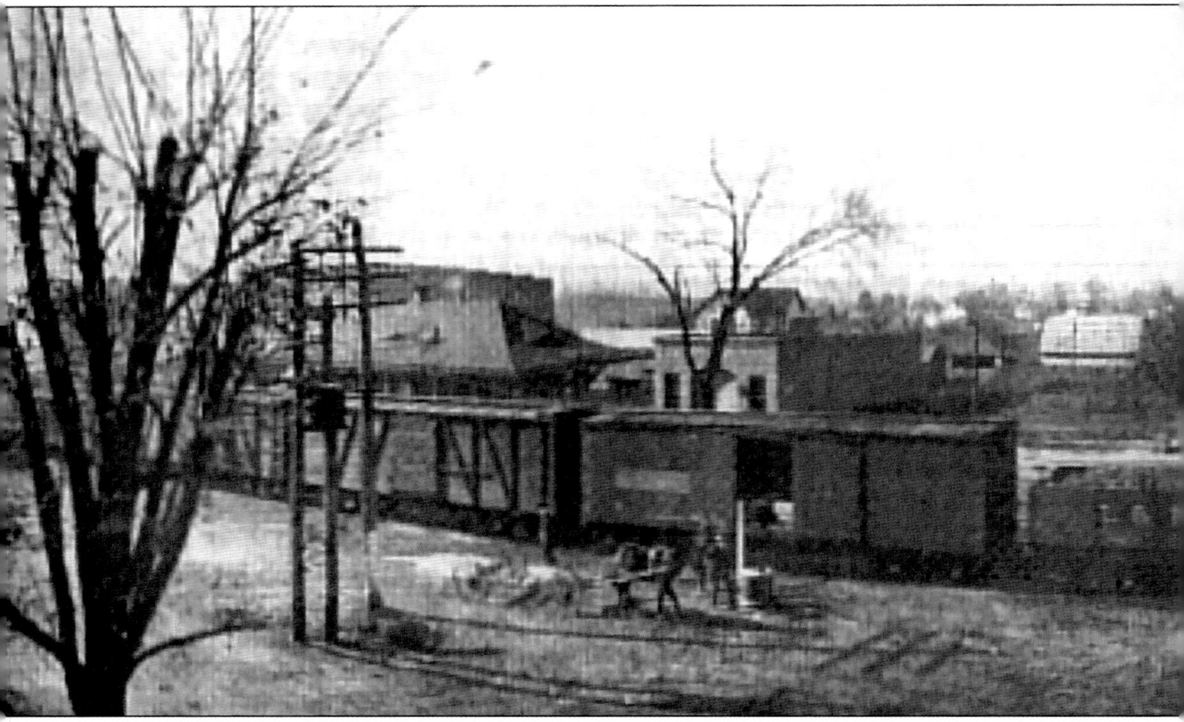

This *c.* 1880 photo of Kings Mountain was taken from Mountain Street looking west across Railroad Avenue towards Battleground Avenue. The Mountain View Hotel is seen in the center across from the railroad tracks. In an era before automobiles, horse-drawn wagons and

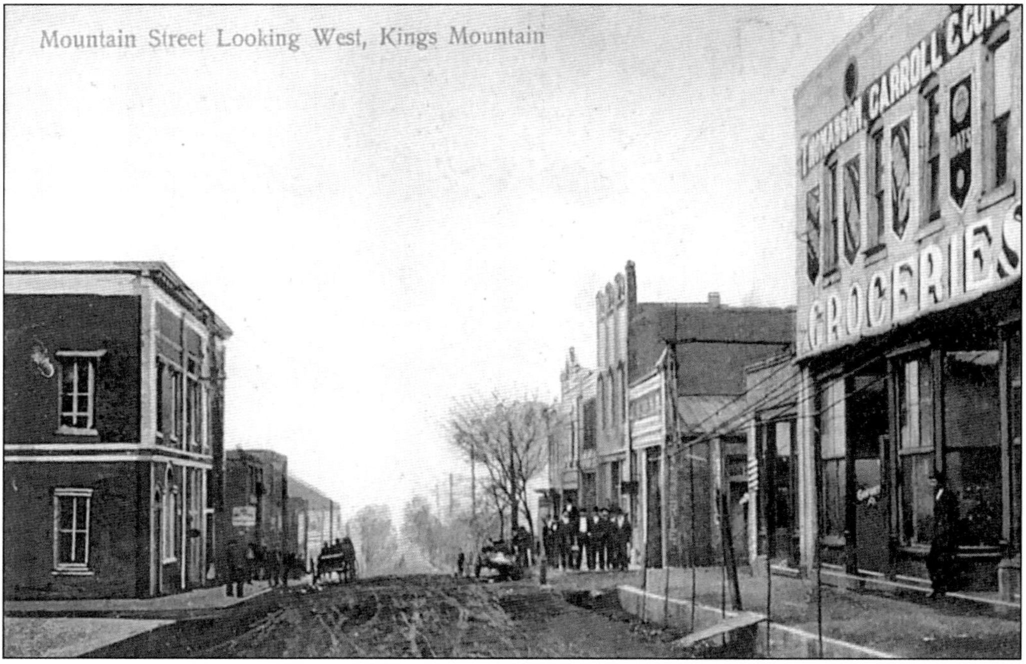

A postcard view of Mountain Street, *c.* 1910, shows the business district before paved roads. Note that the sidewalks were a substantial step to accommodate the height of horse-drawn buggies and wagons.

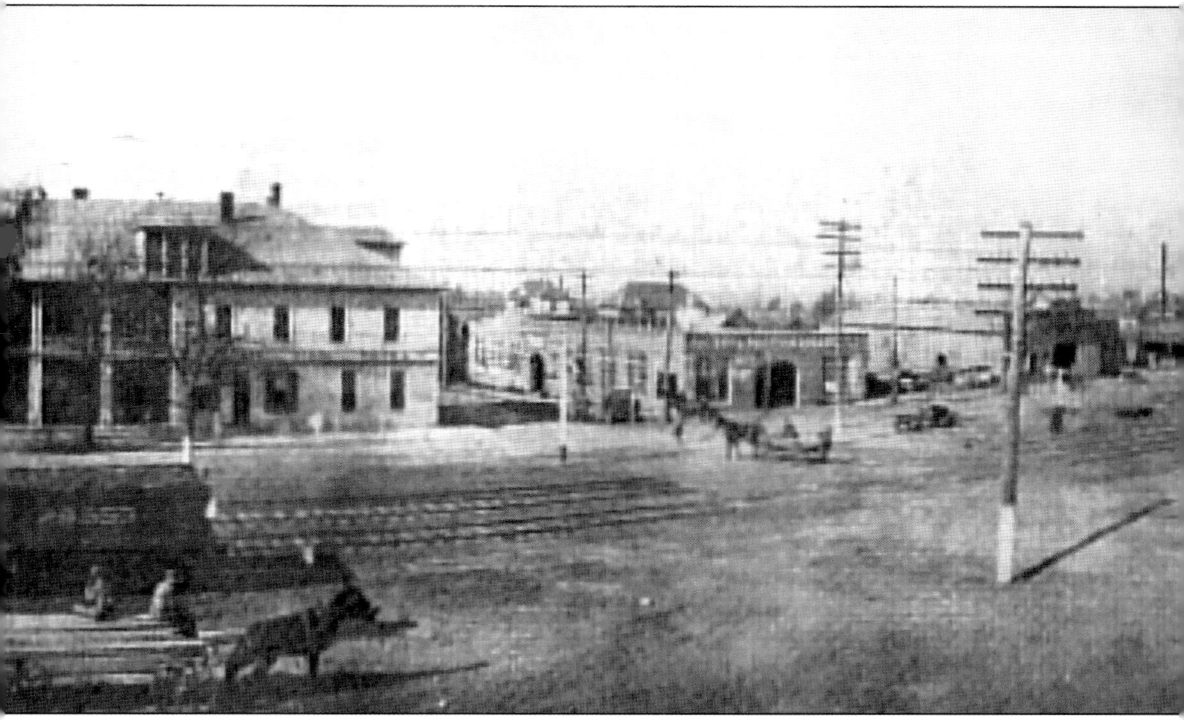

the railroad were the means of transportation. The hotel was a favorite stay for guests traveling by rail.

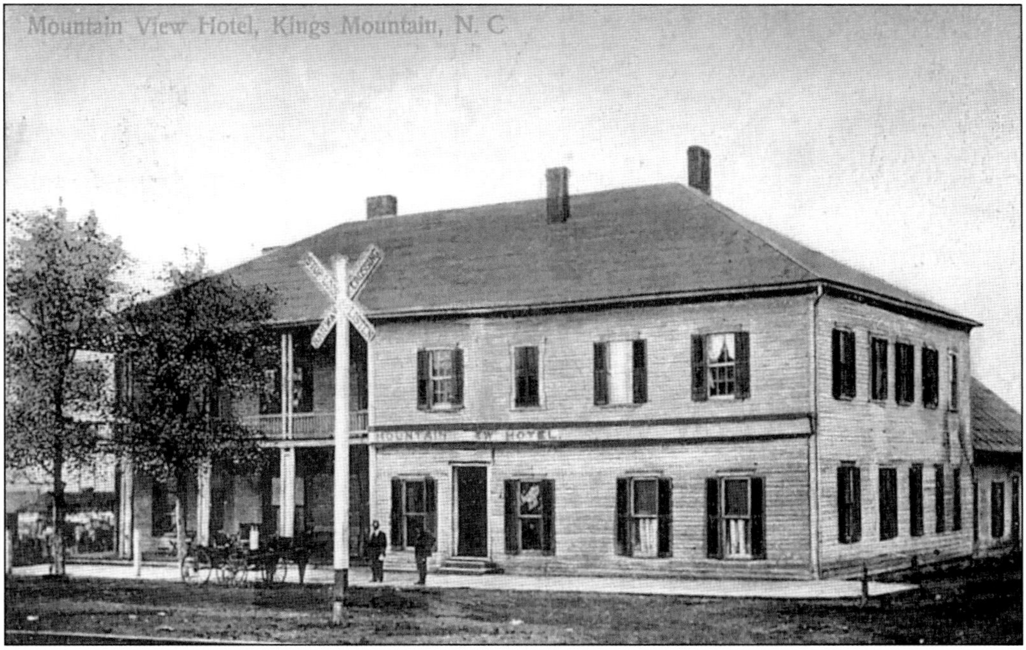

The Mountain View Hotel was a landmark in Kings Mountain for over half a century. Located across from the railroad depot, the hotel was a convenient overnight stop for tourists. The Joy Theater sits on the site of the old hotel today. The theater has recently been restored and houses the local community theater. (Harvey Whisnant.)

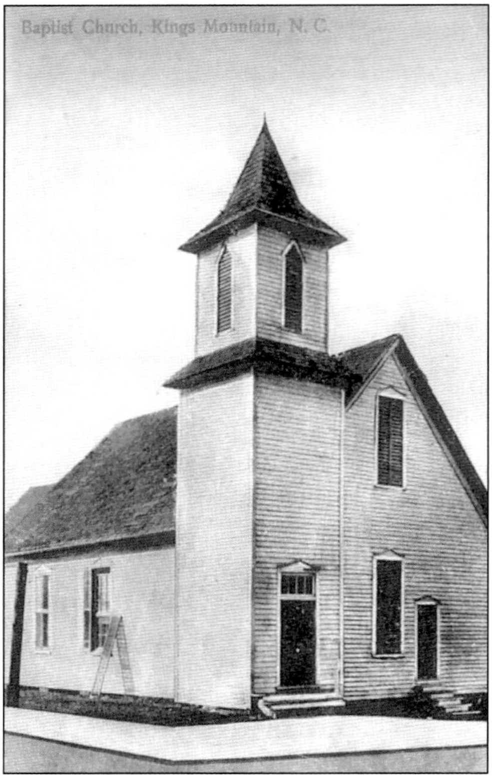

This *c.* 1910 postcard view shows the Baptist Church in Kings Mountain on the southwest corner of Mountain and Piedmont Streets. The church was built in 1890 and served until a new structure was built in 1914.

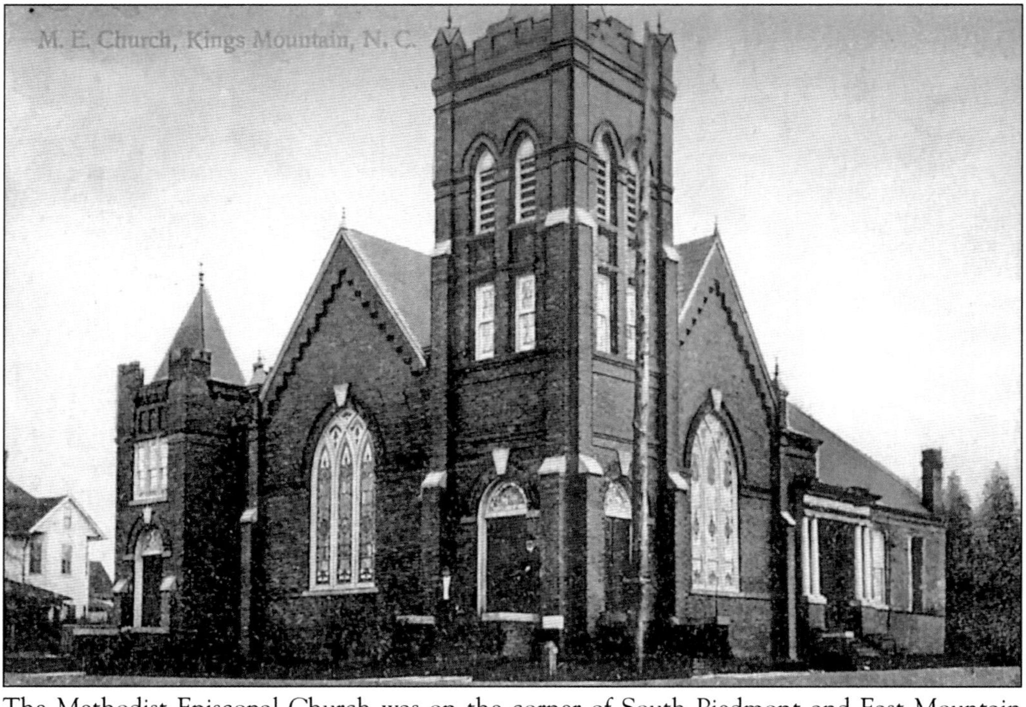

The Methodist Episcopal Church was on the corner of South Piedmont and East Mountain Streets. Built in 1905, the church was replaced in 1967 and today is the home of the Central United Methodist Church.

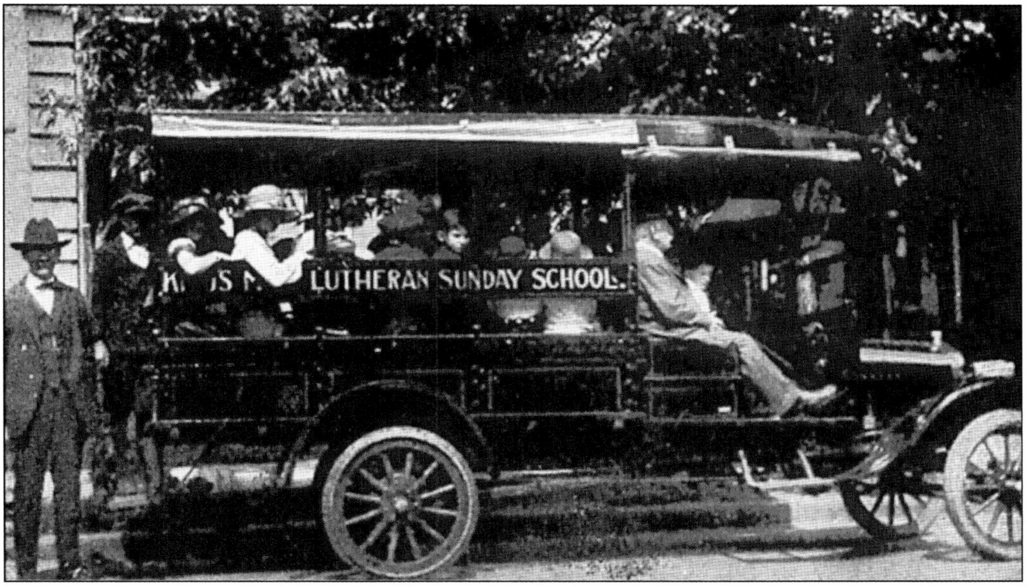

Members of the Saint Mathews Lutheran Church board the church van in this c. 1920 photo. (Dr. John Still.)

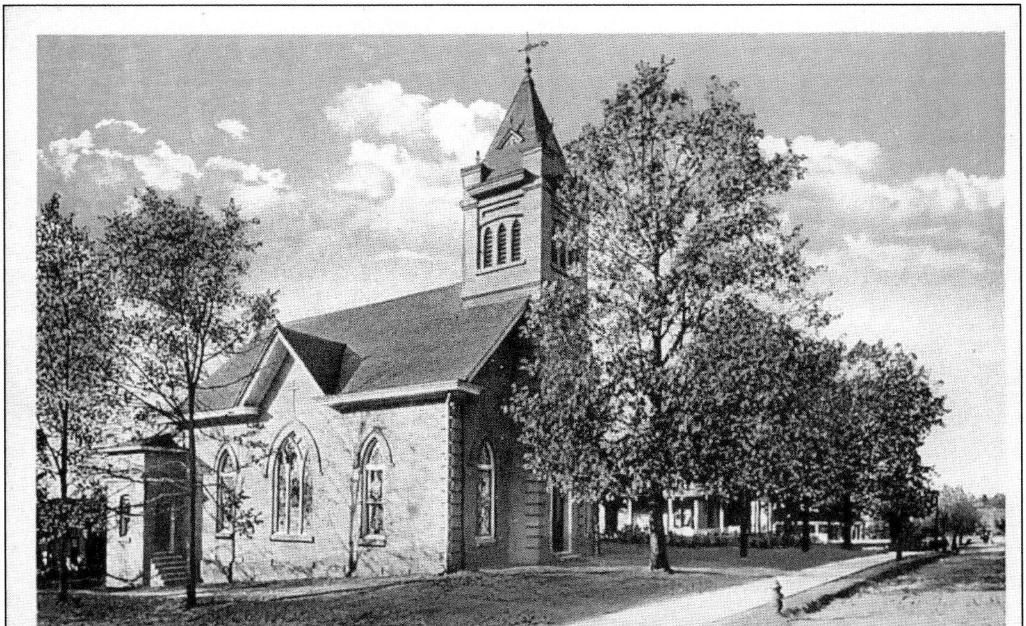

The Saint Mathews Lutheran Church is shown in this postcard view on North Piedmont Street around 1920. The church was organized in 1876.

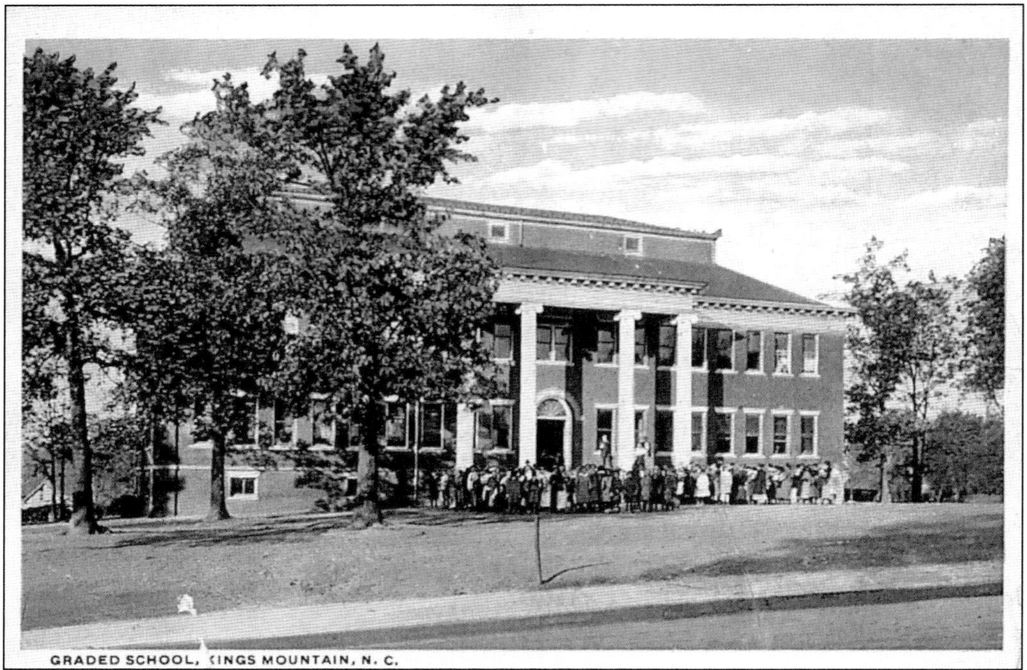

This c. 1920 postcard is of the Kings Mountain Graded High School on Ridge Street. The building burned twice, in 1910 and again in 1932.

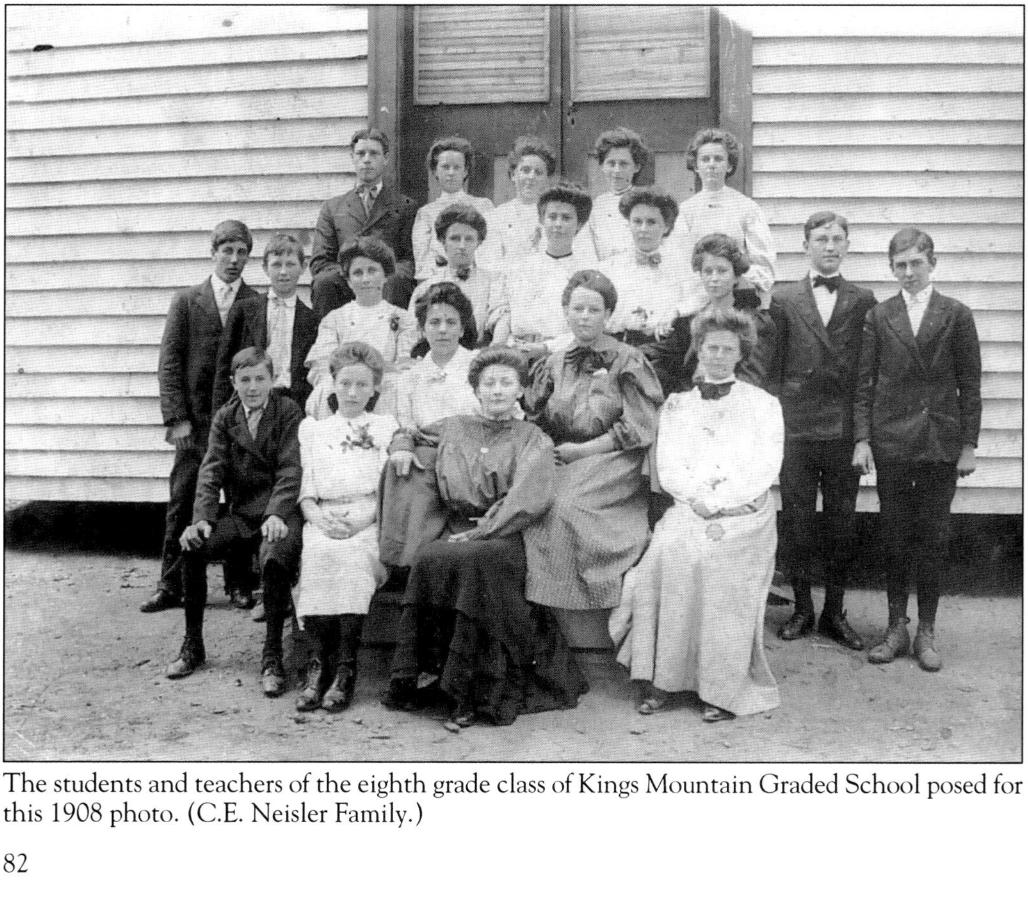

The students and teachers of the eighth grade class of Kings Mountain Graded School posed for this 1908 photo. (C.E. Neisler Family.)

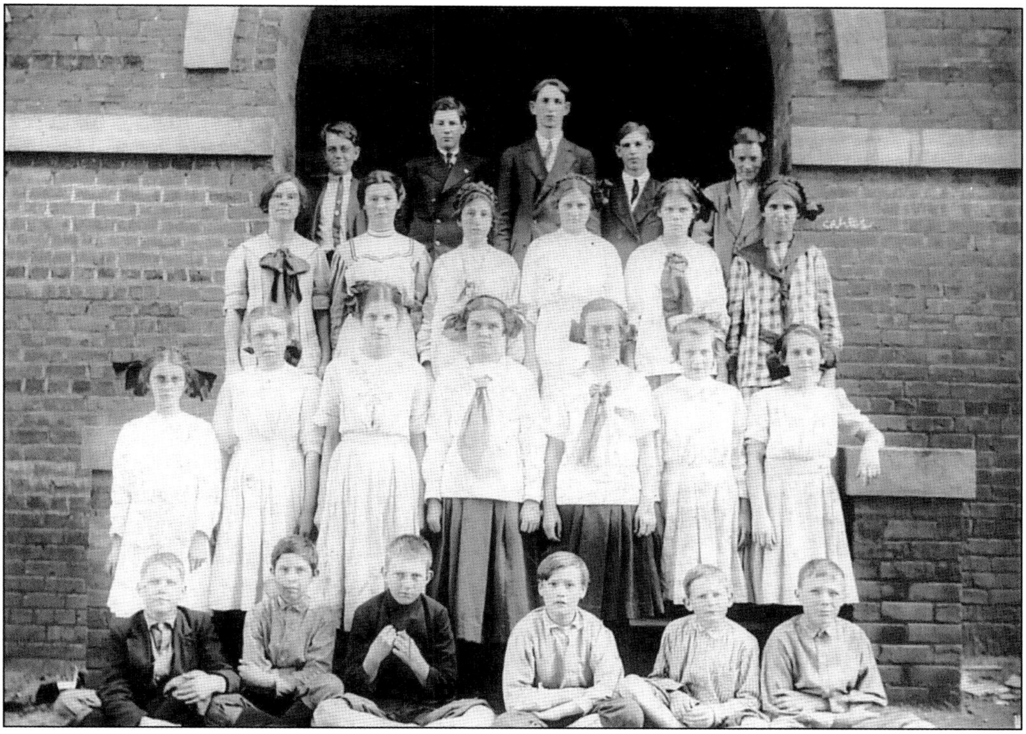

Ms. Eunice Plonk was the seventh grade teacher at Kings Mountain Graded School in this 1912 photo. (C.E. Neisler Family.)

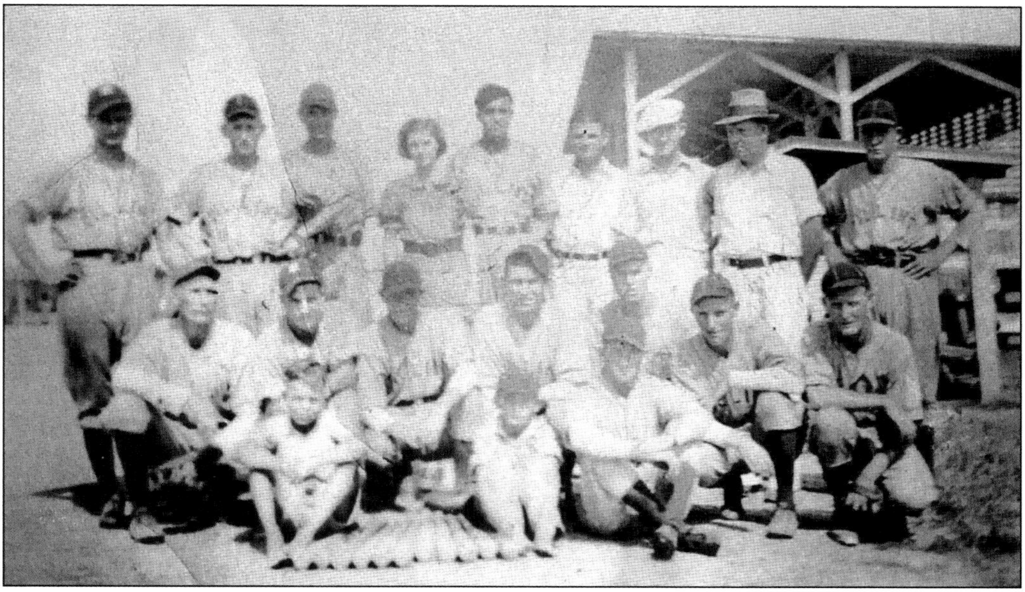

The Dilling Mill Ramblers pose for this 1934 team picture. From left to right are (front row) Robert Ford and Dennis Deese (batboys) and Rabbit Huffstetler; (middle row) Jap Roper, Robert Allen, Grace Davis, Paul Kirby, Smokey York, Olland Pearson, and Tillman Pearson; (back row) Ralph Mitchem, Pot Jackson, Kirt Sanders, Ola Blackwell (ticket sales), Burgin Whitaker, Marsh Grier (business manager), Dink Bennett (manager), Johnny Jones (manager), and Clyde Fite. The team produced a 29 and 5 record that year. (Betty Sue Morris.)

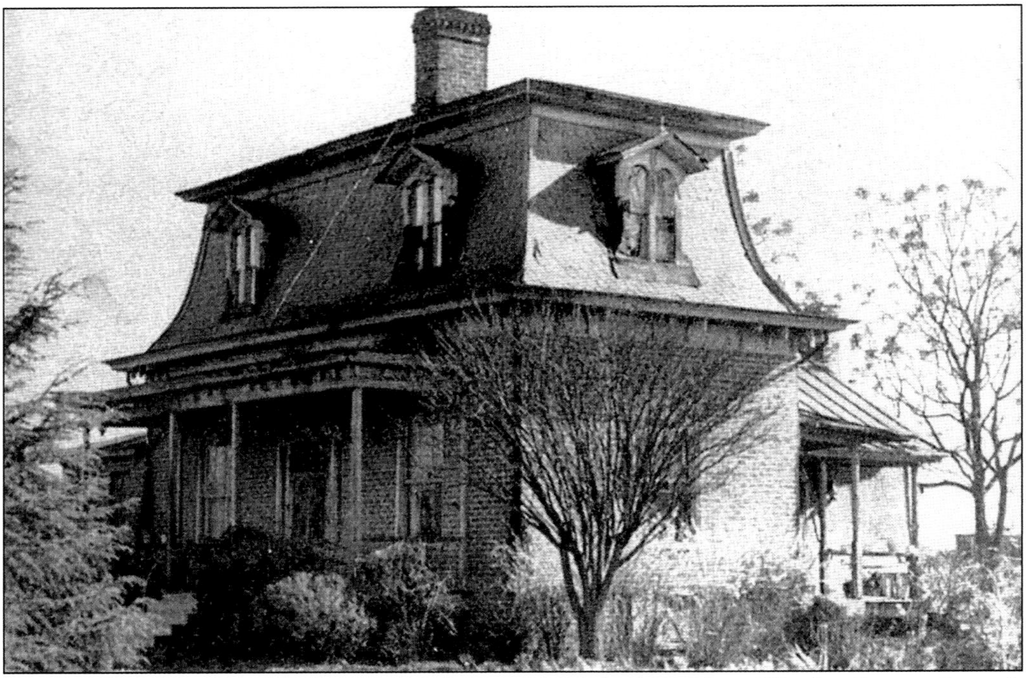

The first known brick home in Kings Mountain was built in the 1870s by George Carruth Herndon. The Bethlehem Road house would later be the home of three well-known Kings Mountain citizens—Marion Elmer, Plato Durham, and James Edward Herndon Sr.

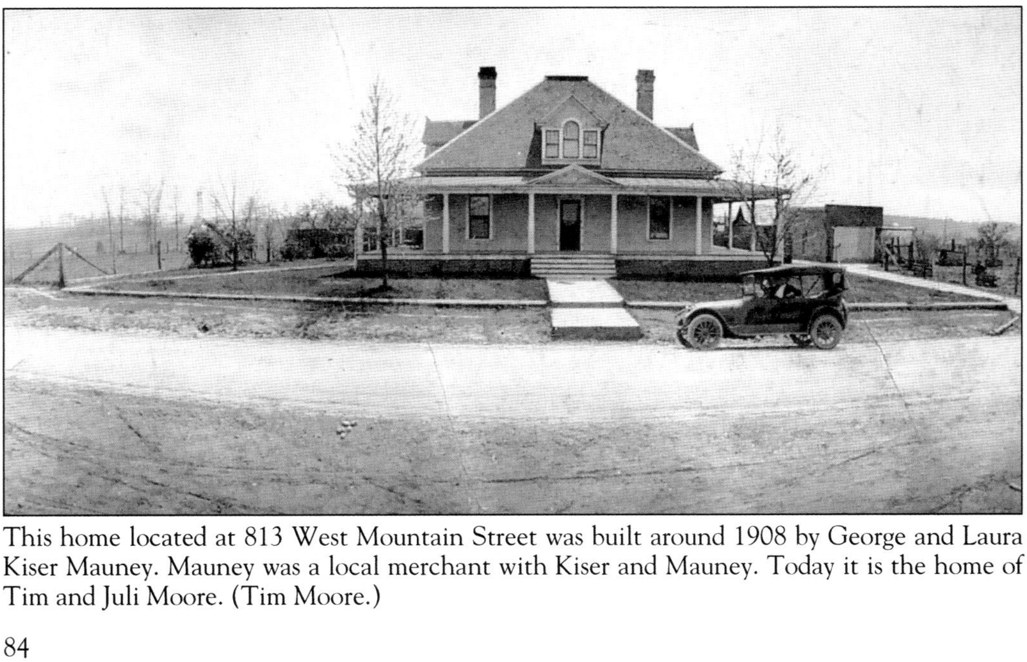

This home located at 813 West Mountain Street was built around 1908 by George and Laura Kiser Mauney. Mauney was a local merchant with Kiser and Mauney. Today it is the home of Tim and Juli Moore. (Tim Moore.)

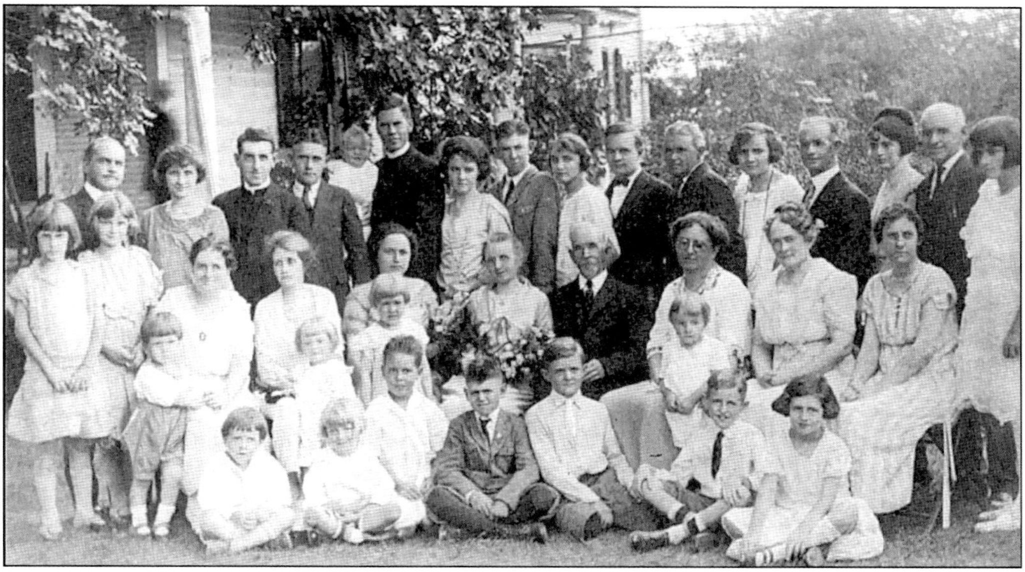

The family of Jacob and Julia Rudisill Mauney pose for this photograph while celebrating Jacob and Julia's 50th wedding anniversary on September 11, 1923. The home is located at 107 North Piedmont Avenue.

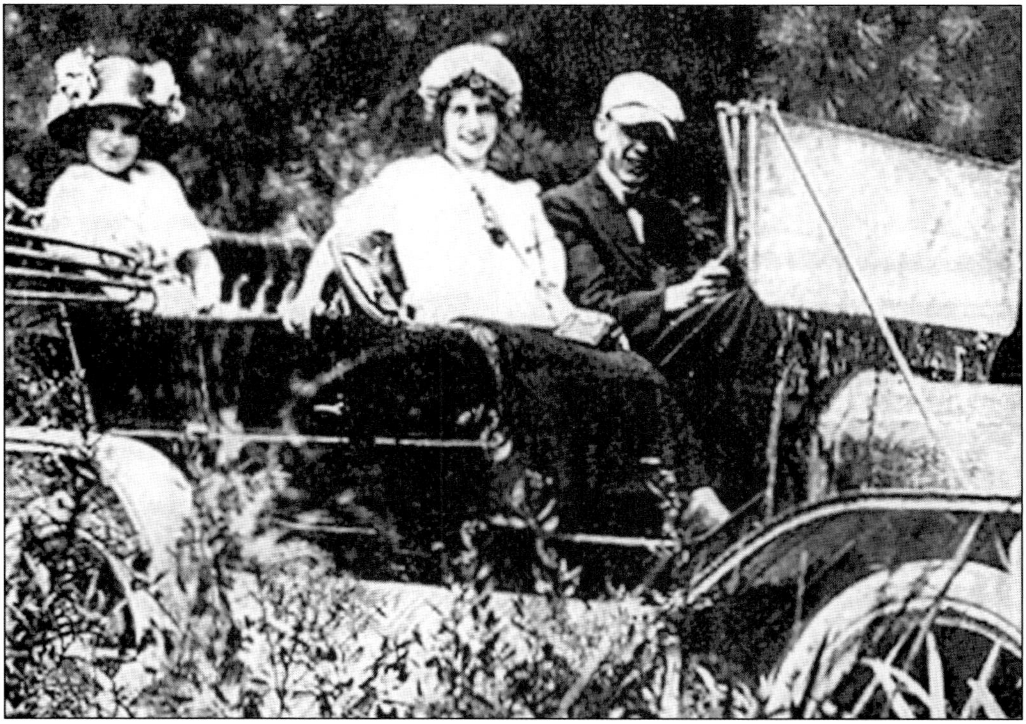

This *c.* 1920 photo shows locals out for a drive. Racing on the streets of Kings Mountain was a regular sporting event in the first part of the century.

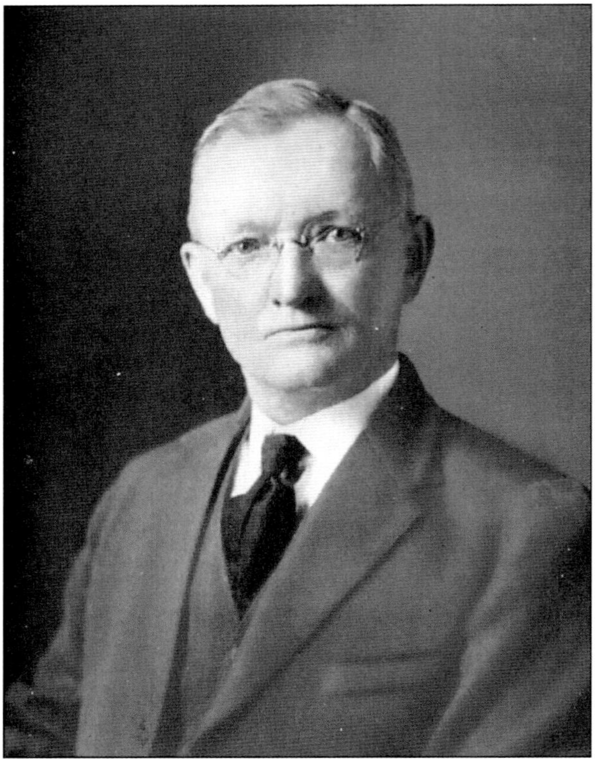

Neisler Mills was founded by C.E. Neisler Sr. in 1910. Neisler had first learned the textile business from his father, Joseph Neisler, who operated a textile mill in Concord. He managed mills owned by his father-in-law, W.A. Mauney, who built the first textile mill in Kings Mountain in 1888. (C.E. Neisler Family.)

C.E. and Ida Pauline Neisler's sons, pictured from left to right, are Paul, Joe, C.E. Jr., Hugh, and Hunter. (C.E. Neisler Family.)

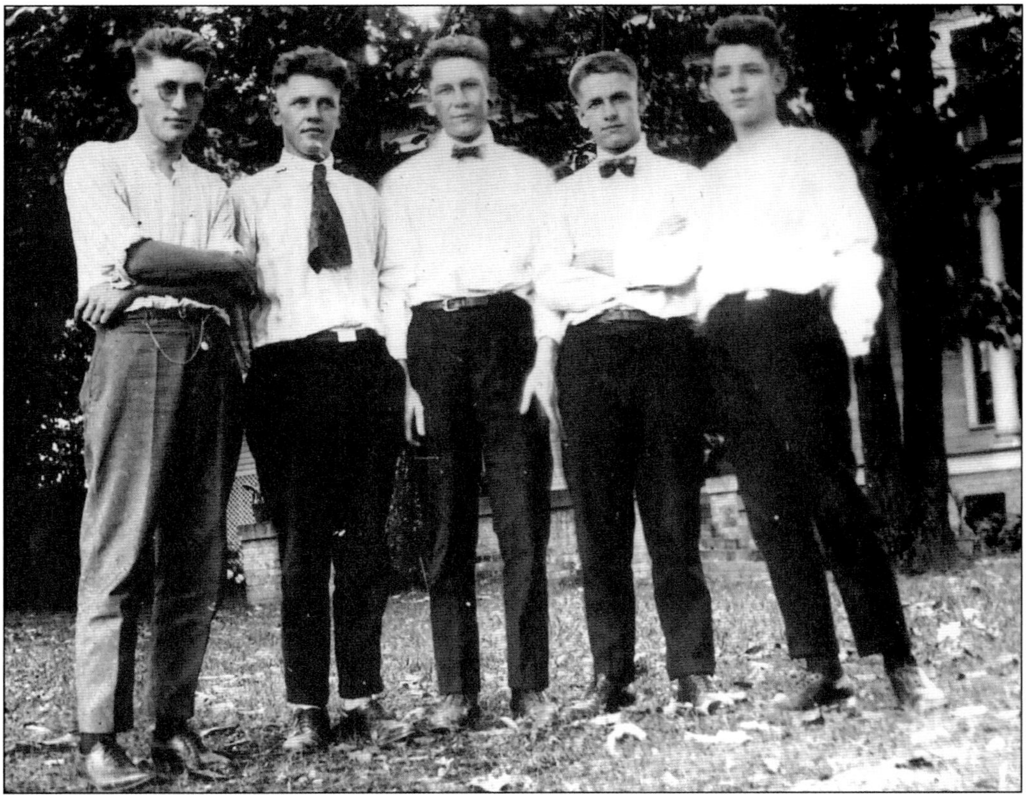

Sisters Pauline Nesiler Brewer and Grace Neisler Page learned the sport of skeet shooting from their brothers. Grace became an accomplished shooter competing in a sport that, at the time, was made up almost entirely of men. For her accomplishments, Grace was inducted into the Kings Mountain Sports Hall of Fame. (C.E. Neisler Family.)

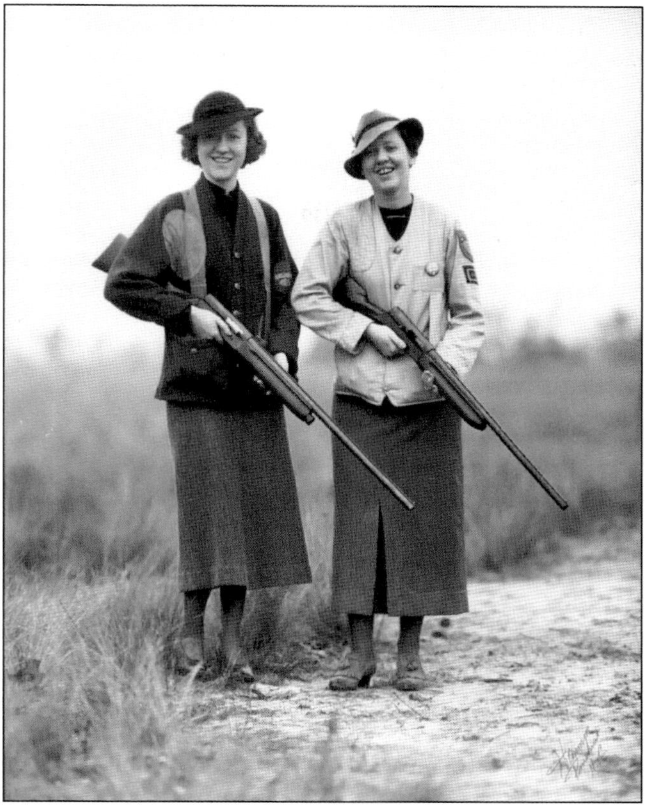

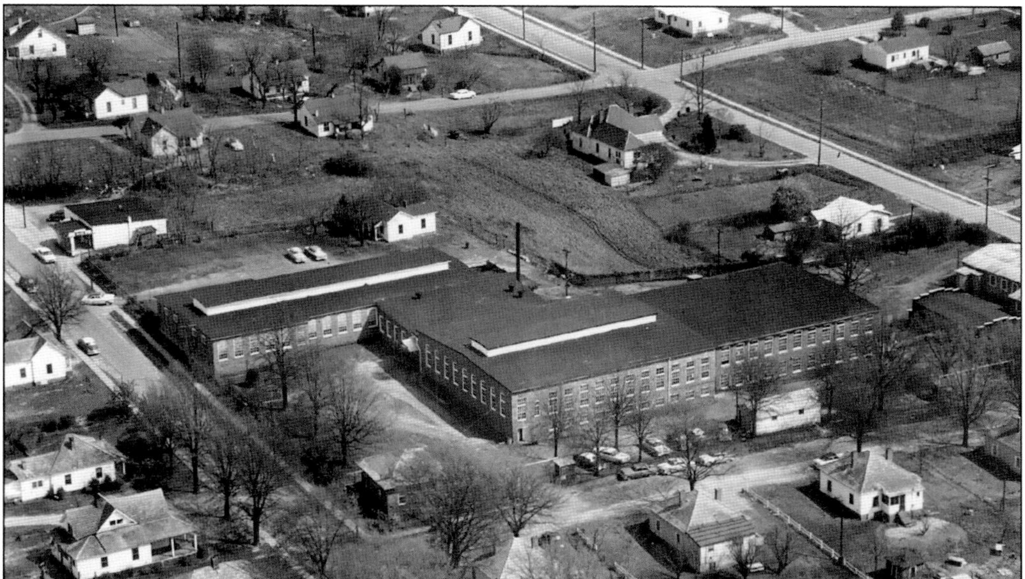

The Pauline Mill is pictured in this *c.* 1955 photo. The image shows how the mill was at the center of a community with homes surrounding the mill. The Pauline Store is seen to the upper left. (C.E. Neisler Family.)

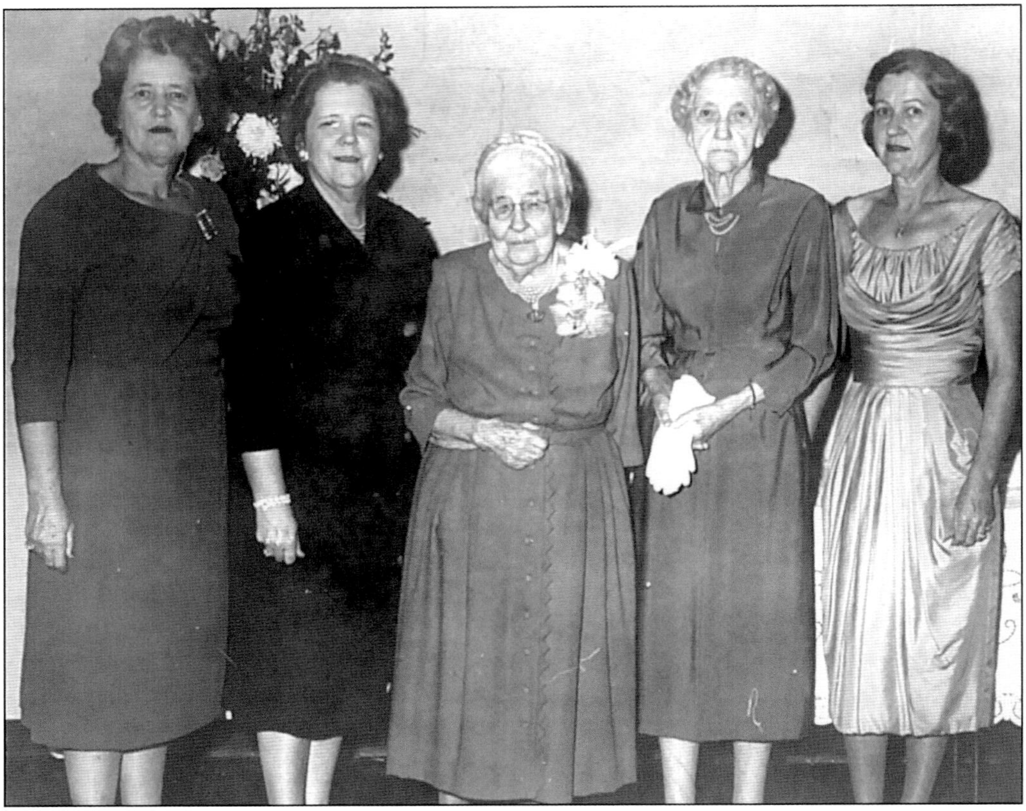

Gathered for a celebration honoring Mrs. Ida Pauline Mauney Neisler are daughters Grace Neisler Page, Margaret Neisler Hunnicutt, family friend Jennie Lee Kerr, and daughter Pauline Neisler Brewer. (C.E. Neisler Family.)

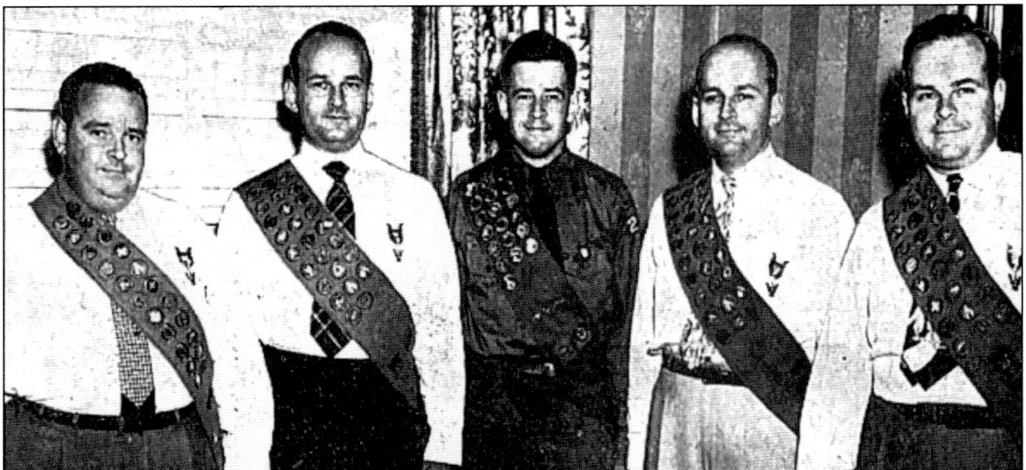

The five sons of Mr. and Mrs. W.K. Mauney all earned the Eagle Scout award. Pictured in this 1952 photo are, from left to right, W.K. Jr., Miles, David, Ernest, and George. (C.E. Neisler Family.)

Jake Early played for Kings Mountain High School in 1935. Early was a catcher who threw right-handed and batted left-handed. He went on to play professional baseball for Washington in the late 1930s and 1940s.

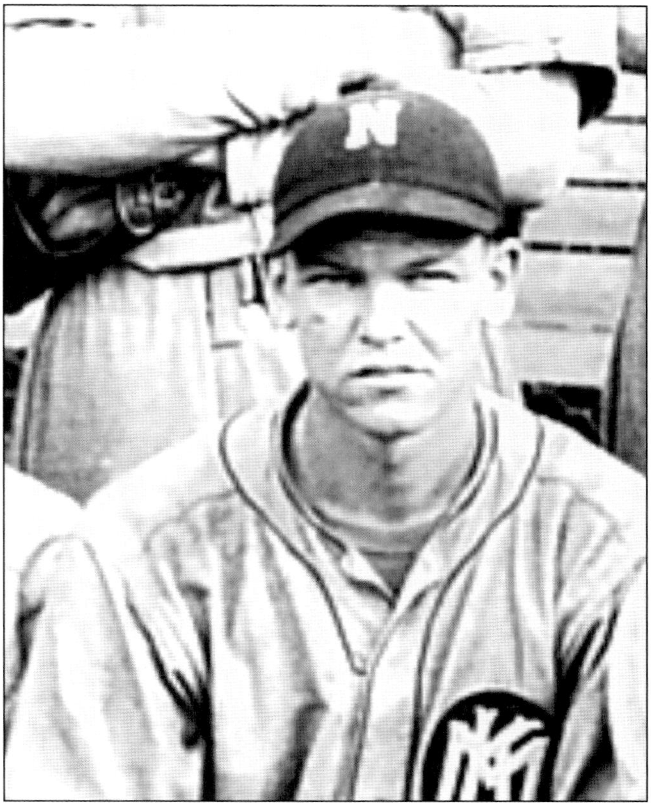

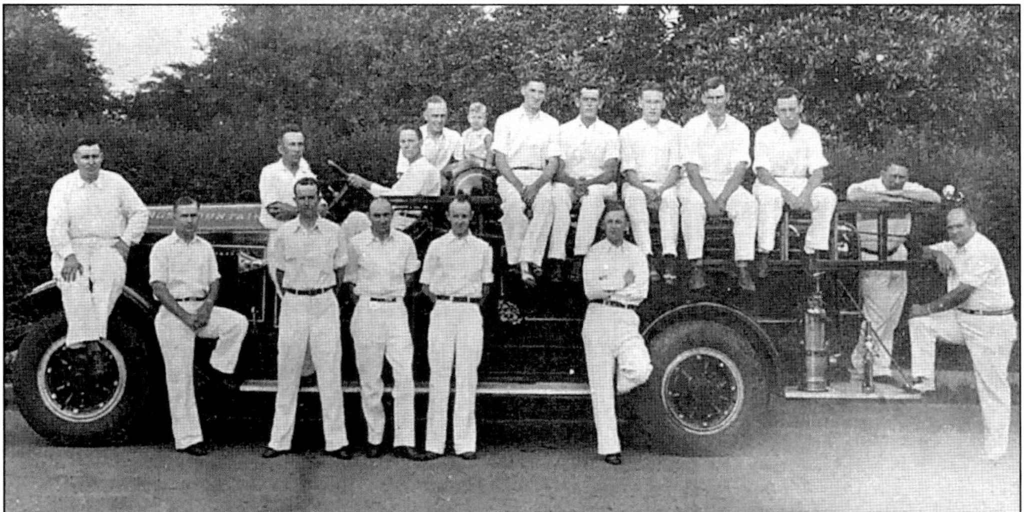

Members of the first organized fire department in Kings Mountain pose with their new fire engine. The department was formed in 1931.

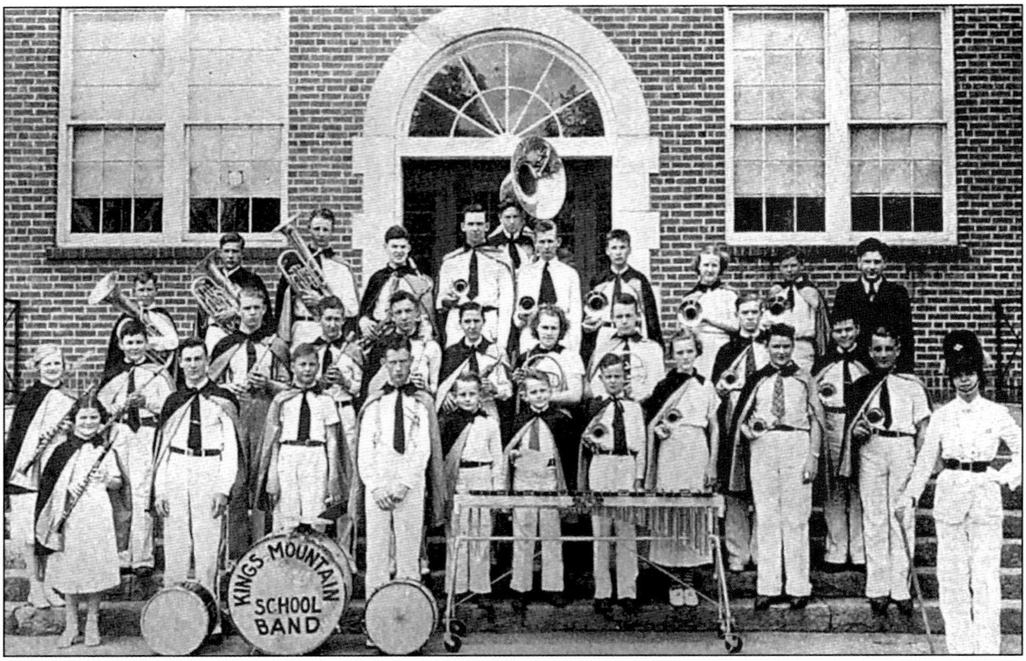

The Kings Mountain High School Band posed for this 1936 photo. Note the band uniforms included capes and neckties for the boys.

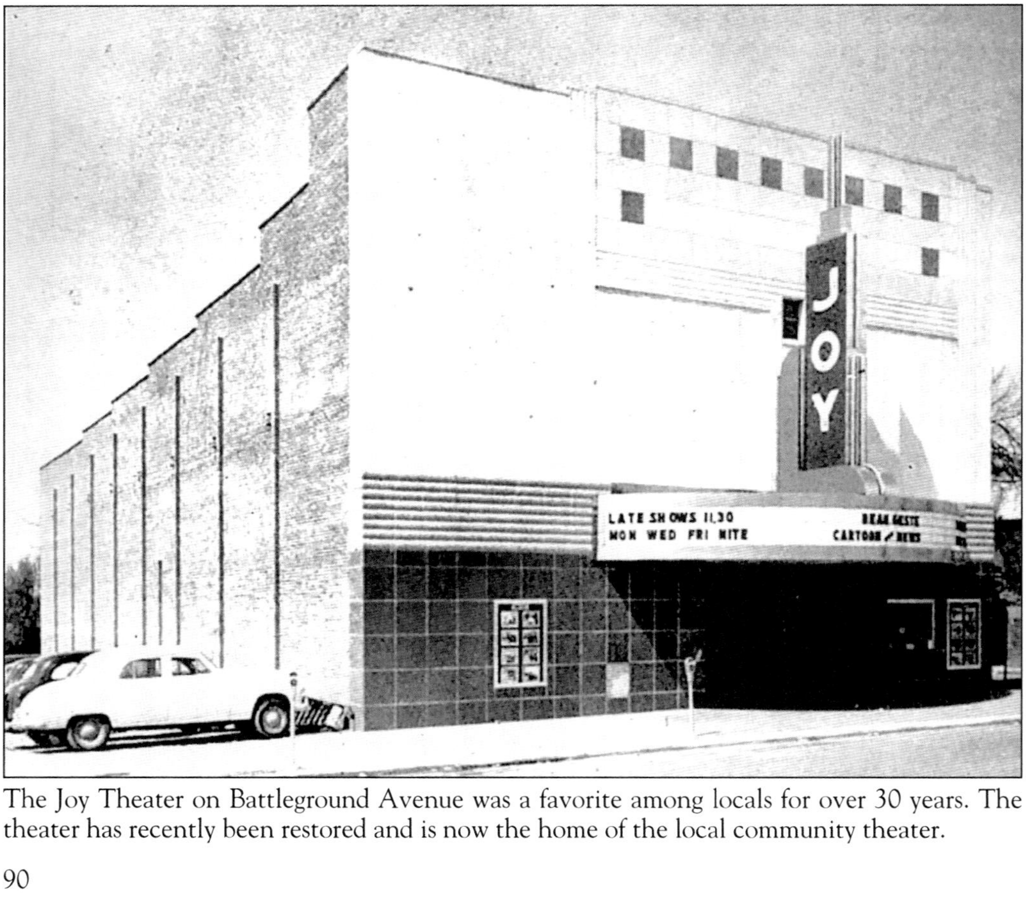

The Joy Theater on Battleground Avenue was a favorite among locals for over 30 years. The theater has recently been restored and is now the home of the local community theater.

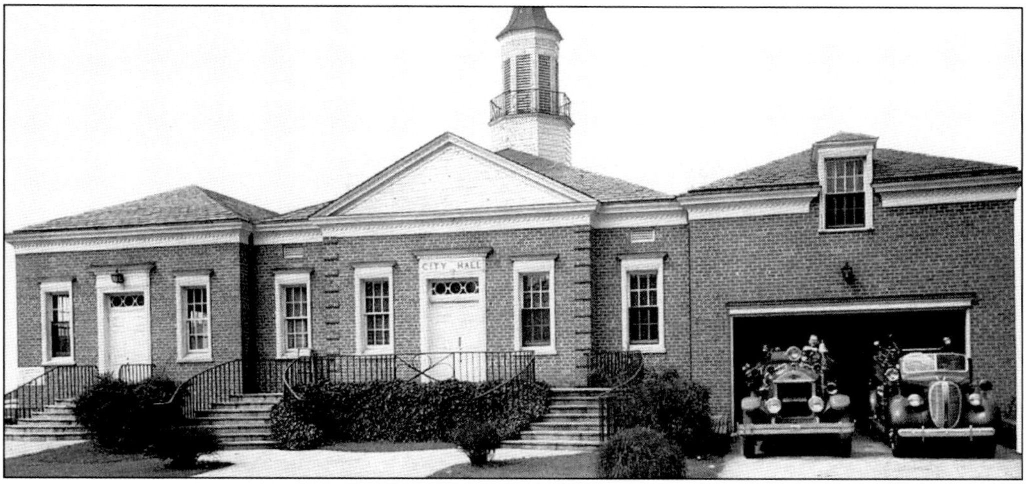

The Kings Mountain City Hall housed the city fire department through the middle of the 20th century.

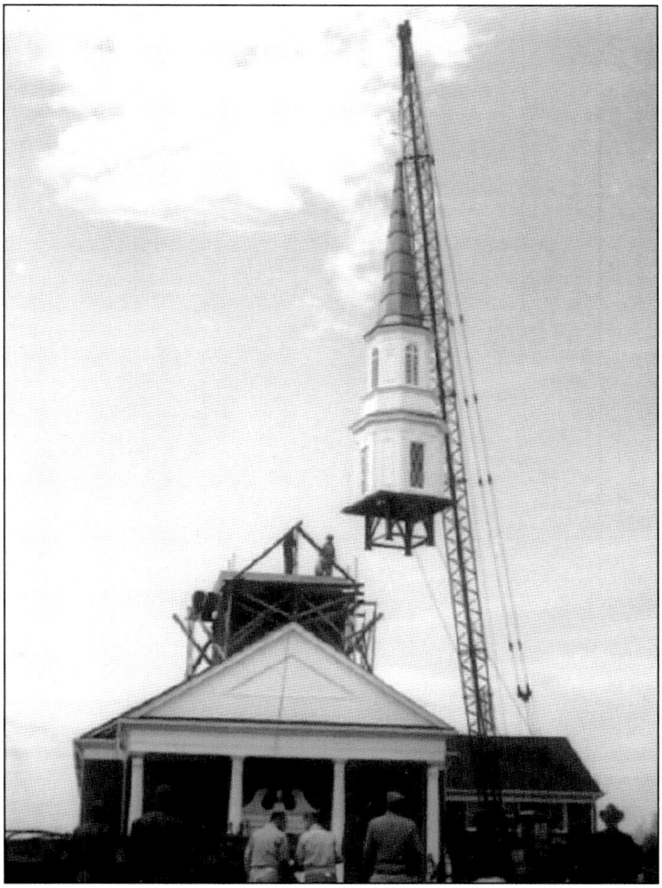

Resurrection Lutheran Church on Crescent Hill celebrated their steeple raising in April 1961. (Resurrection Lutheran Church.)

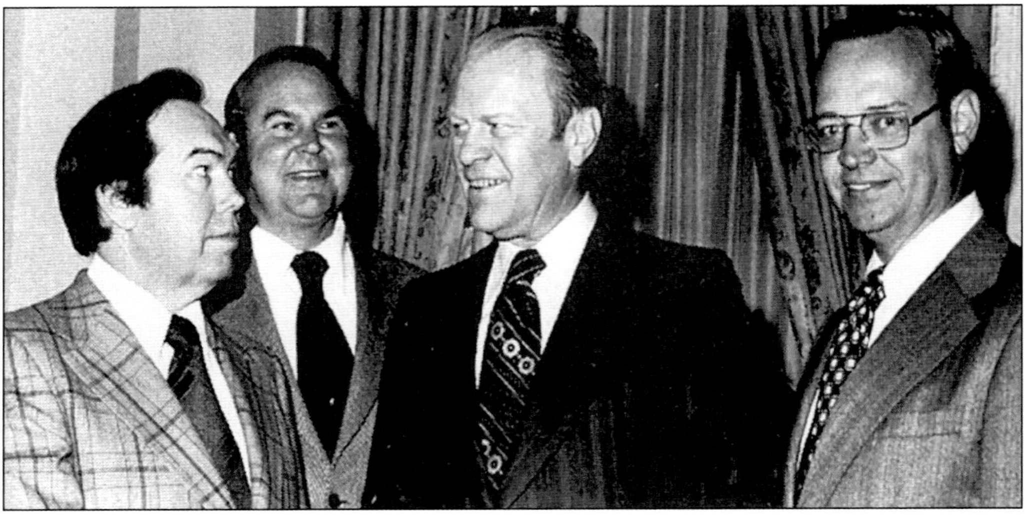

One of the most influential citizens in Kings Mountain history is former mayor John Henry Moss. Moss is pictured with Charles Mauney in a 1974 meeting with then Vice President Gerald Ford and North Carolina congressman James Broyhill.

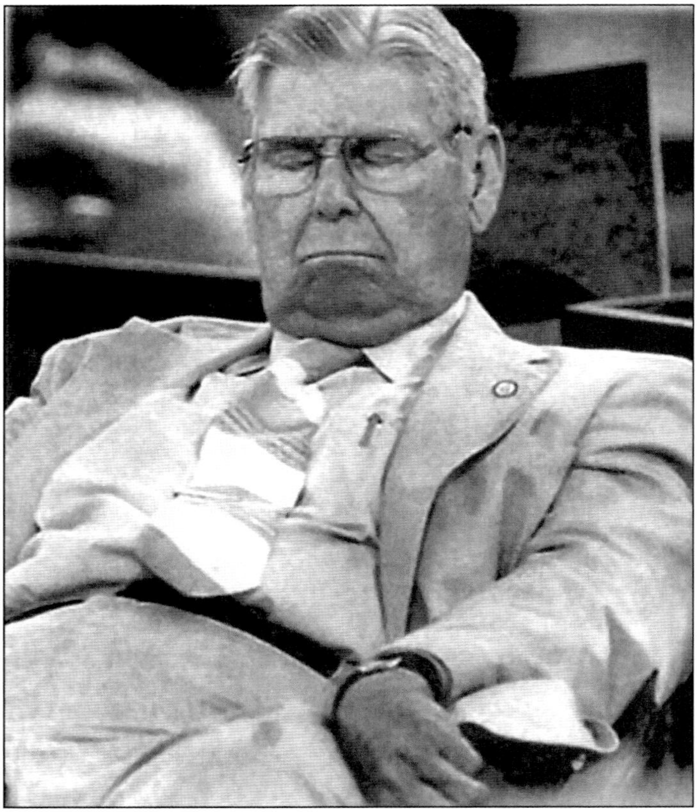

This famous Associated Press photo catches North Carolina senator Ollie Harris "resting his eyes" during a session of the North Carolina General Assembly. Harris served for approximately 20 years as coroner of Cleveland County and then 20 years as a state senator.

Four

Boiling Springs

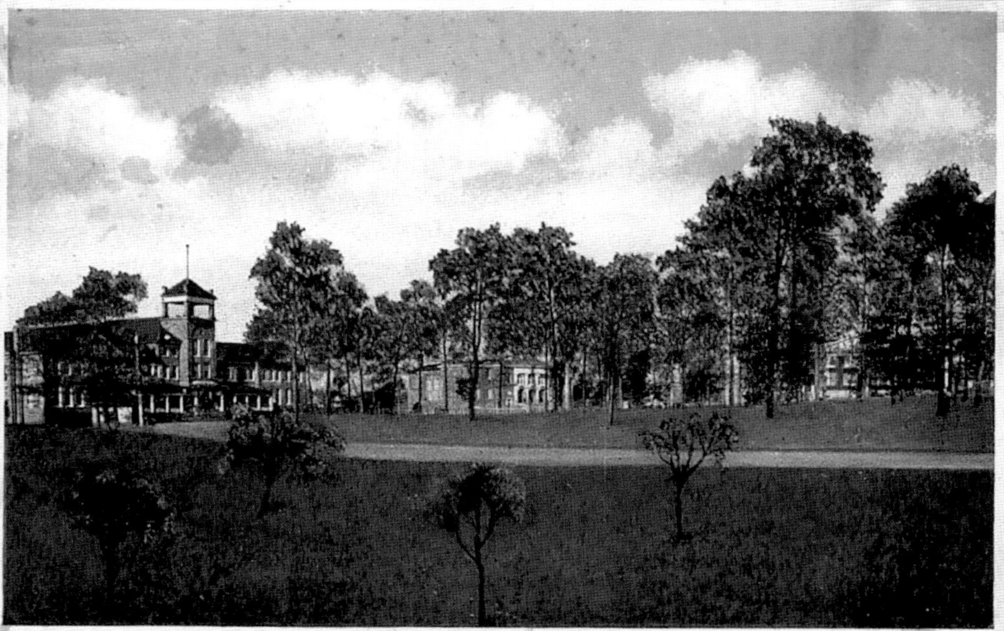

BOILING SPRINGS HIGH SCHOOL, BOILING SPRINGS, CLEVELAND CO., N. C. 110288

Boiling Springs was named for a spring that appeared to boil at the earth's surface and was located near the center of town. The town was incorporated in 1911 and was by then the business center of the southwestern part of the county. The town was surrounded in all directions by rolling farmland. In the first decade of the 20th century, local Baptists opened a boarding high school. This postcard shows the campus of the high school in the early years.

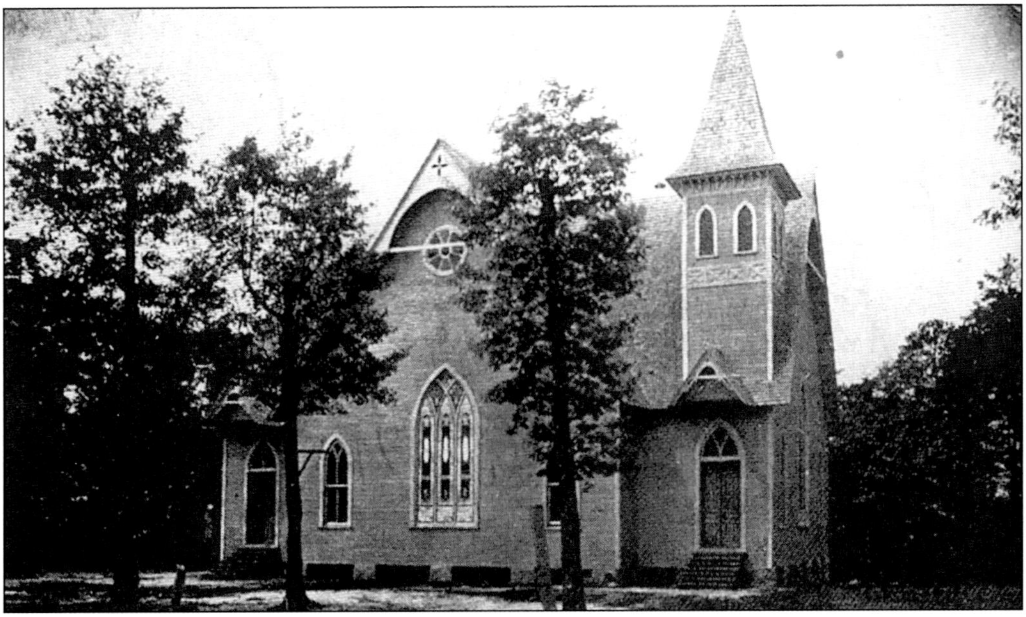

Baptists have been the largest religious group in Boiling Springs since its beginning. This early building served the Boiling Springs Baptist Church until 1924.

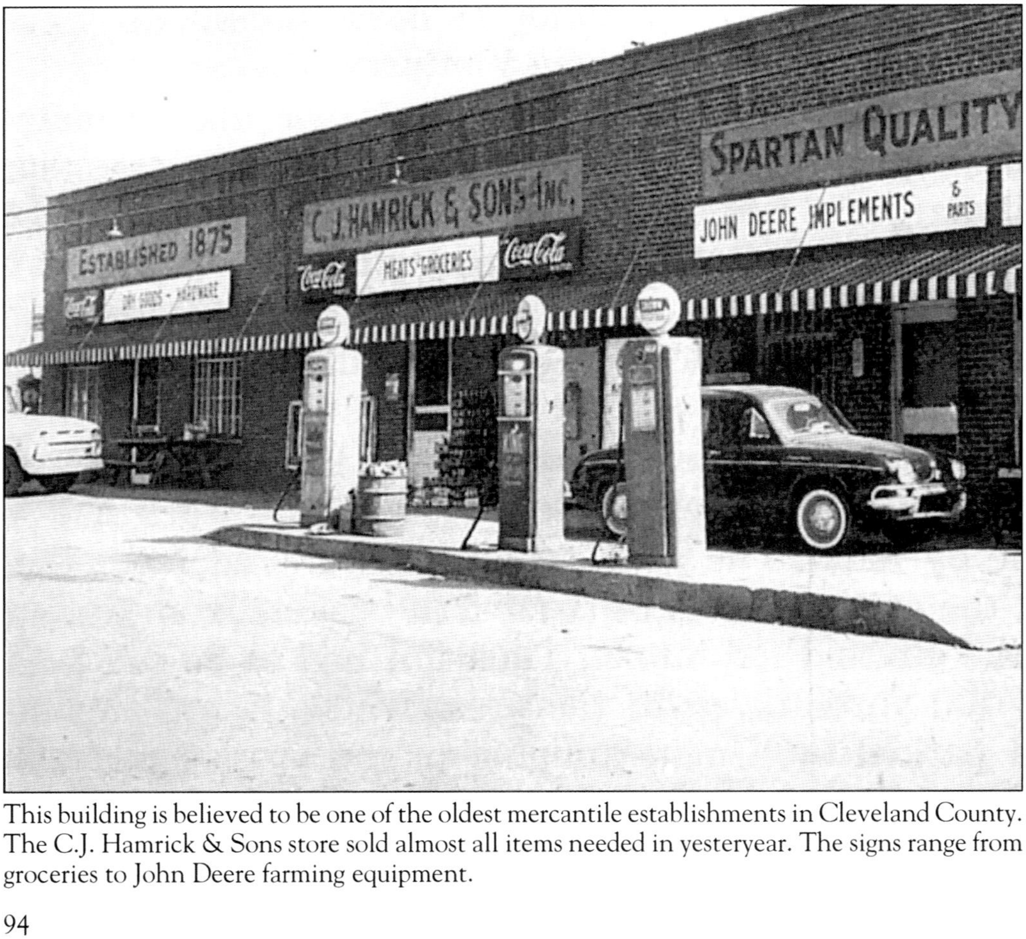

This building is believed to be one of the oldest mercantile establishments in Cleveland County. The C.J. Hamrick & Sons store sold almost all items needed in yesteryear. The signs range from groceries to John Deere farming equipment.

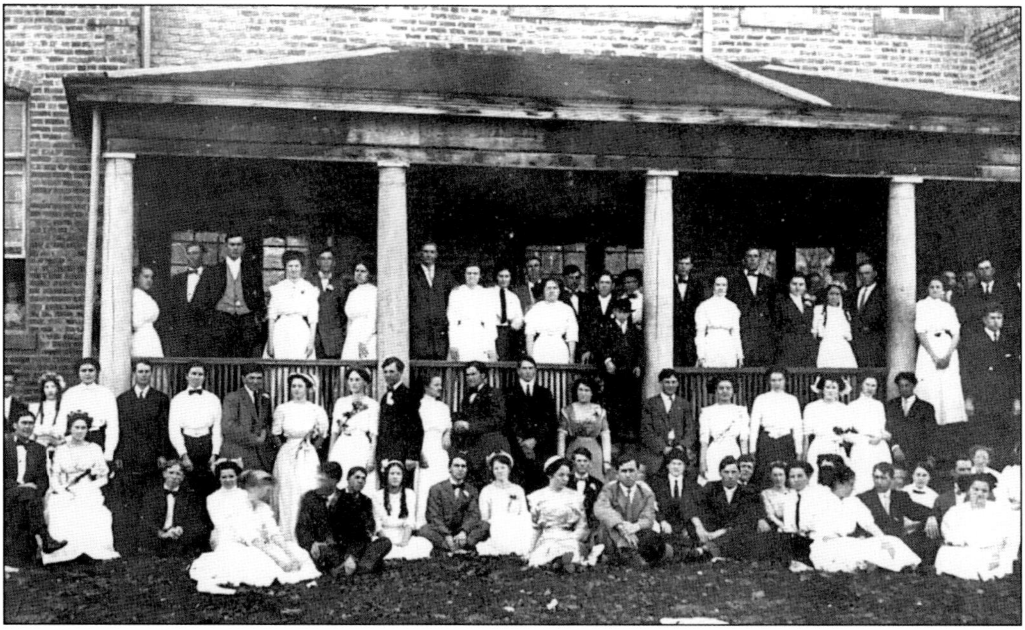

Until it burned in 1957, the main building on the high school campus and later junior college was the Huggins-Curtis Building, named in honor of professors J.D. Huggins and Etta Curtis. Here, students dress up for a May Day picture at the female entrance to the building. (*The Anchor*, GWC Annual.)

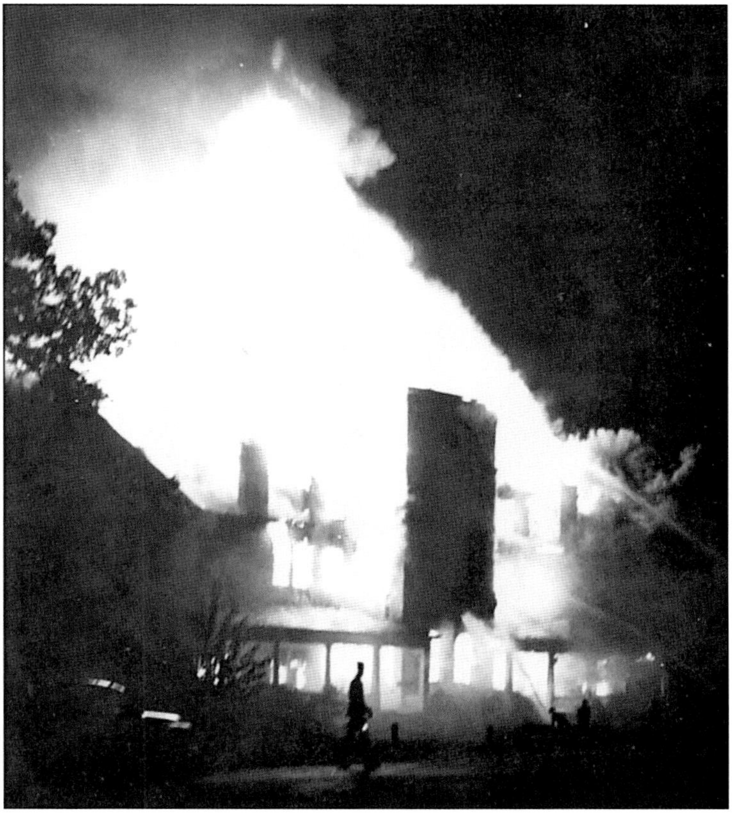

The high school became Boiling Springs Junior College in 1928 and Gardner-Webb Junior College in 1942. By 1957, the Huggins-Curtis Building served many purposes including housing the administration. A nighttime fire destroyed the historic structure in 1957. (*The Anchor*, GWC Annual.)

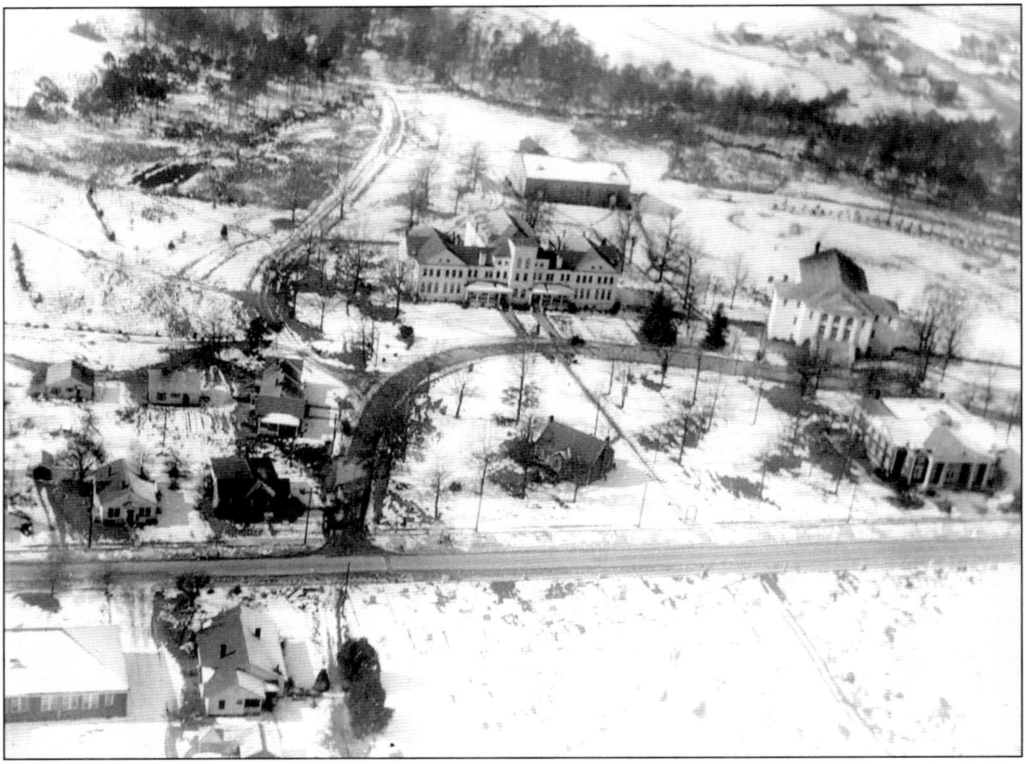

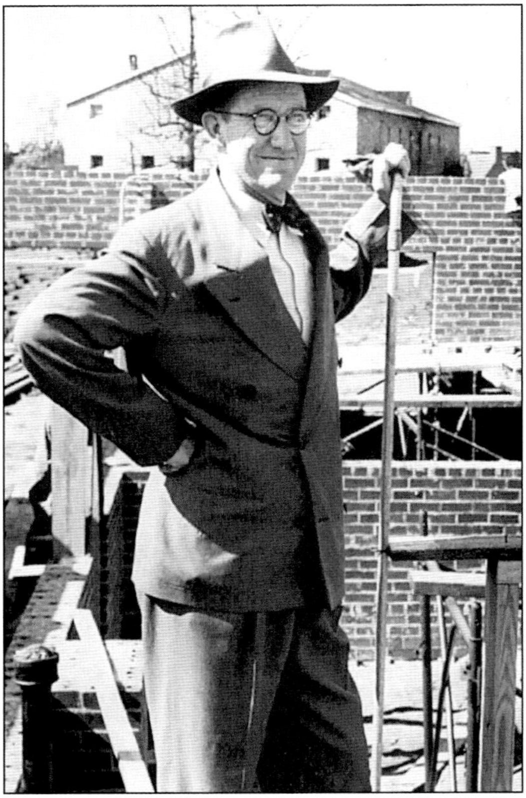

This snowy, aerial photo of the early 1940s looks across South Main Street at the college. The Huggins-Curtis Building is in the center with the Hamrick Building at the right. The Boiling Springs Baptist Church is to the far right. (Madge Harris.)

The struggling junior college gained a new president in 1943, at the time it was beginning the era as Gardner-Webb College. Dr. Phillip Lovin Elliott had taught English at Mars Hill and Western Carolina Colleges. He became a widely respected leader and guided the college for a record 18 years. He died in his office in 1961 just two months before his retirement. (*The Anchor*, GWC Annual.)

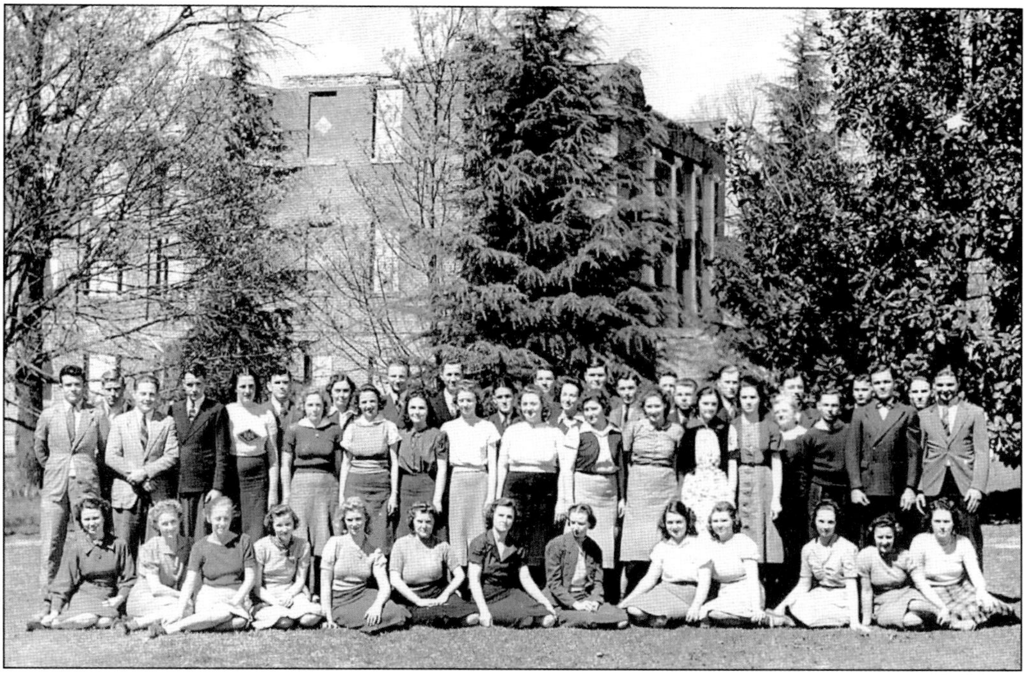

Fire had hit the college long before 1957. The 1937 class of Boiling Springs Junior College poses with the burned out Memorial Building in the background. (*The Anchor*, GWC Annual.)

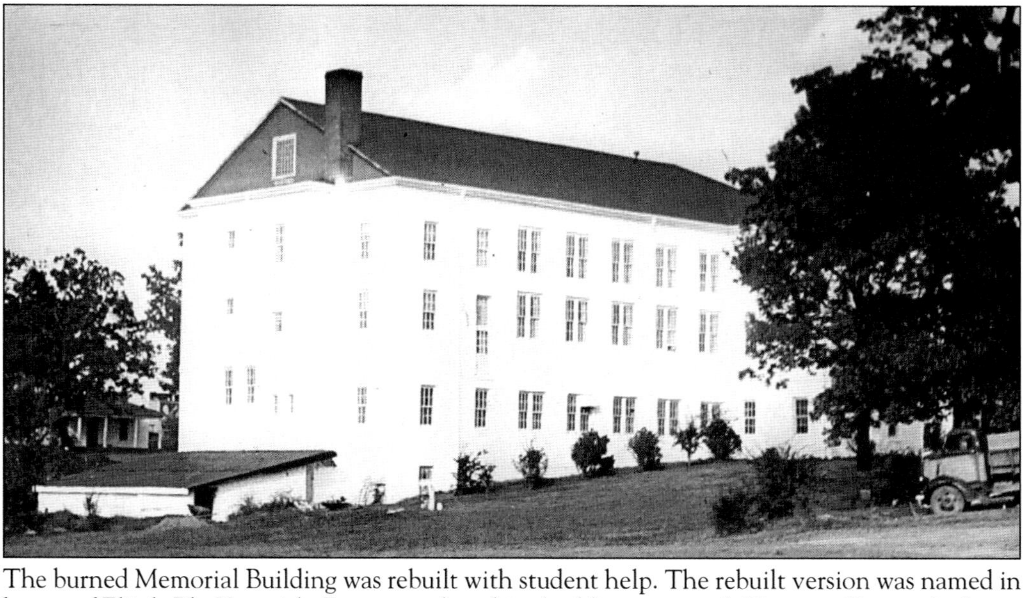

The burned Memorial Building was rebuilt with student help. The rebuilt version was named in honor of Elijah Bly Hamrick. For years, the white building was, with Huggins-Curtis, the heart of the campus. (*The Anchor*, GWC Annual.)

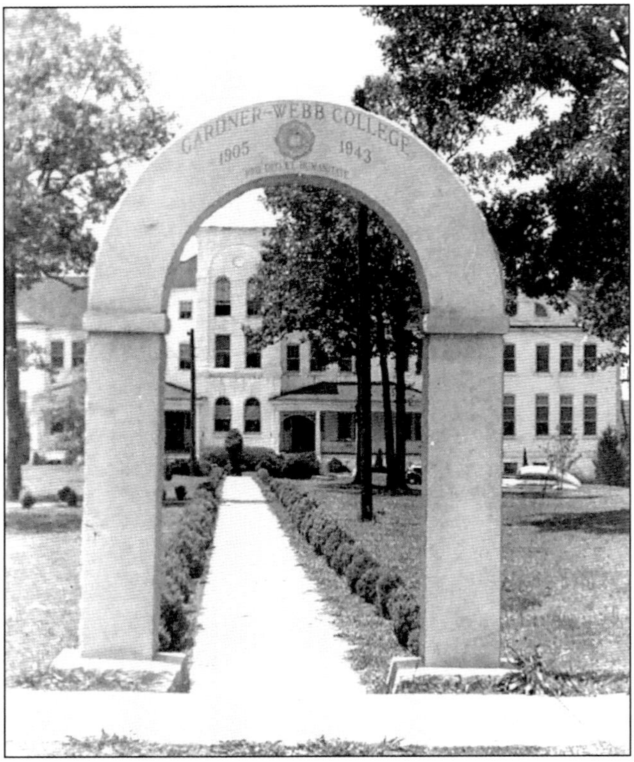

The arch carrying the college motto "Pro Deo et Humanitate" (for God and humanity) was built in 1943. In this picture, it stood on South Main Street with Huggins-Curtis in the background. For years, all graduates marched through the arch on their way to the graduation ceremony. (*The Anchor*, GWC Annual.)

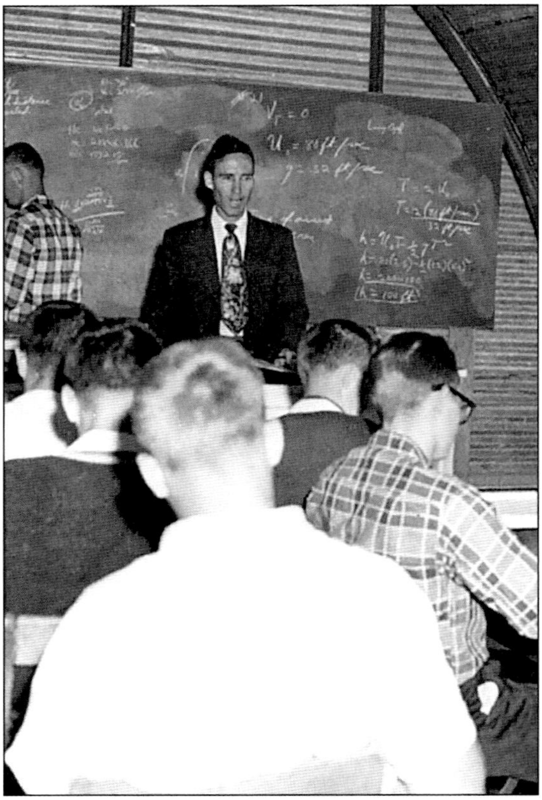

In the 1950s, a quonset hut served as a classroom. The hut was located just north of the Hamrick building. Here, Prof. Seth L. Washburn teaches physics. (*The Anchor*, GWC Annual.)

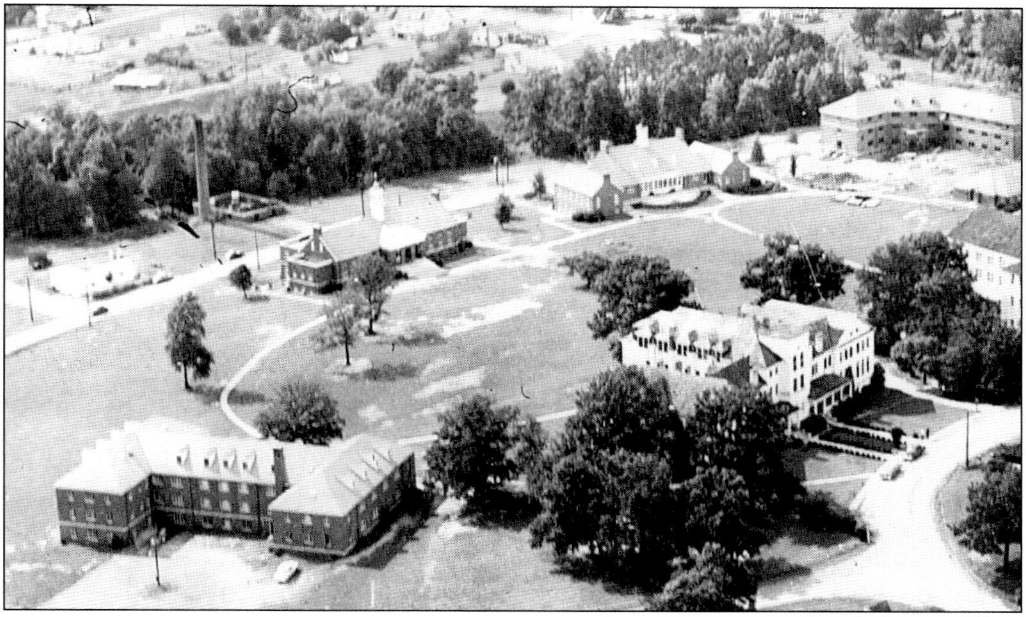

This photo was taken a year before Huggins-Curtis burned. At the upper right, Stroup Dormitory for girls was under construction. The seven major buildings on the quad are, from left to right, Huggins-Curtis, Hamrick, H.A.P.Y. Dormitory, Stroup, O. Max Gardner Memorial, John R. Dover Library, and Decker Dormitory for boys. Decker was named for O. Max Gardner's son. (*The Anchor*, GWC Annual.)

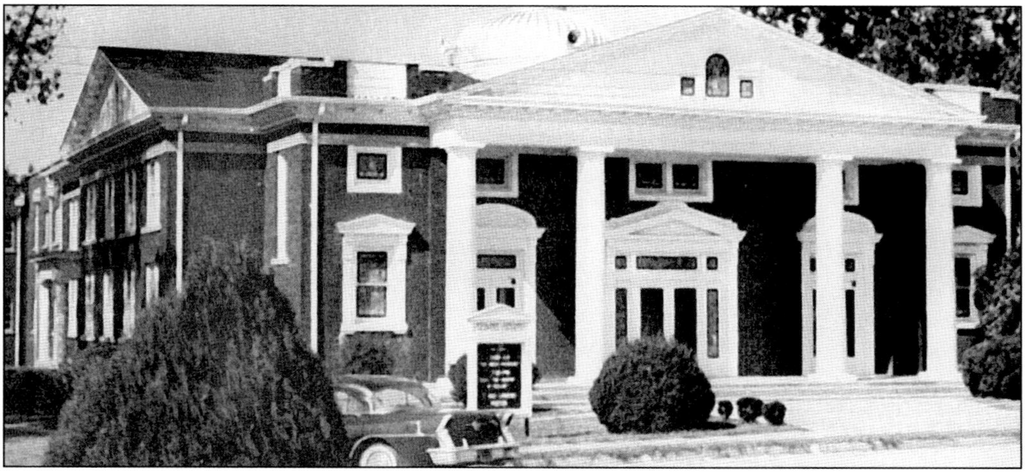

This picture of the Boiling Springs Baptist Church on South Main Street is from the 1950s. The church occupied this structure from 1924 until 1969. After the college bought the property, the auditorium served briefly as an opera house until the building was razed to make way for the Dover Chapel. (*The Anchor*, GWC Annual.)

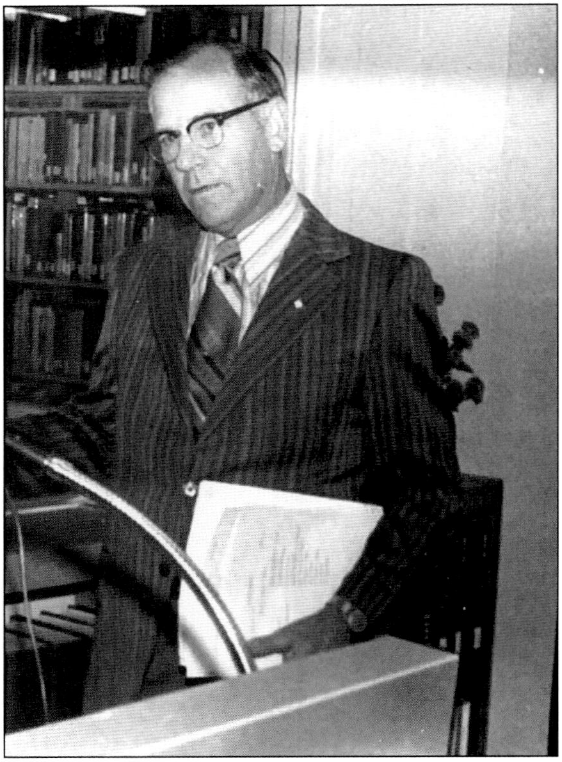

Students remember professors and have stories about those who made an impression on them. Hubert C. Dixon taught math from 1935 (with time off to serve in World War II) until his sudden death in April 1976. Dixon was, in the language of the past, a gentleman and a scholar. His tenure is the longest of any Gardner-Webb professor. Thousands of students remember his firm but gentle demeanor in math class. (*The Anchor*, GWC Annual.)

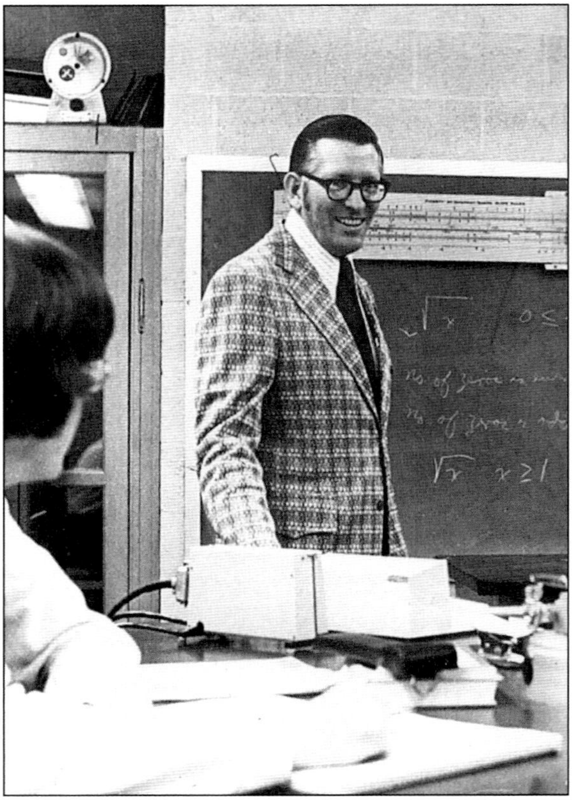

Dr. Paul Jolley joined Professor Dixon in 1962 and became department chairman when Dixon died. Jolley led the mathematics department until his retirement in 1995. The overlapping careers of the two men spanned well over half a century. (*The Anchor*, GWC Annual.)

The Washburn family has had a great impact on Boiling Springs and Gardner-Webb. Drs. Wyan and Gene Washburn served the community as medical doctors for decades. Their sister, Dorothy Hamrick Edwards, was registrar of Gardner-Webb for over 25 years. She is loved and respected by all who worked with her. (*The Anchor*, GWC Annual.)

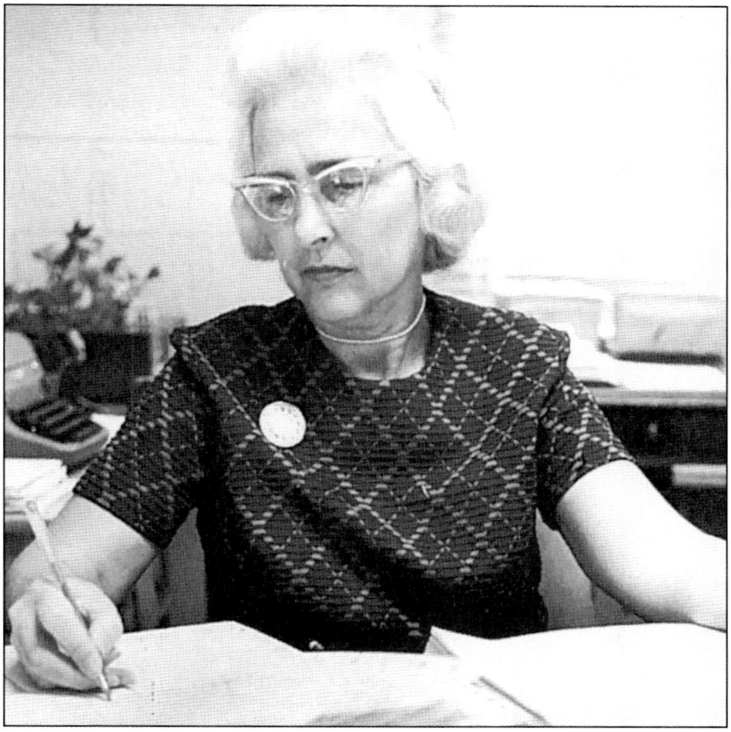

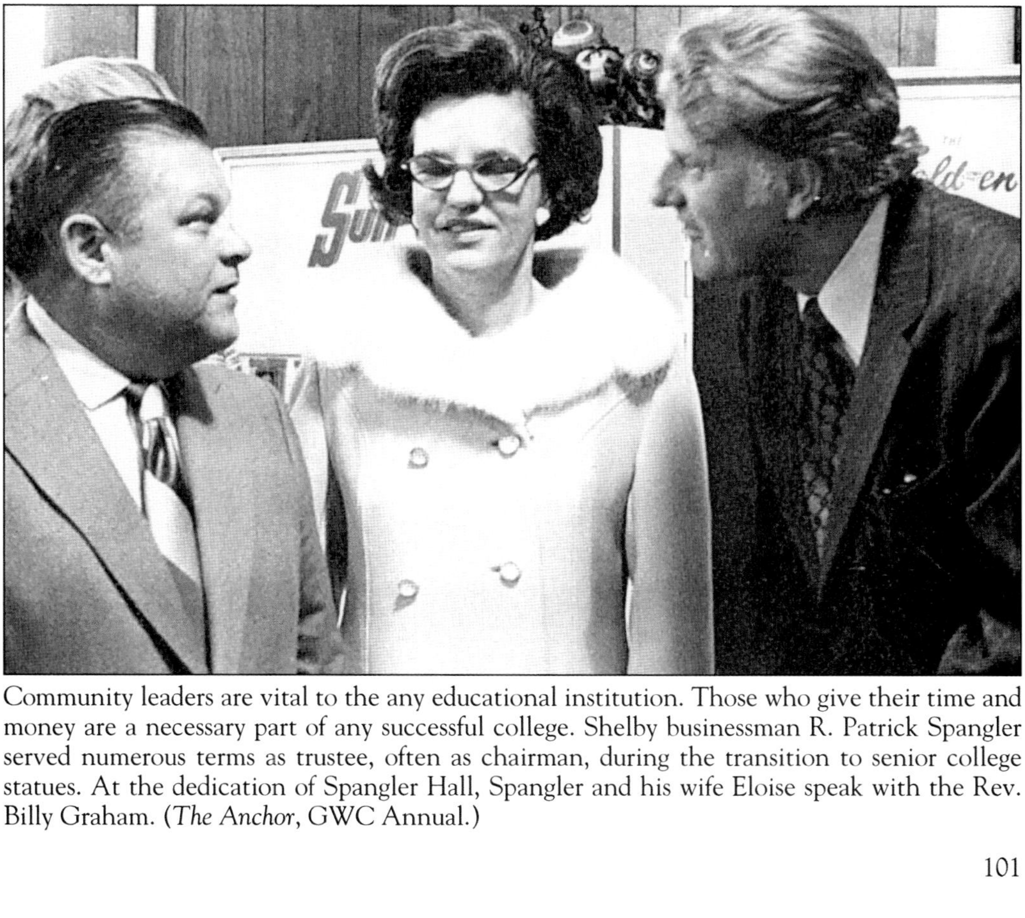

Community leaders are vital to the any educational institution. Those who give their time and money are a necessary part of any successful college. Shelby businessman R. Patrick Spangler served numerous terms as trustee, often as chairman, during the transition to senior college statues. At the dedication of Spangler Hall, Spangler and his wife Eloise speak with the Rev. Billy Graham. (*The Anchor*, GWC Annual.)

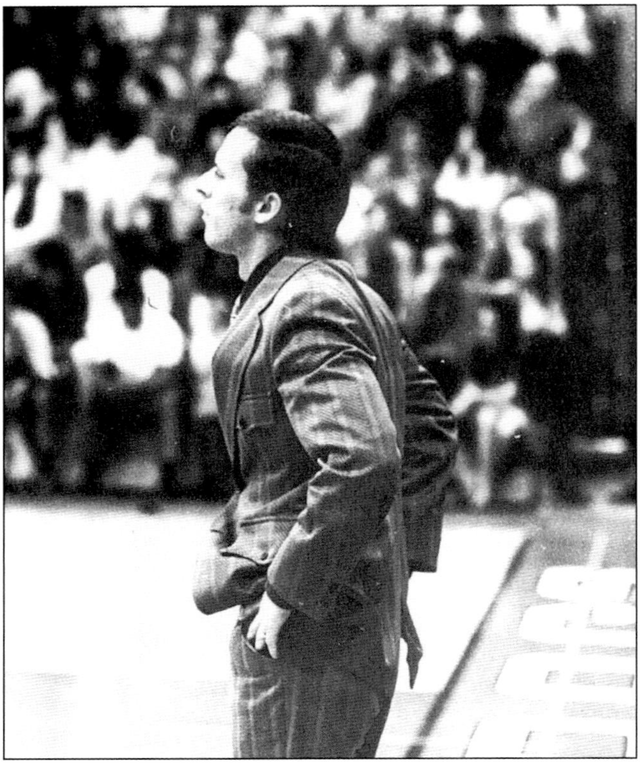

During the 1960s, as Gardner-Webb moved toward senior college status, basketball brought name recognition to the school. Coach Eddie Holbrook led the Bulldogs to national tournaments in both junior college and senior college competition. (*The Anchor*, GWC Annual.)

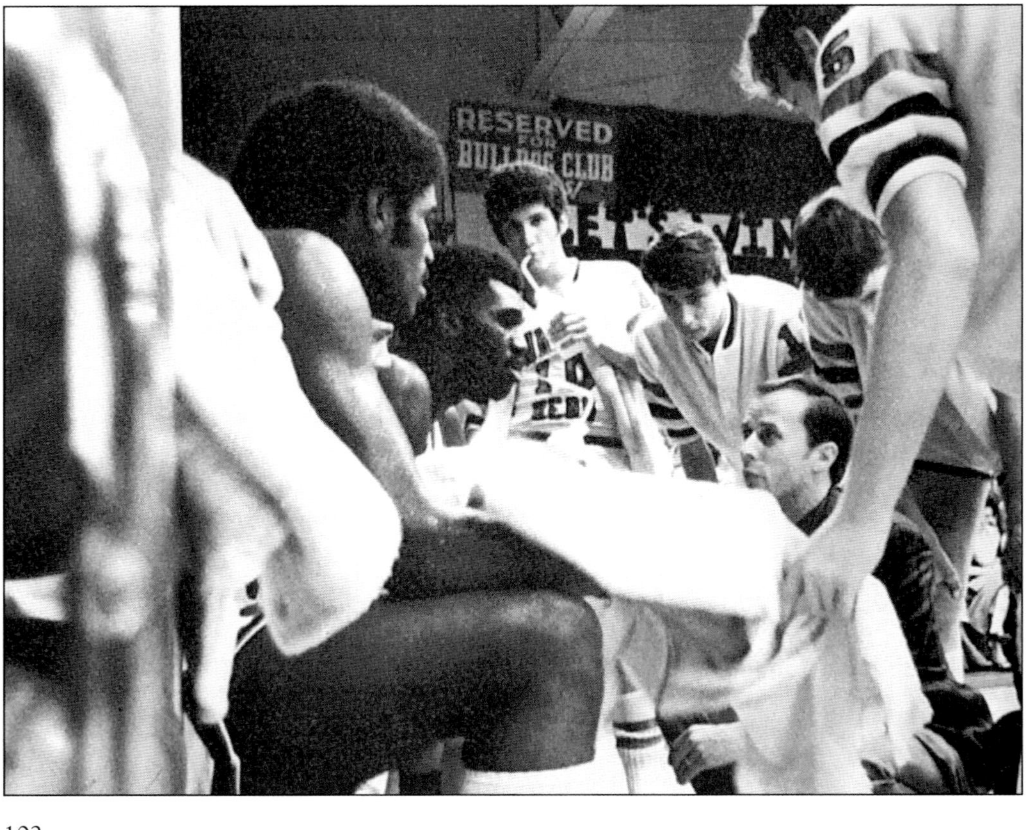

Coach Holbrook talks to his team during a time-out in Bost Gymnasium. Former Kings Mountain High School star and future ABA professional star George Adams is seated at the left. (*The Anchor*, GWC Annual.)

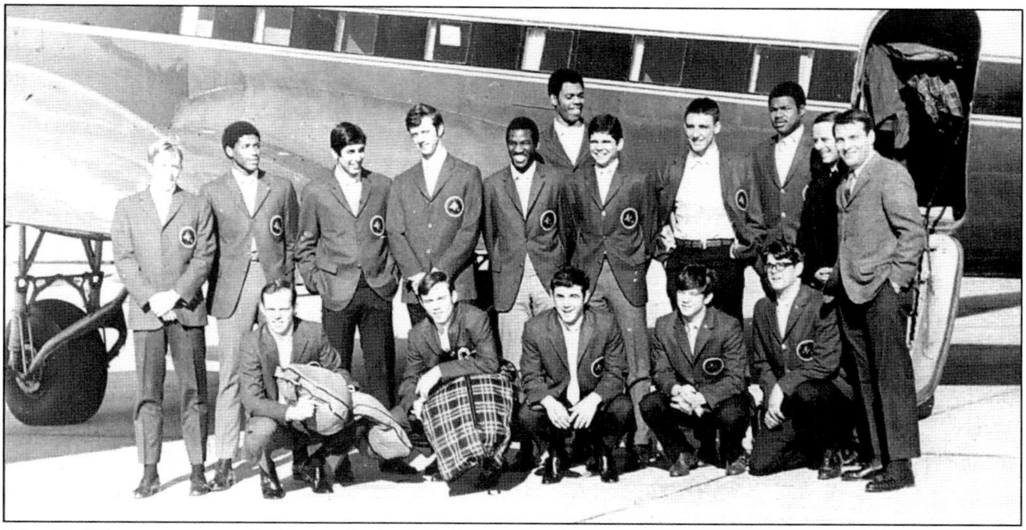

The Bulldogs pose just before a flight to Hutchinson, Kansas, for the National Championships. From left to right are (kneeling) Steve Kubeck, Jack McGill, Alan Ladd, David Crisp, and Larry Thomas; (standing) Kevin Cantwell, ABA star George Adams, Tony Spagnola, Willie Rogers, Joe Brookins, ABA and NBA standout Artis Gilmore, Gerry Vallaincourt (later WBT's Gerry V.), Meriedith Scruggs, Ernie Fleming, Coach Holbrook, and Assistant Coach Ron Hooper. (*The Anchor*, GWC Annual.)

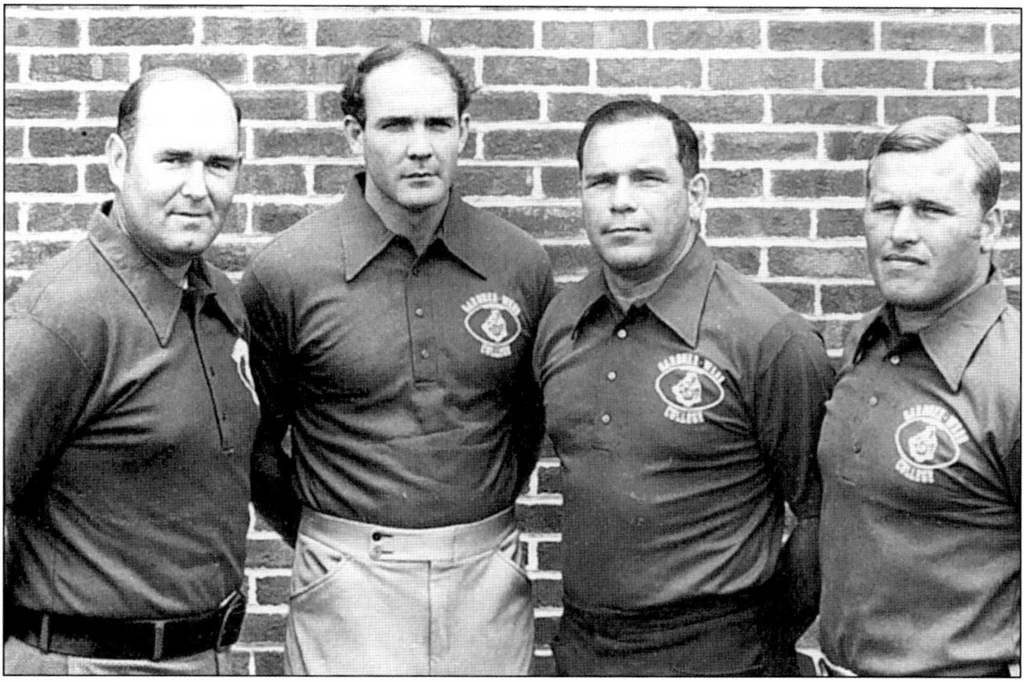

Although these coaches led the Gardner-Webb 1973 football team to its first bowl game as a senior college, many will remember them as leading area educators. Head Coach George Litton (left) went on to lead Crest High School as principal, Ken Sanford (second from left) later became principal at Chase High School, and Steve Curtis (far right) became superintendent for Shelby City Schools. Richard Mayes left Gardner-Webb to coach at Tennessee Tech. (*The Anchor*, GWC Annual.)

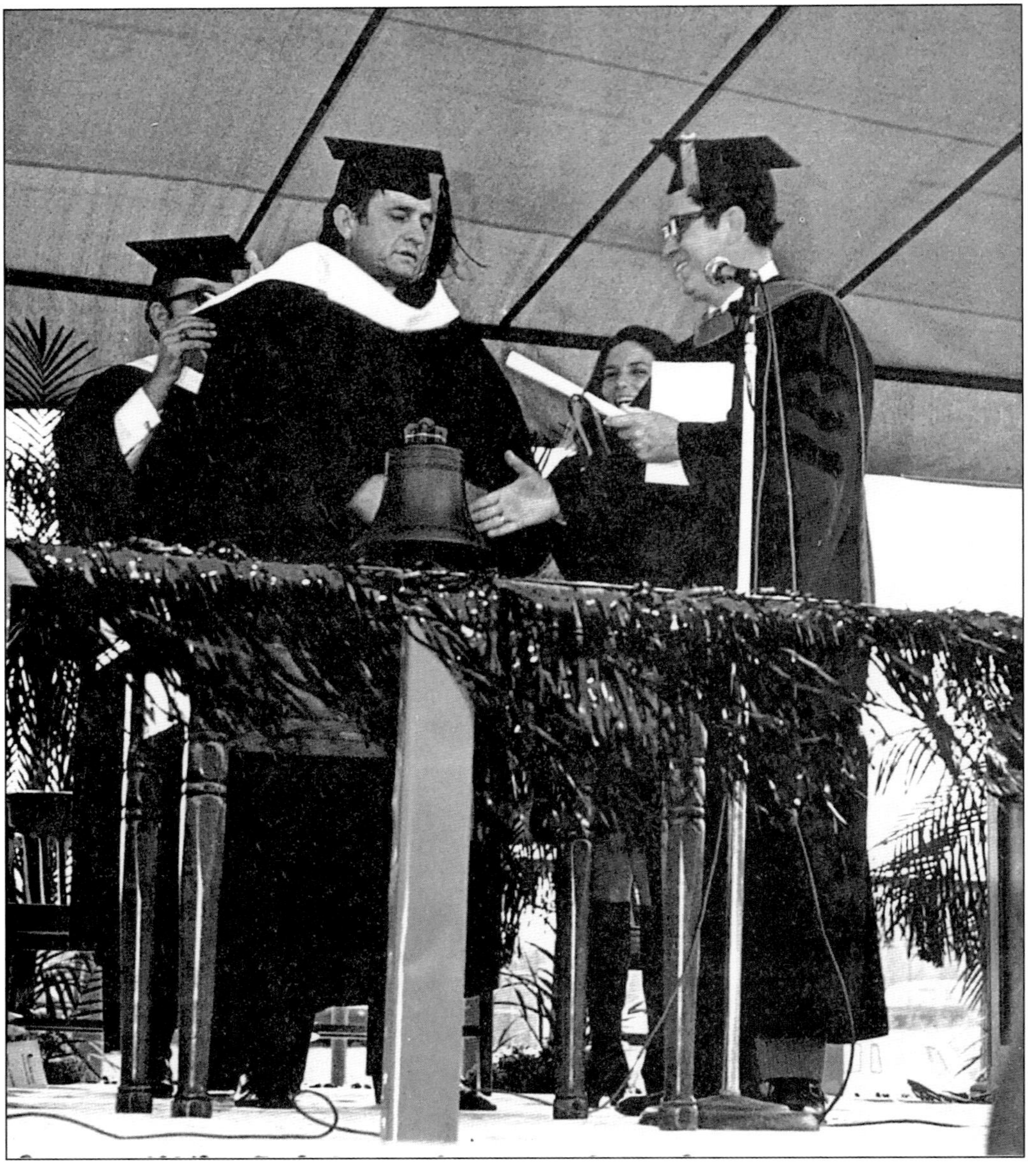

After the passing of Dr. Phil Elliott in 1961, the college had a smooth transition since Dr. Eugene Poston had already been selected as the new president. Dr. Poston led a "decade of advance," which resulted in the college reaching four-year status. Dr. Poston served 15 years as president. Here he presents an honorary doctorate to singer Johnny Cash. (*The Anchor*, GWC Annual.)

Five

Around the County

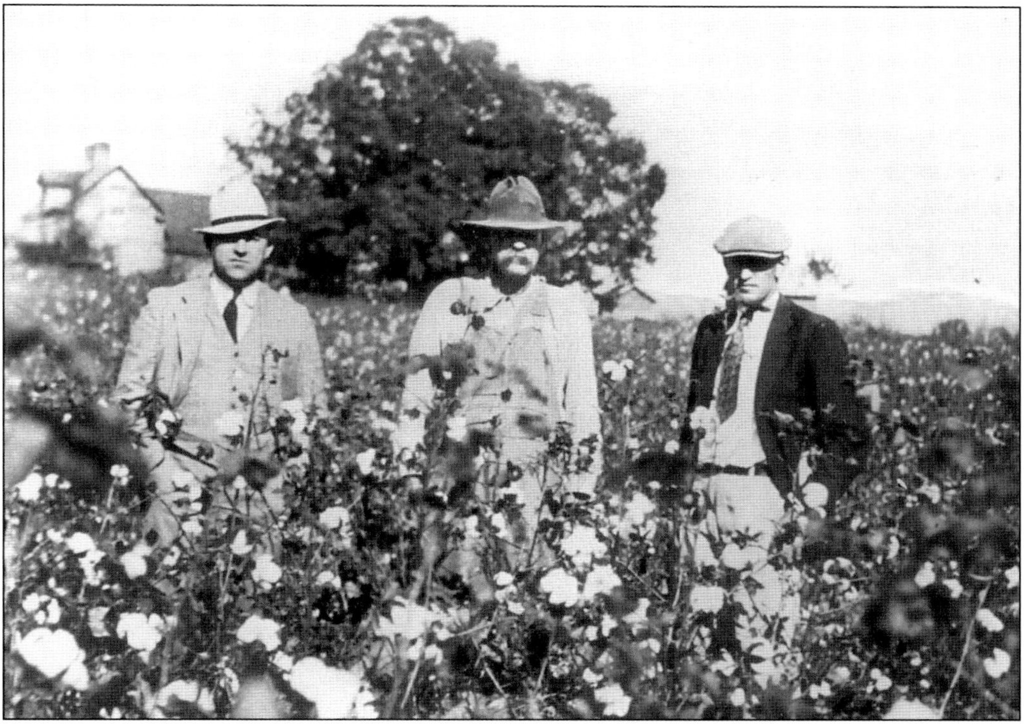

O.Z. Morgan was a leader and pioneer in agriculture extension in Cleveland County and North Carolina. John D. Honeycutt and R.P. Weathers are pictured with O.Z. examining a cotton field west of Shelby. The Burwell and Francis Doggett Blanton home seen in the background was built before the Civil War. The house still stands today west of Shelby on Highway 74. (Jack Morgan Family.)

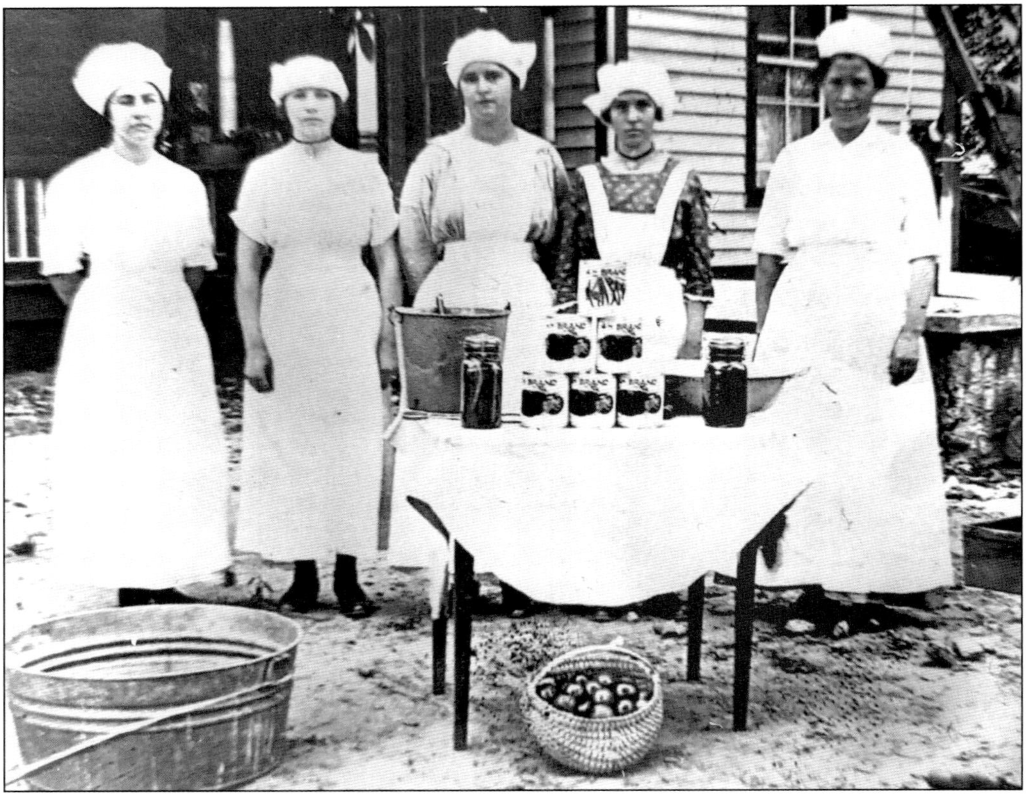

The Tomato Club in Belwood is the first known organization of agriculture extension in Cleveland County. Pictured from left to right in this 1915 photo are Hattie Bingham, Ora Sain, Carrie Willis, Jettie Hicks, and Susan Elliott Weathers. (Cleveland County Agriculture Extension.)

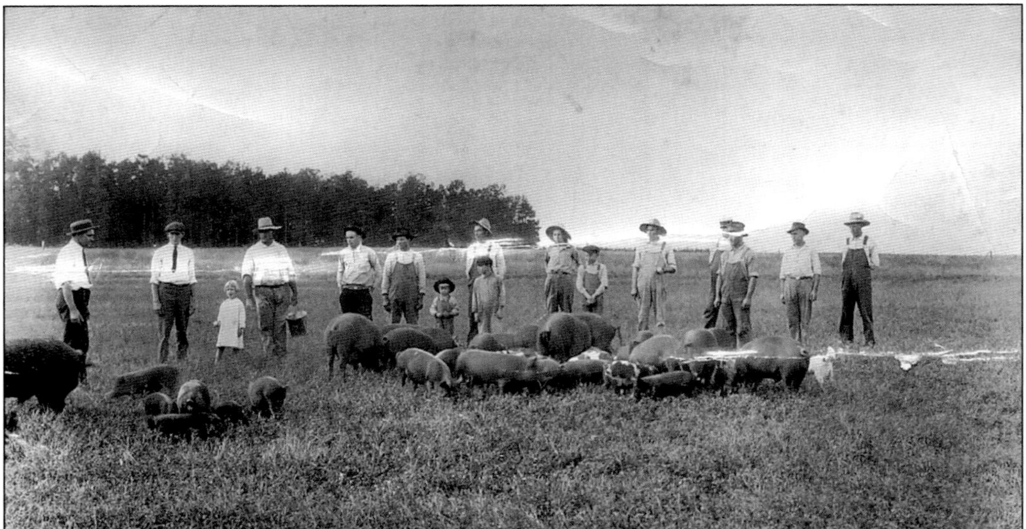

This United States Department of Agriculture photo shows a swine specialist (left) visiting Cleveland County and talking with area farmers. Second from left is local farmer O.Z. Morgan. (Jack Morgan Family.)

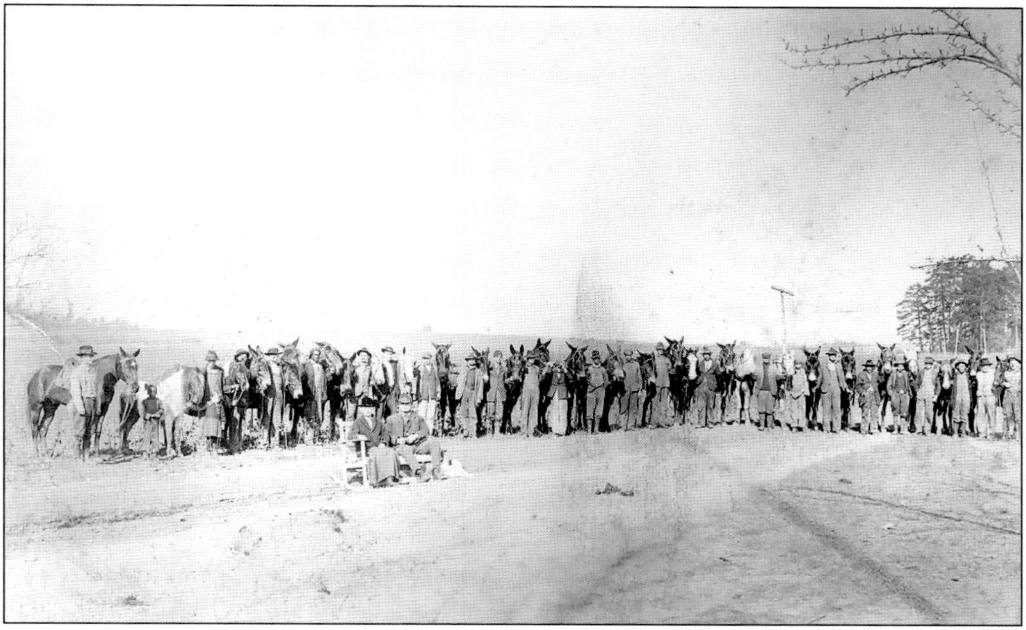

William A. and Mary Elliott Lattimore posed for this c. 1920 photo with a group of tenant farmers and their mules. The Lattimores' son Sam is the first gentleman on the left. The Lattimore farm was located southwest of Shelby where Riverbend Acres is today. (Bill Lattimore.)

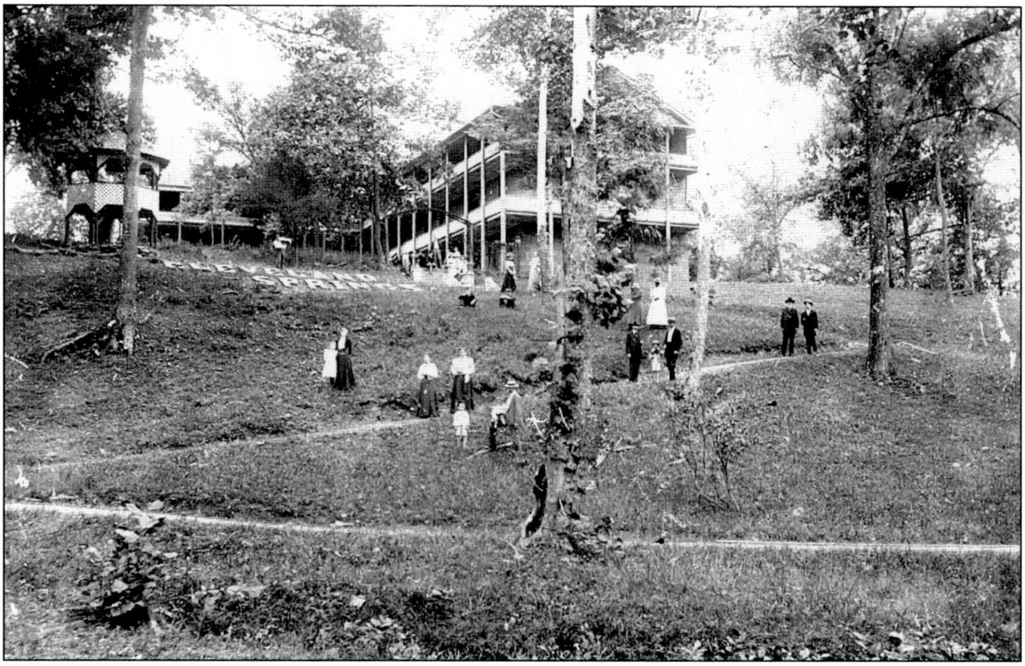

Visitors to the area pose along the path to the three springhouses of the famed Cleveland Springs Hotel in this c. 1900 photo. The second of three hotels built on the site can be seen in the background. When the county was formed in 1841, the state legislature noted that the county seat should be located within four miles of the springs. This hotel was built in 1866 and burned September 9, 1909 because of a lightning strike. (Mike Royster.)

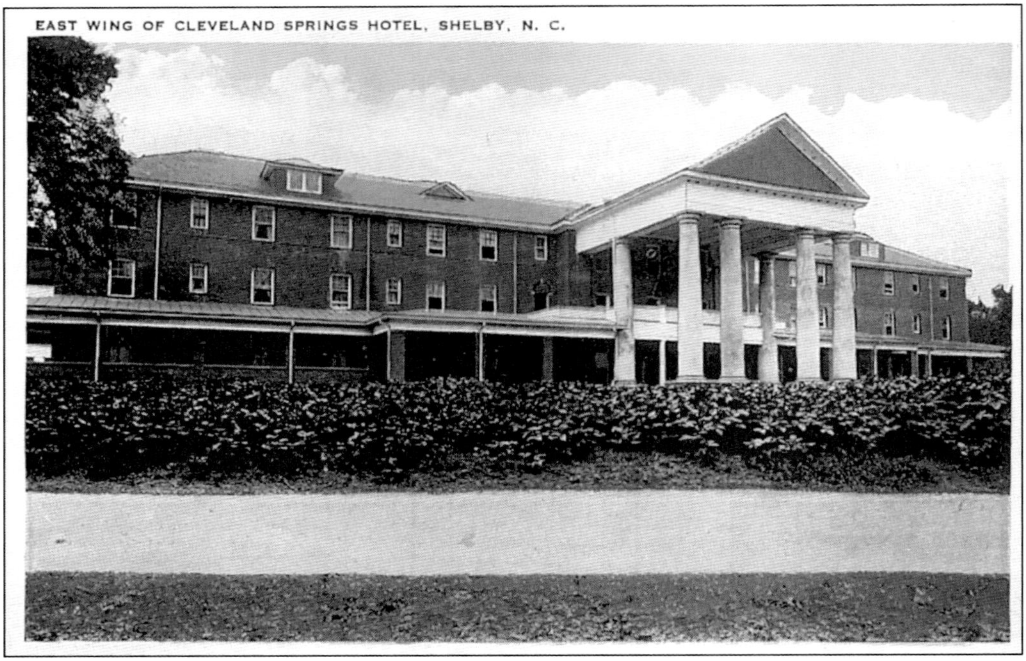

The third of three hotels built at Cleveland Springs was constructed in 1921 at a cost of $250,000. Horse riding trails led from the hotel towards Shelby near the Belvedere community. All three hotels were destroyed by fire, this one in 1928.

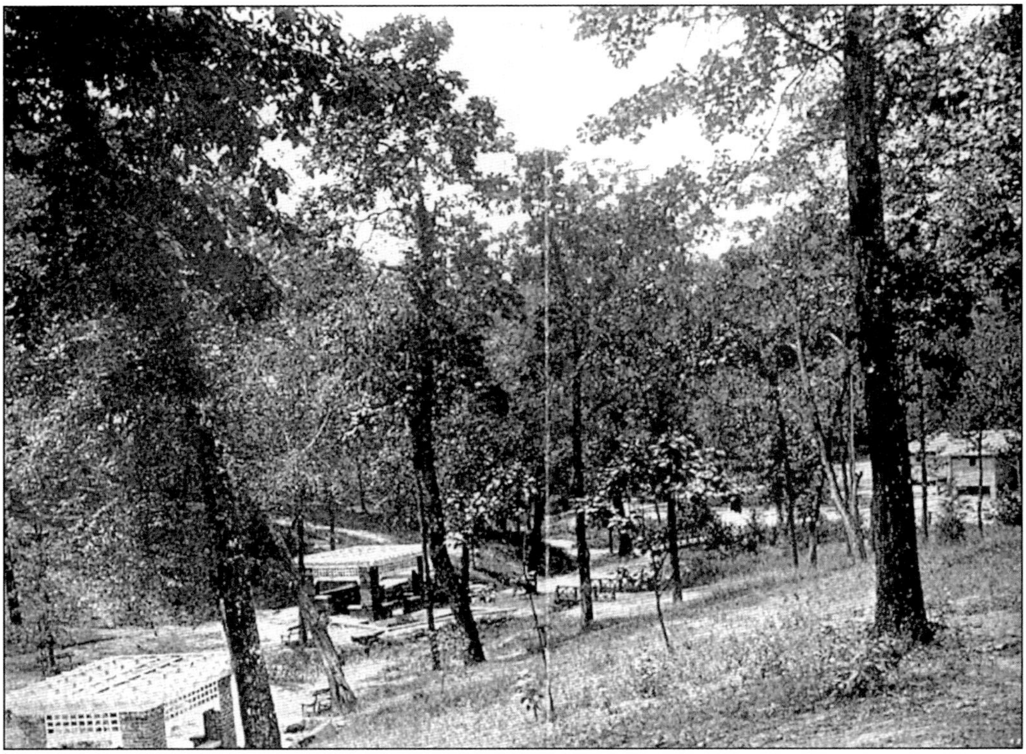

The Cleveland Springs consisted of three individual springs including white sulfur, red sulfur, and carbonate of lime. The bath house is seen in the background of this c. 1925 photograph.

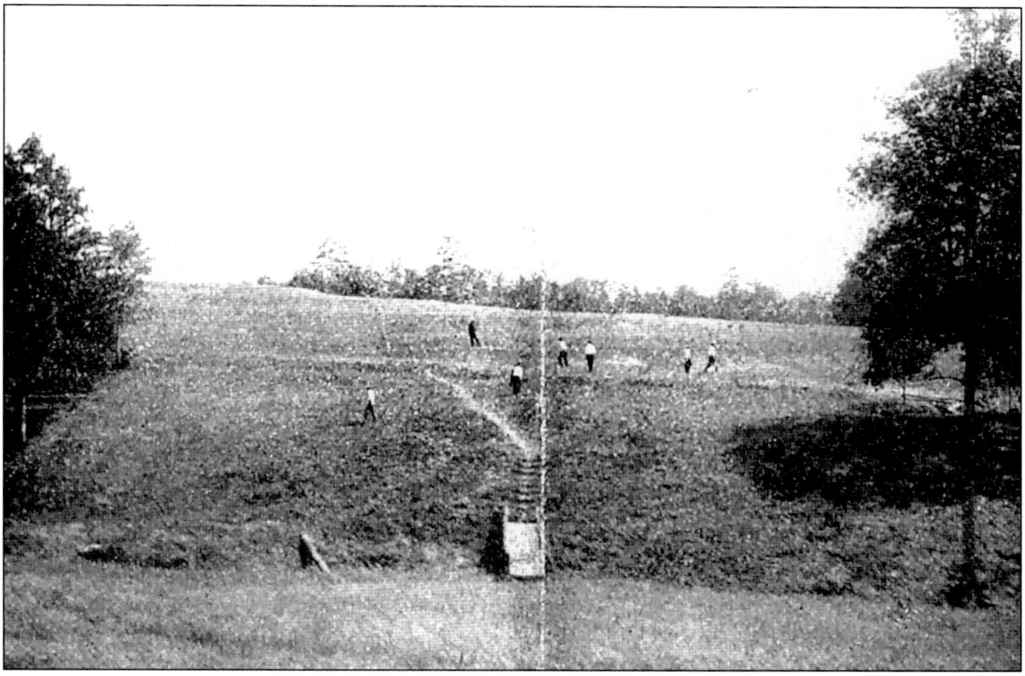

A 1920s brochure detailing the recreation facilities surrounding the hotel included a picture of a nine-hole golf course. This photo notes the fairway from the first tee. The same fairway today is a part of the 16th hole of the Cleveland Country Club.

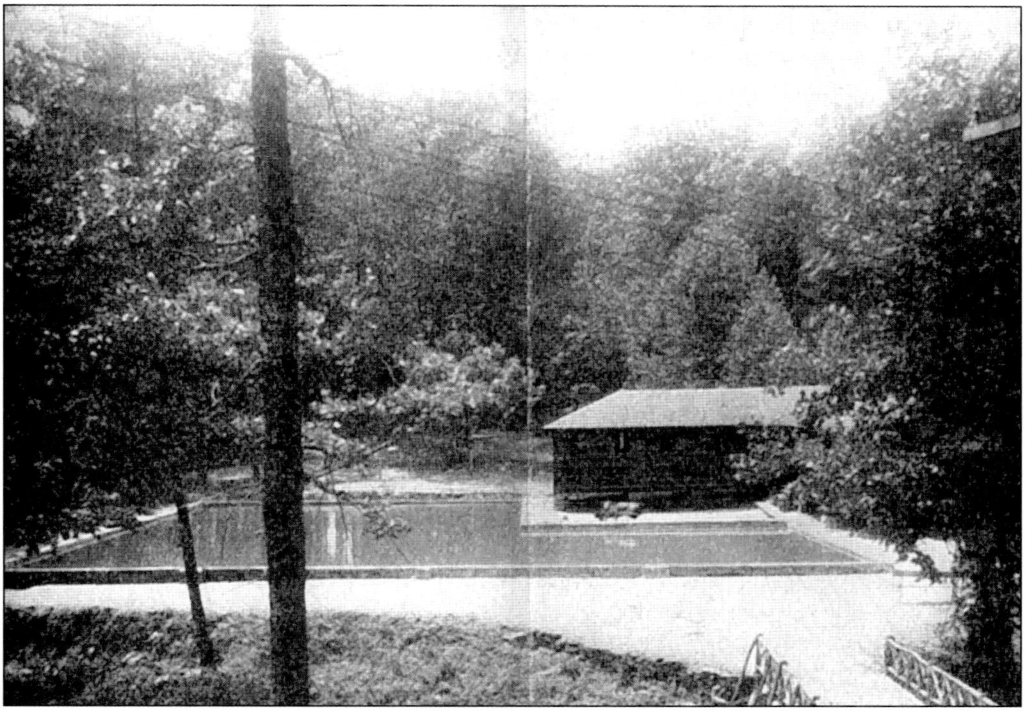

The resort included a bathhouse and a swimming pool, pictured here. A portion of the concrete foundation of the pool remains today just west of the condominiums that are named for the columns of the hotel that stood for 50 years after the last hotel was destroyed.

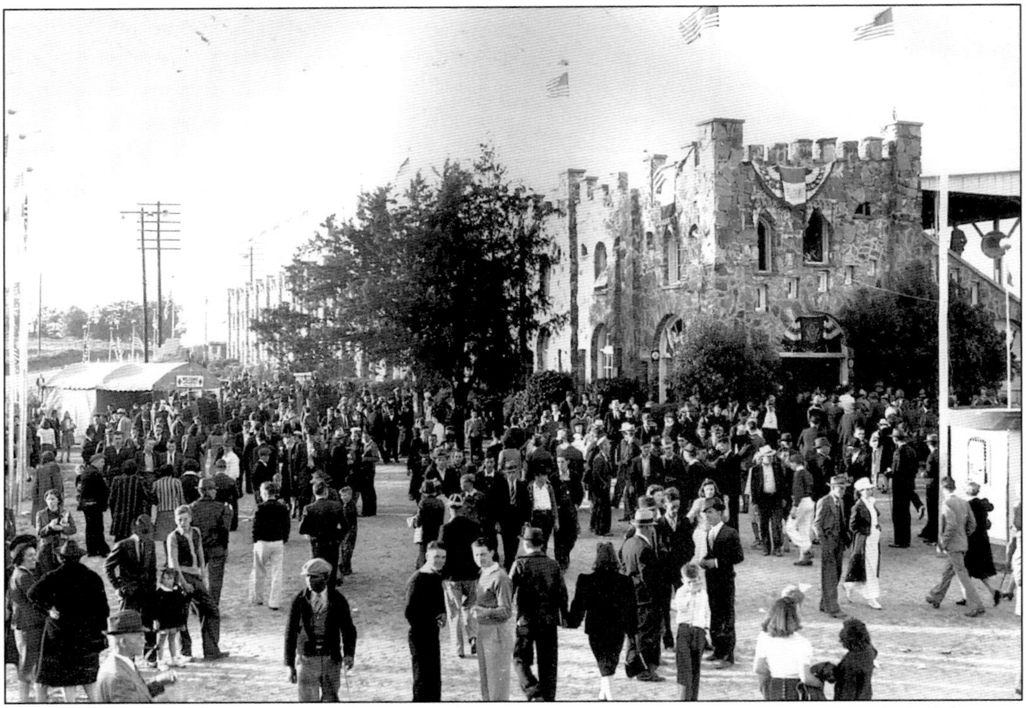

This 1948 photo shows the entrance to the Cleveland County Fairgrounds. The old stone grandstand can be seen to the right. City and county came together in the fall of the year to celebrate the harvesting of crops. (Joe A. Goforth.)

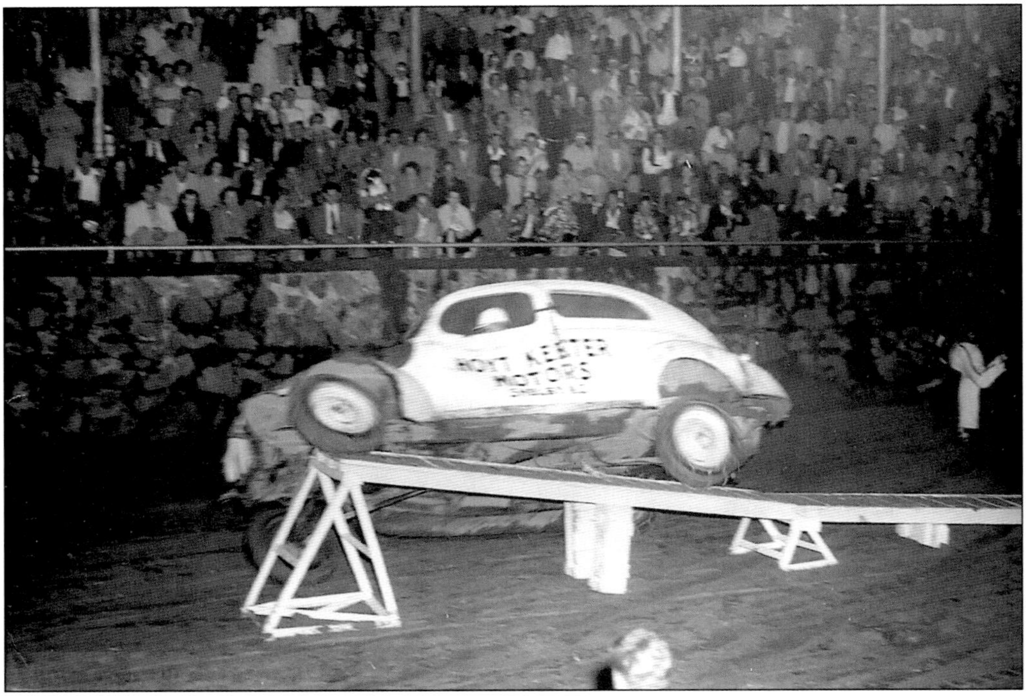

Automobile thrill shows have long been a favorite attraction at the fair. Hoyt Keeter Motors sponsored this auto used in what looks to be a role over demolition. (Joe A. Goforth.)

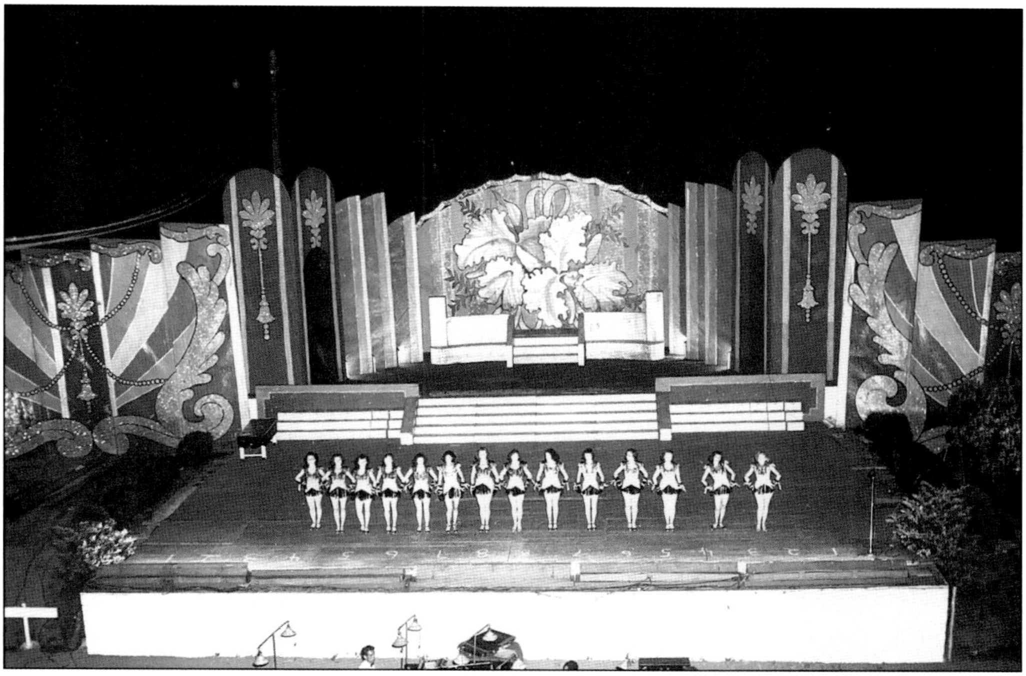

Elaborate stage shows were produced in the main grandstand. Here the "Roxyettes" perform before the audience. Note the orchestra in the foreground of what would later be the front straight of the racetrack. (Joe A. Goforth.)

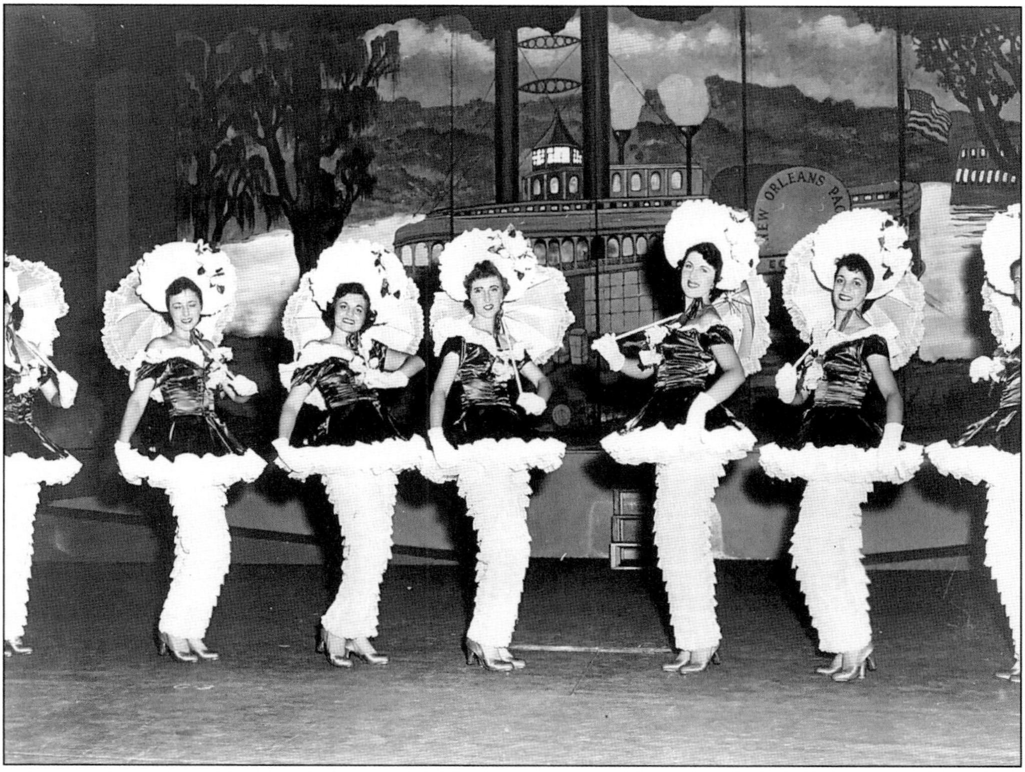

This close-up of the performers shows the elaborate details of the costumes. (Joe A. Goforth.)

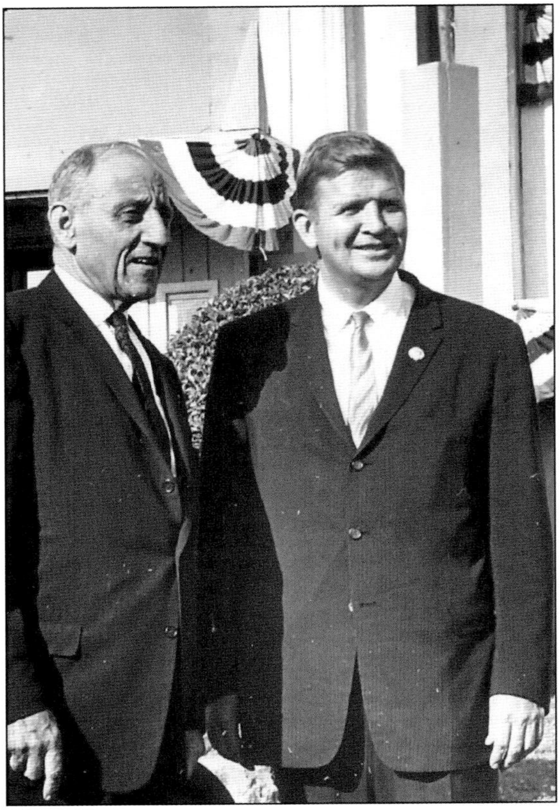

This 1960s photo shows North Carolina governor Terry Sanford touring the fairgrounds with "Mr. Fair," Dr. J.S. Dorton. (Joe A. Goforth.)

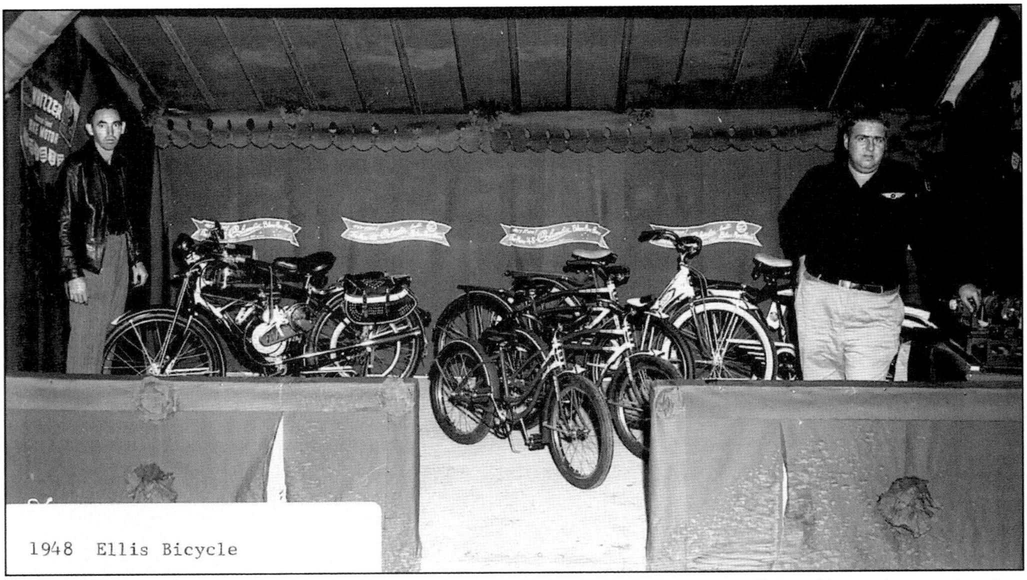

This 1948 photo shows the Ellis Bicycle Shop displaying the new models of bicycles at the fair just in time for Christmas. How many thousands of local youth had their dream of a new bicycle realized through a purchase from Ellis? (Joe A. Goforth.)

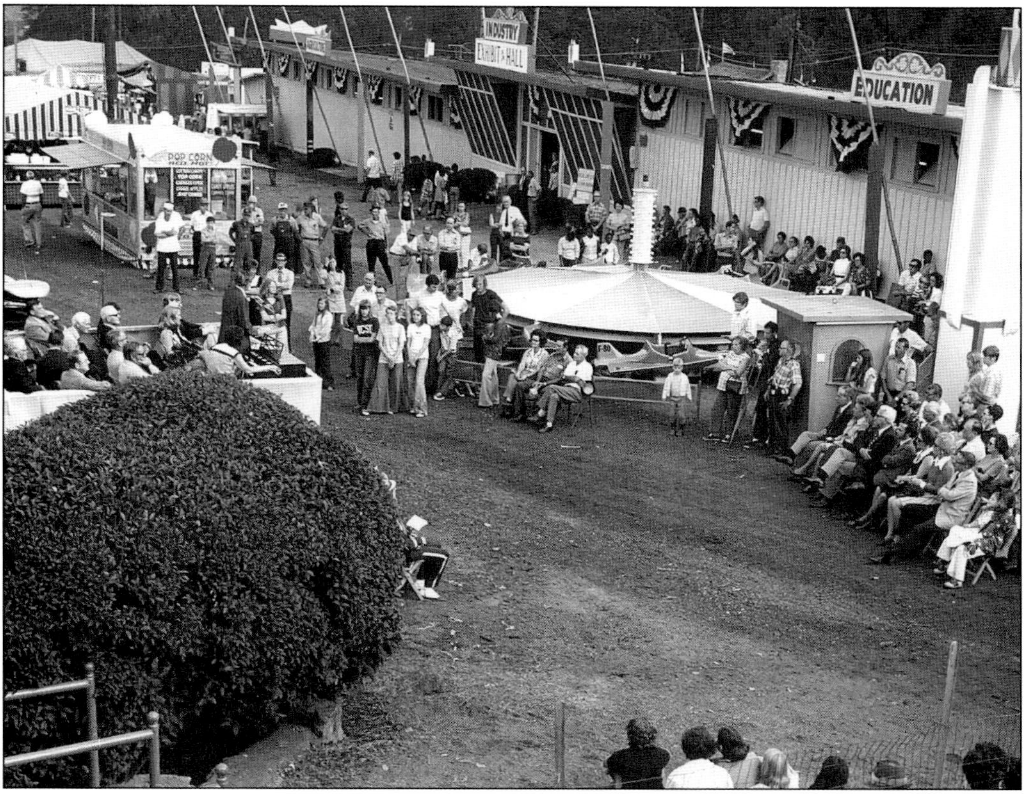

A crowd has gathered in front of the Exhibit Hall to hear speakers gathered on a stage to the left of this 1960s photo. Among the dignitaries gathered is George Blanton, president of First National Bank. (Joe A. Goforth.)

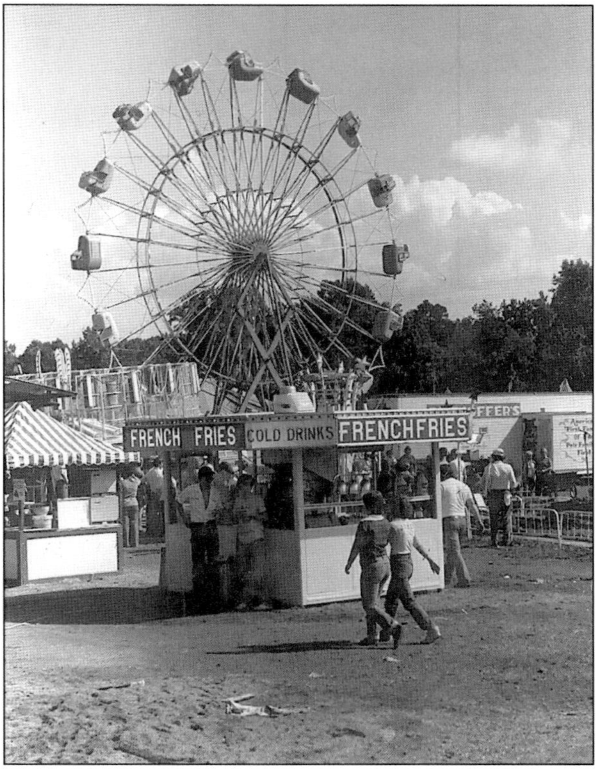

You can almost smell the vinegar fries in this photo leading to the midway of rides and entertainment at the fair. Do you remember the days when sawdust lined the midway? (Evan Thompson.)

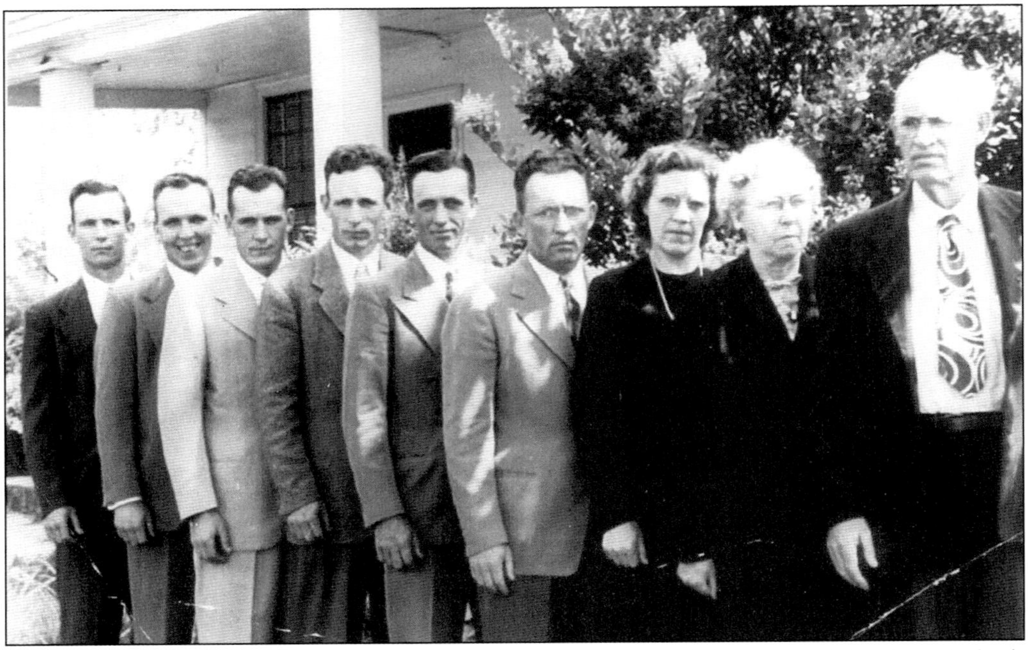

The family name Goforth is synonymous with management of the county fair. Sam Goforth managed the fair in the 1970s and turned over management duties to his brother Joe who remains as manager today. The George E. Goforth family gathered for this Mother's Day photo in 1949. Pictured, from left to right, are Coleman, Joe, Sam, George M., Charles, John, Zella Goforth Sweezy, Elizabeth Pannell Goforth, and George E. Goforth. (Joe A. Goforth.)

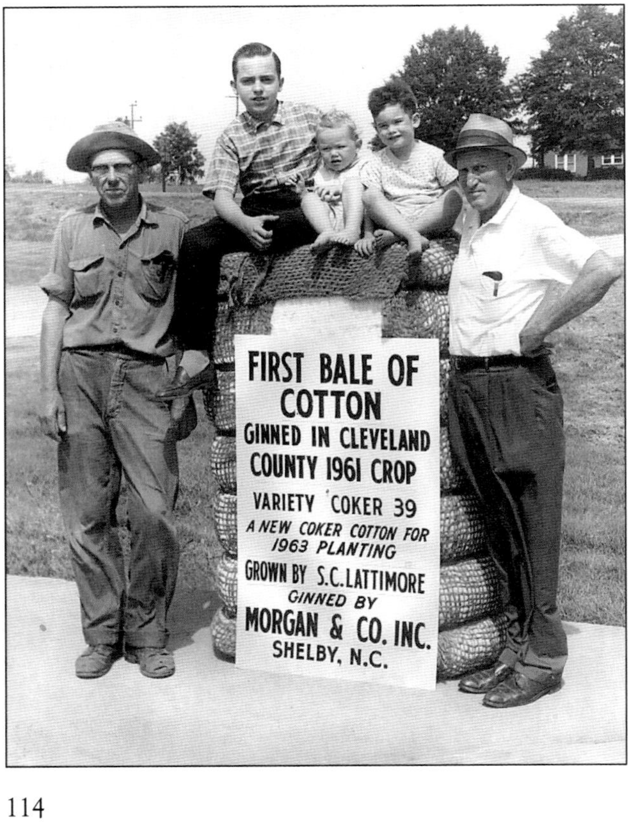

Cleveland County was for many years the leading producer of cotton in North Carolina, reaching a high of 72,000 bales in 1948. Max Camp (left) poses with O.Z. Morgan in this 1961 photo. Sitting on the bale of cotton are Buck Lattimore, who today serves as the industrial commissioner for the state of North Carolina; Neel Lattimore, who served as press secretary for former first lady Hilary Clinton; and Talley Lattimore, an attorney in Columbia, South Carolina. (Jack Morgan Family.)

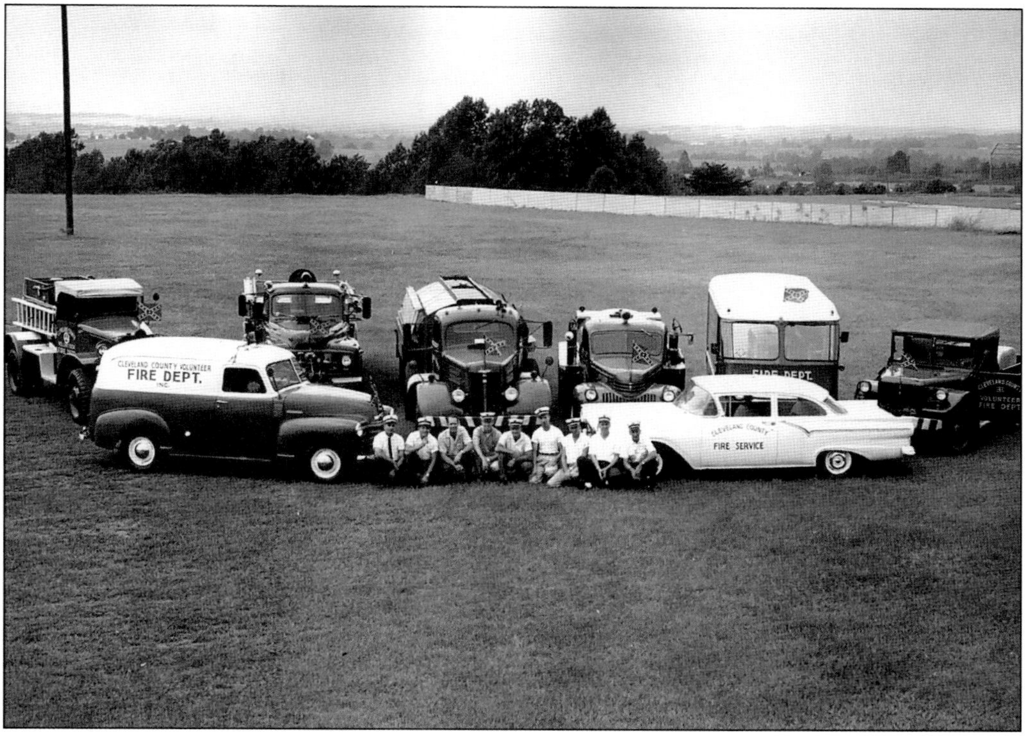

This 1961 photograph shows the Cleveland County Volunteer Fire Department vehicles. (Delane Davis.)

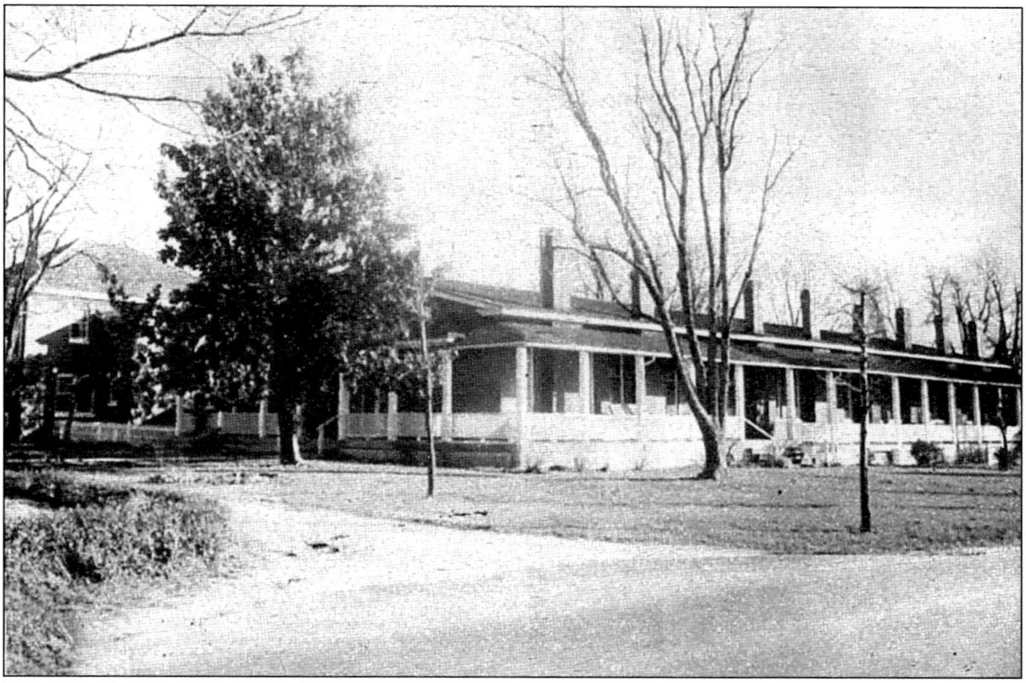

The old County Home building on South Post Road was converted to classrooms in the late 1960s in order to become the new home for Cleveland County Technical Institute.

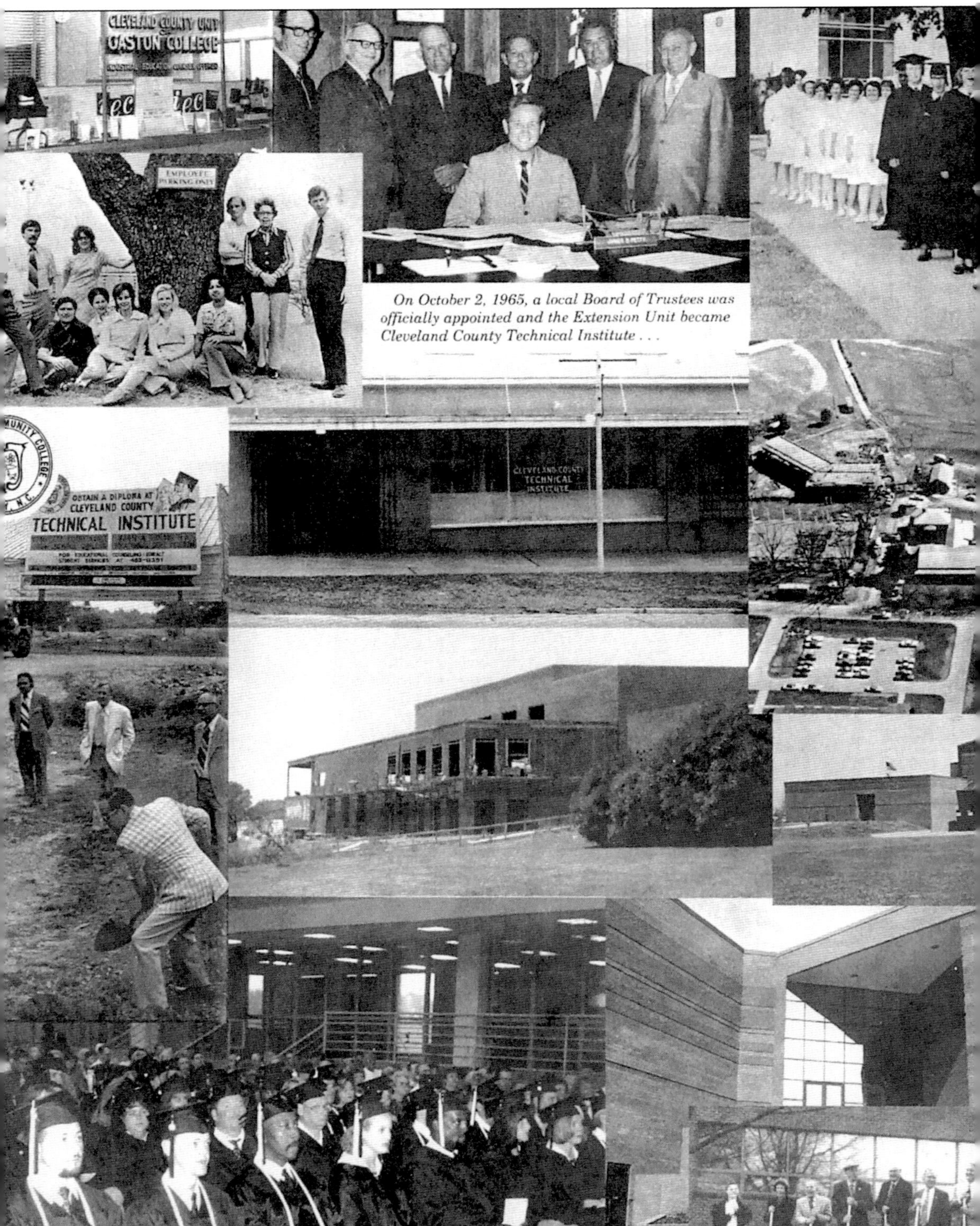

On October 2, 1965, a local Board of Trustees was officially appointed and the Extension Unit became Cleveland County Technical Institute . . .

Through the leadership and guidance of Dr. James Petty (1965–1990) and Dr. L. Steve Thornburg (1990–present), Cleveland County Technical Institute has evolved into Cleveland

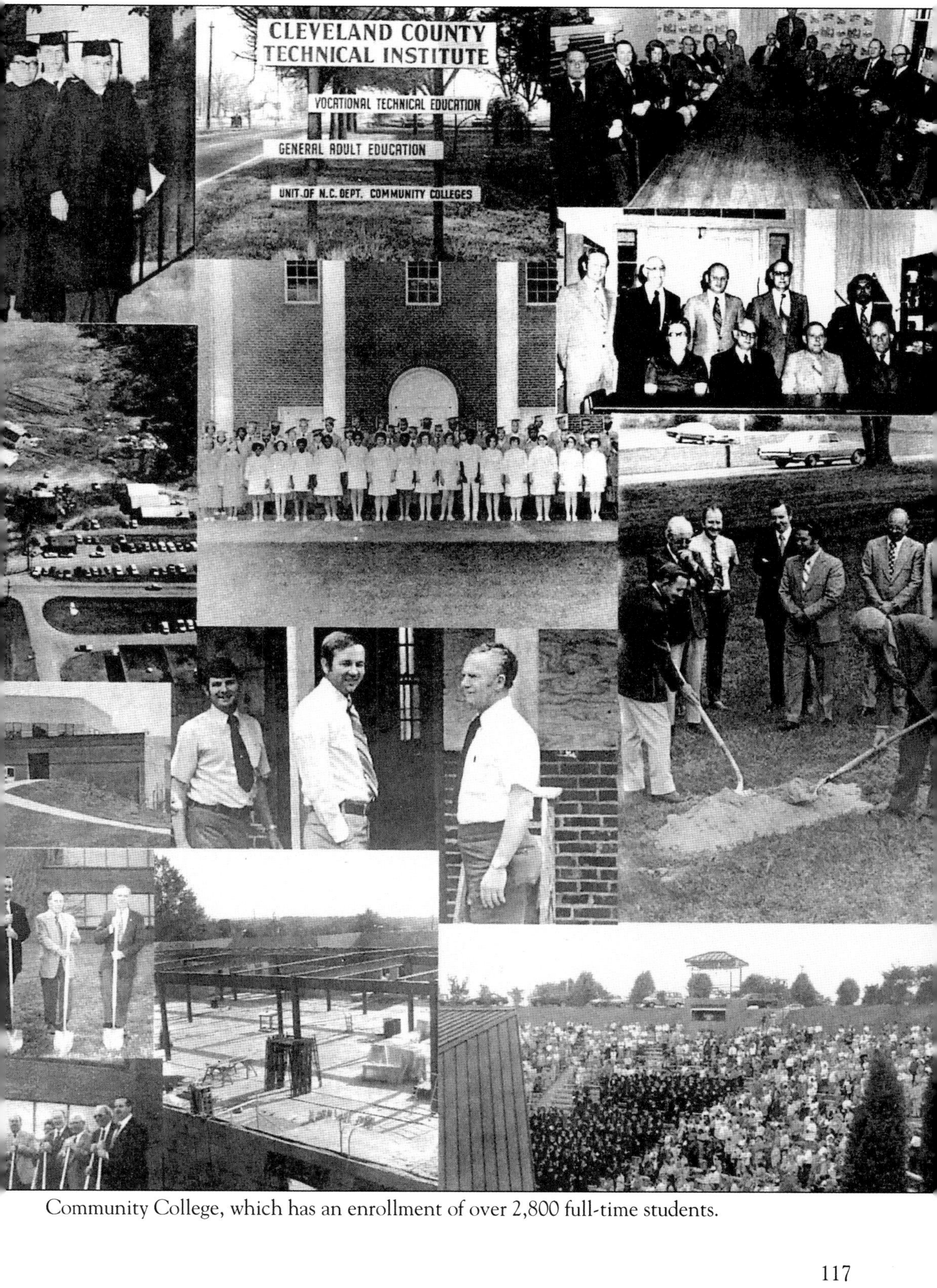

Community College, which has an enrollment of over 2,800 full-time students.

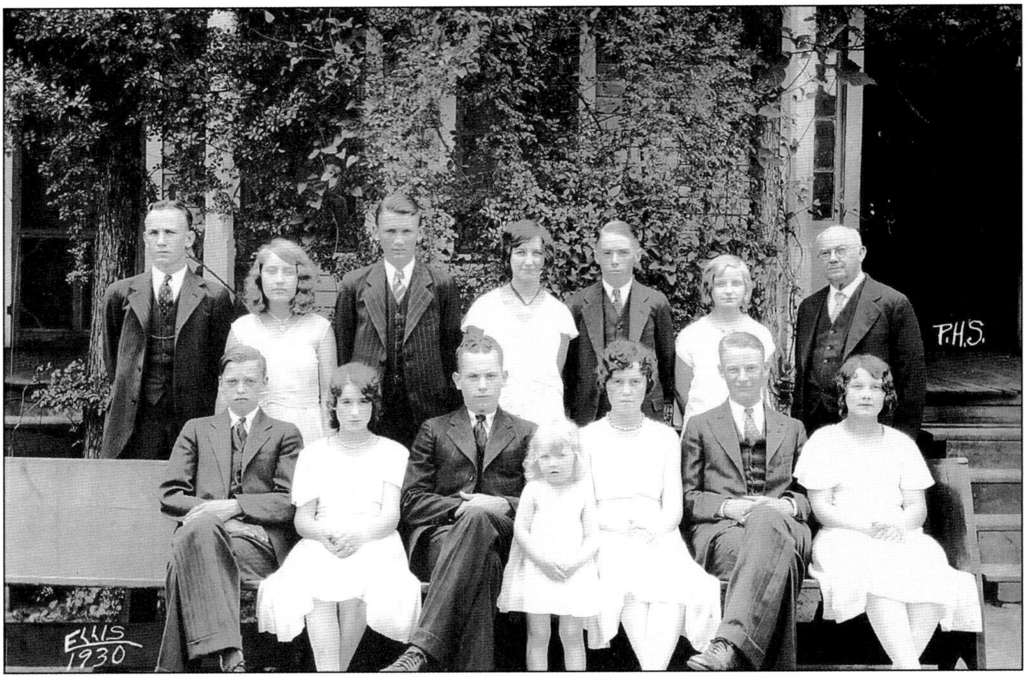

Lawndale grew as a textile village on the First Broad River in upper Cleveland County. Maj. H.F. Schenck built textile plants in the 19th century and then developed a railroad that ran from Lawndale to Shelby. A private high school known as Piedmont High School served Lawndale for decades. The class of 1930 had less than a dozen students. Here, they are dressed for their class photo made by Ellis Studio. (Uptown Shelby Association.)

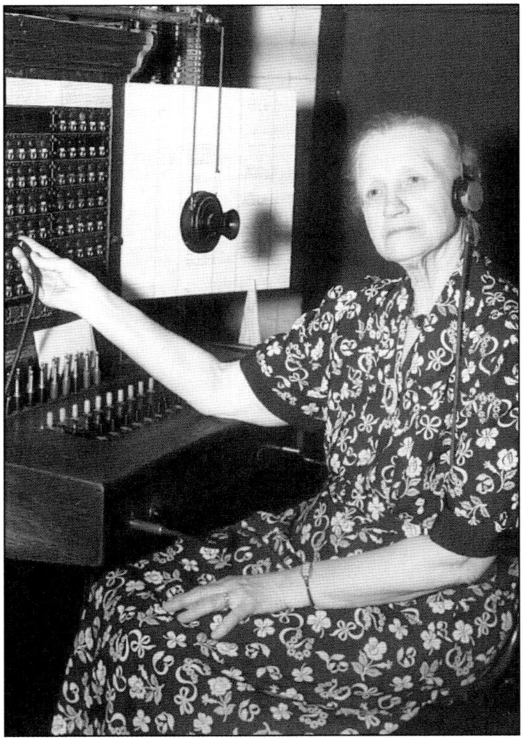

"Miss Josie" Eaker operated the Lawndale switchboard telephone exchange from her home, starting in 1907 and continuing through 1950, when the switchboard was replaced by a Southern Bell dialing system.

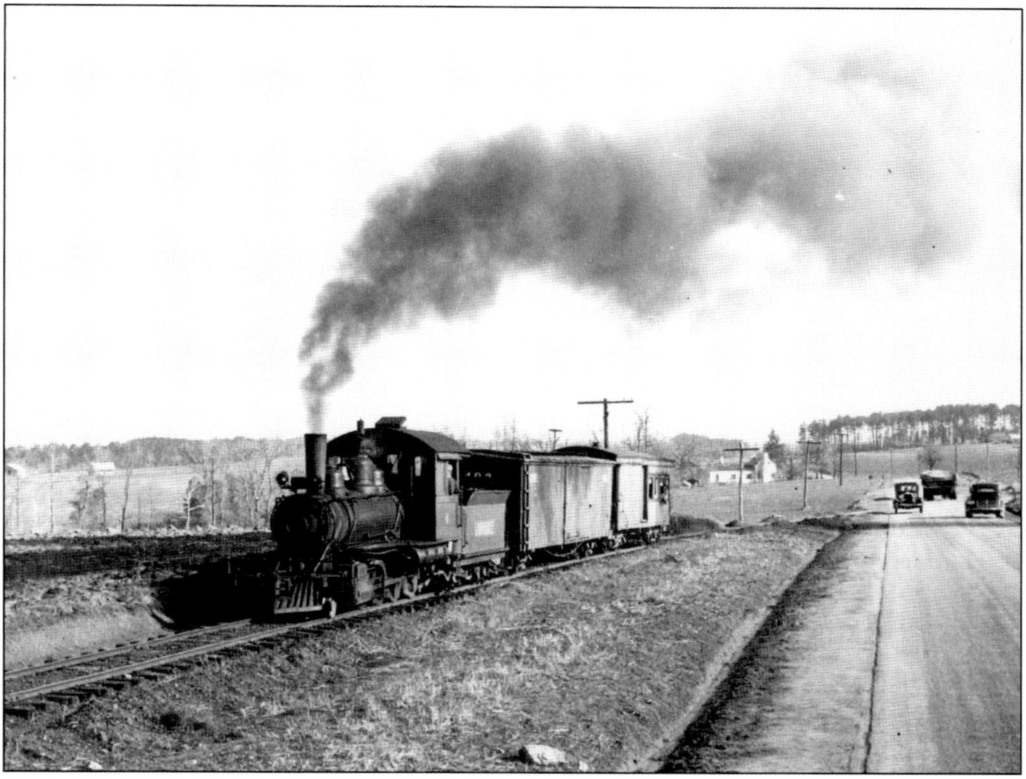

One of Major Schenck's railroad engines is pictured with the crew. The engine operated on a narrow gauge track transporting both people and goods along the 11.7-mile line from Lawndale to Shelby. (R.W. Richardson.)

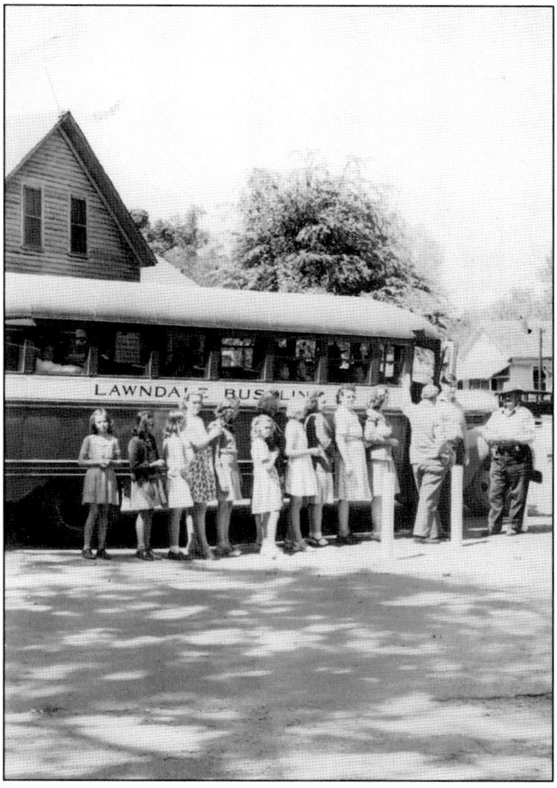

Before many families had automobiles, small communities such as Lawndale had private bus services. This scene shows a group ready to board the Lawndale Bus Line for the short drive to Shelby. (Tommy Forney.)

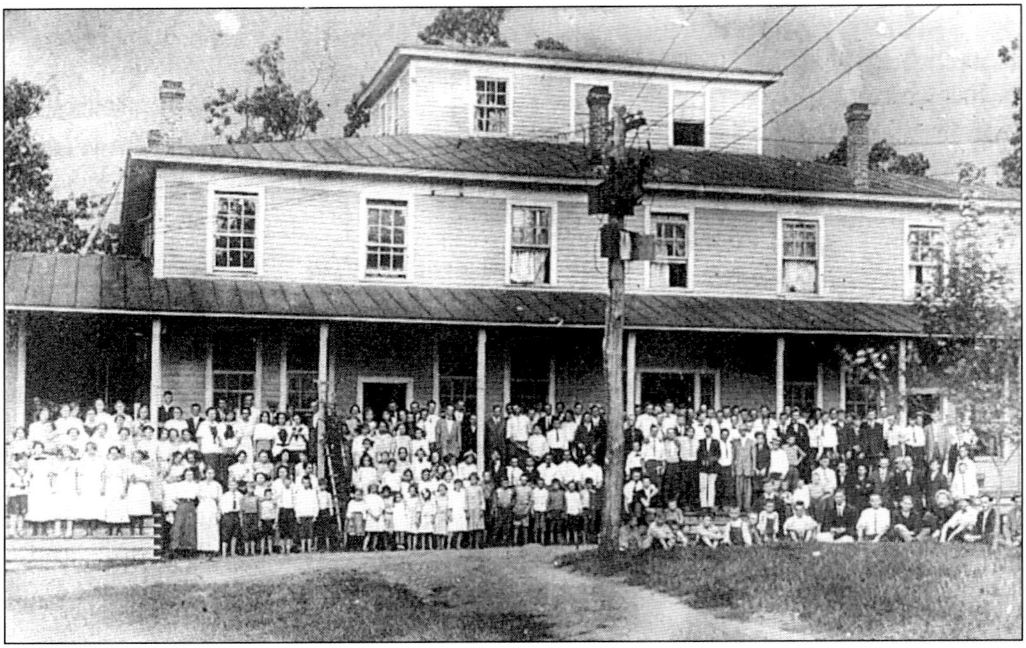

This photograph shows the students from all grades standing in front of Schenck Hall at Piedmont High School.

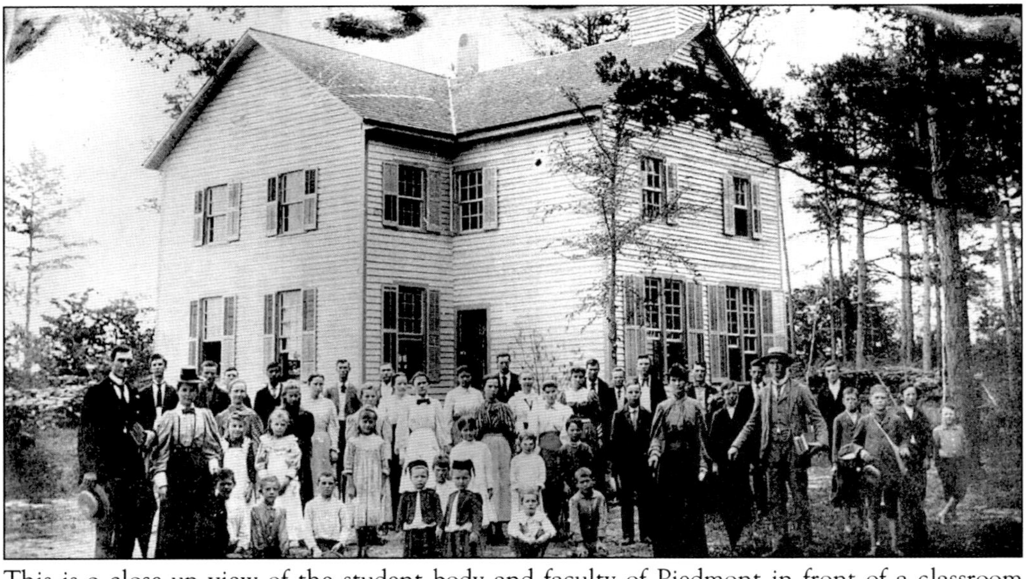

This is a close-up view of the student body and faculty of Piedmont in front of a classroom building. (Joe Southards.)

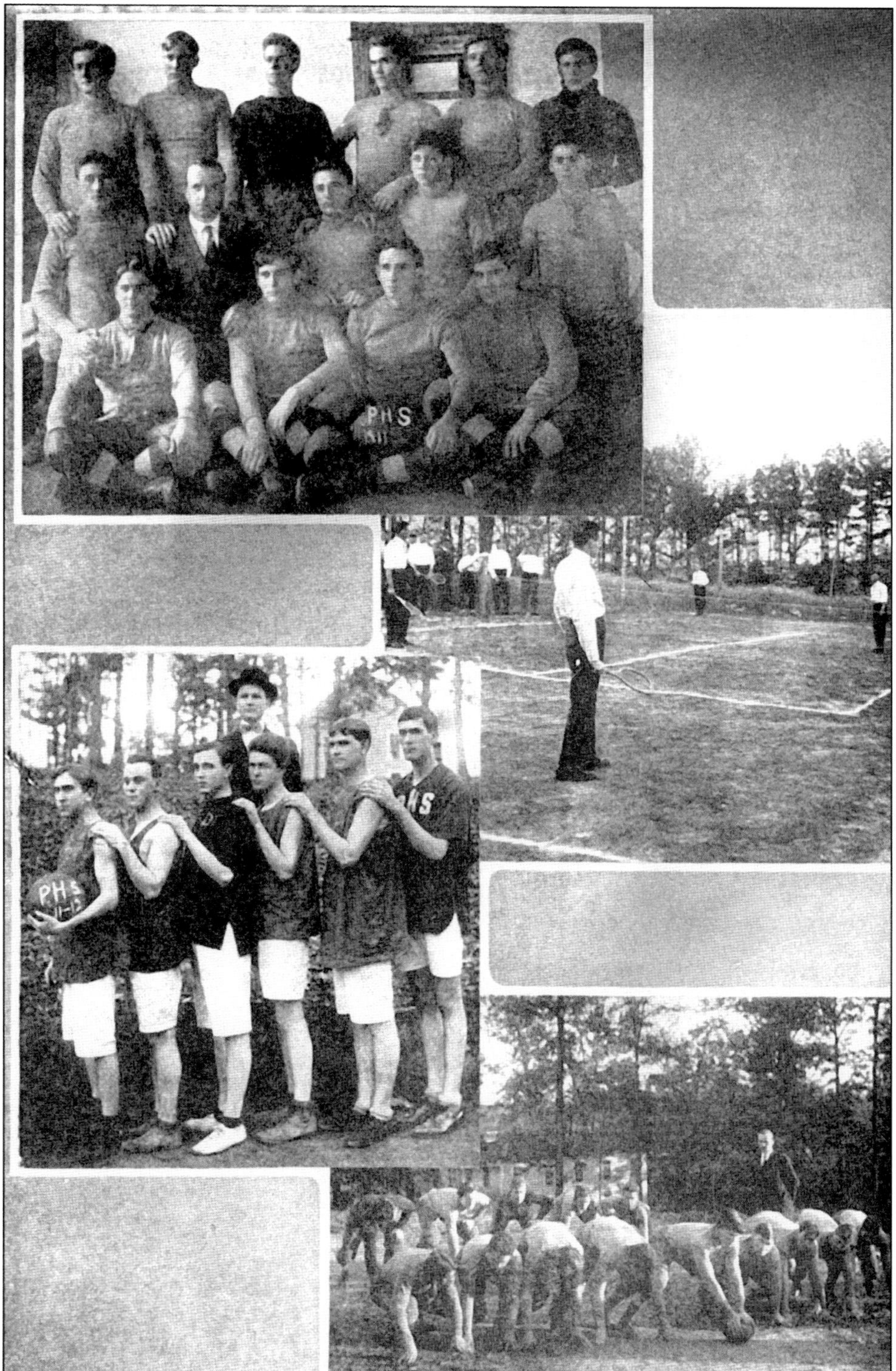

Piedmont offered a variety of sports before 1920. Football and basketball required just enough players for teams. The tennis picture is quite different from today in dress, racquets, and surface of the courts. (Joe Southards.)

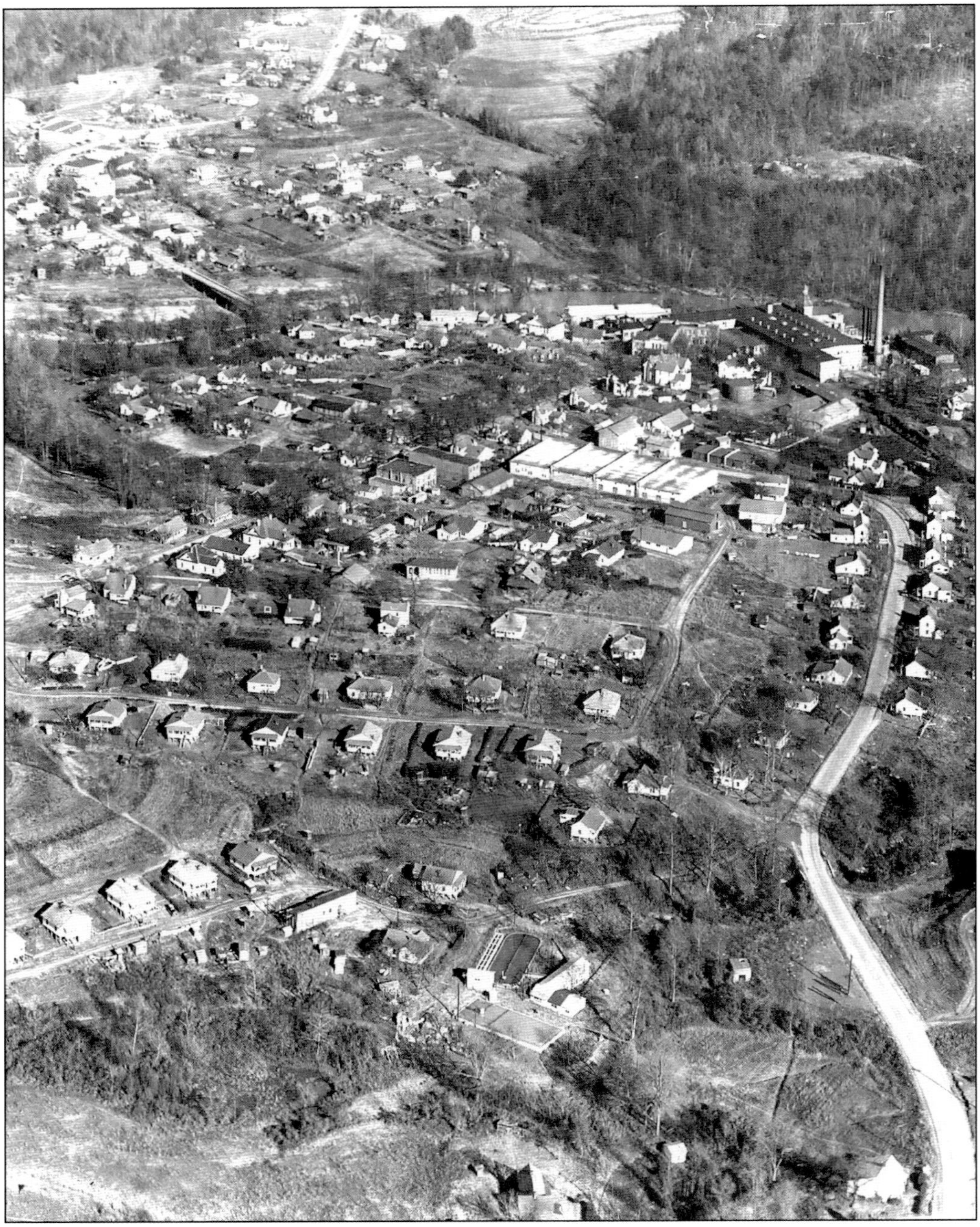

This aerial view shows Lawndale after the new bridge was built across the First Broad River in the 1940s. The current downtown Lawndale is at the top on the north side of the river. This photo could represent numerous mill villages of the 20th century. Note the houses, which are similar to each other and within walking distance of the mill. (Dean Floyd.).

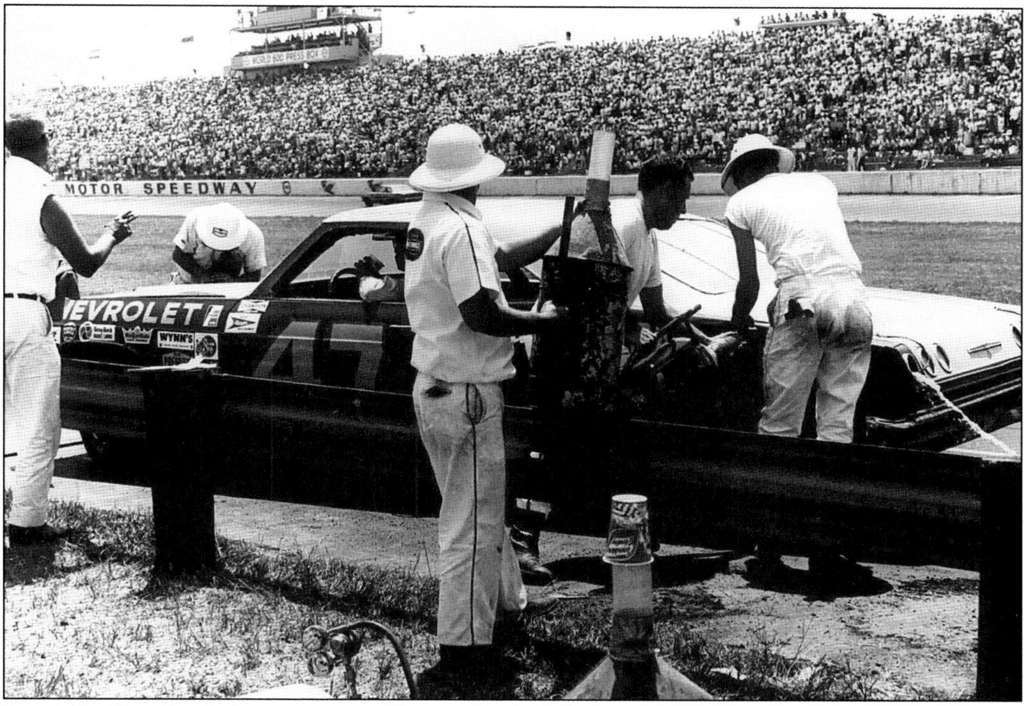

In 1967, Cleveland County native Gene "Stick" Elliott was a regular on the stock car racing scene. He is pictured here with his pit crew in action at Charlotte Motor Speedway.

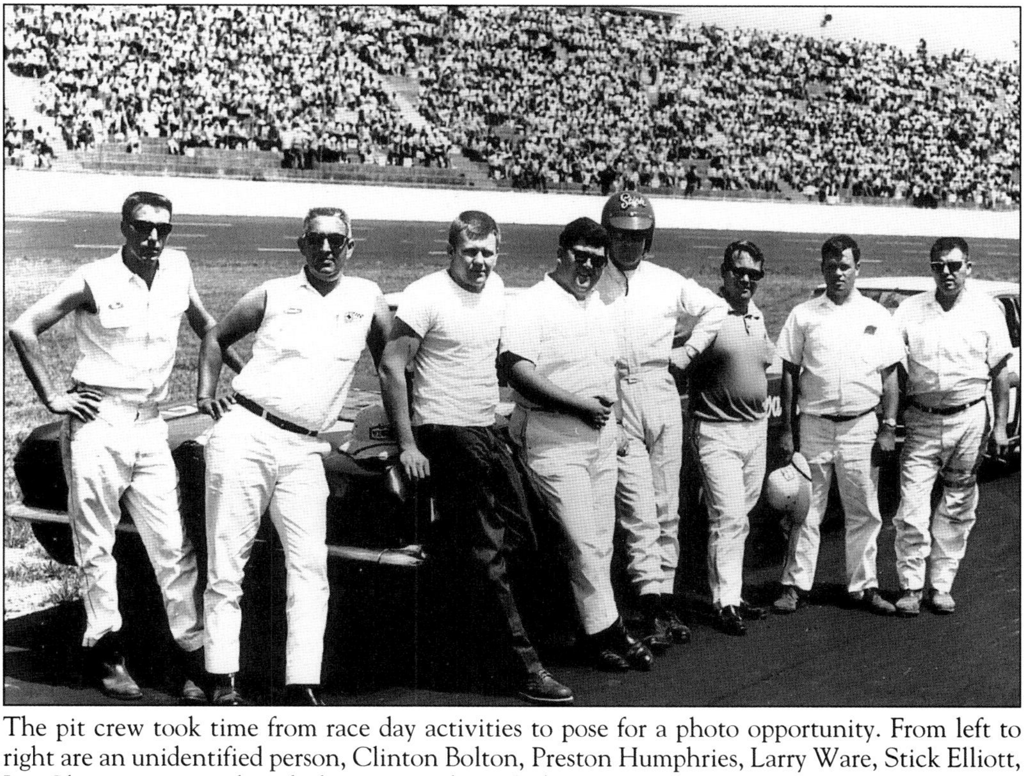

The pit crew took time from race day activities to pose for a photo opportunity. From left to right are an unidentified person, Clinton Bolton, Preston Humphries, Larry Ware, Stick Elliott, Jim Clemmer, an unidentified person, and Toy Bolton.

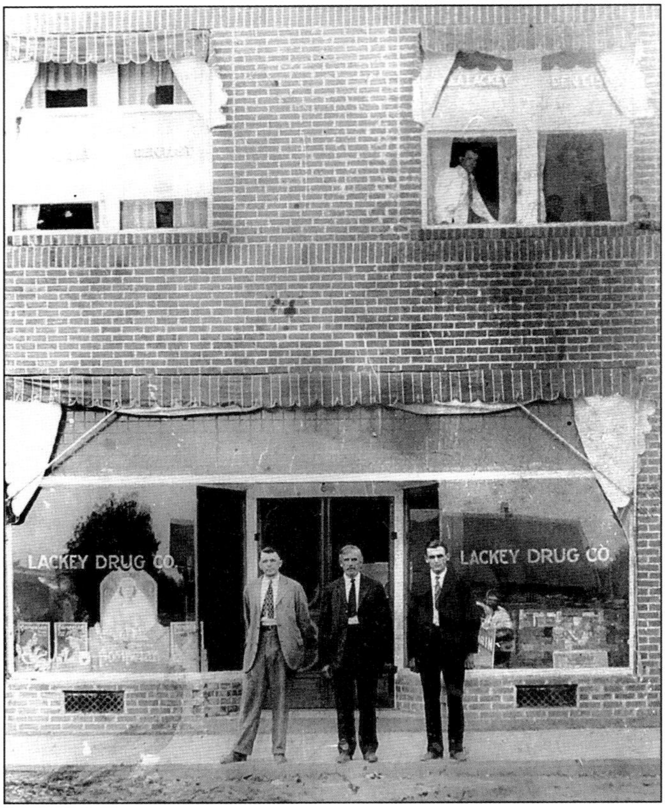

Pictured in front of the Lackey Drug Co. in Fallston are Dr. Frank Lackey, Dr. Rufus Lackey, and Dr. Walter Lackey. Dr. Austin Lackey can be seen in the second floor window of this 1920s photo. (Helen Lackey.)

This photo inside the Lackey Drug Store gives a feel for the time. Pictured from left to right are Drs. Austin, Rufus, Frank, and Walter Lackey. (Helen Lackey.)

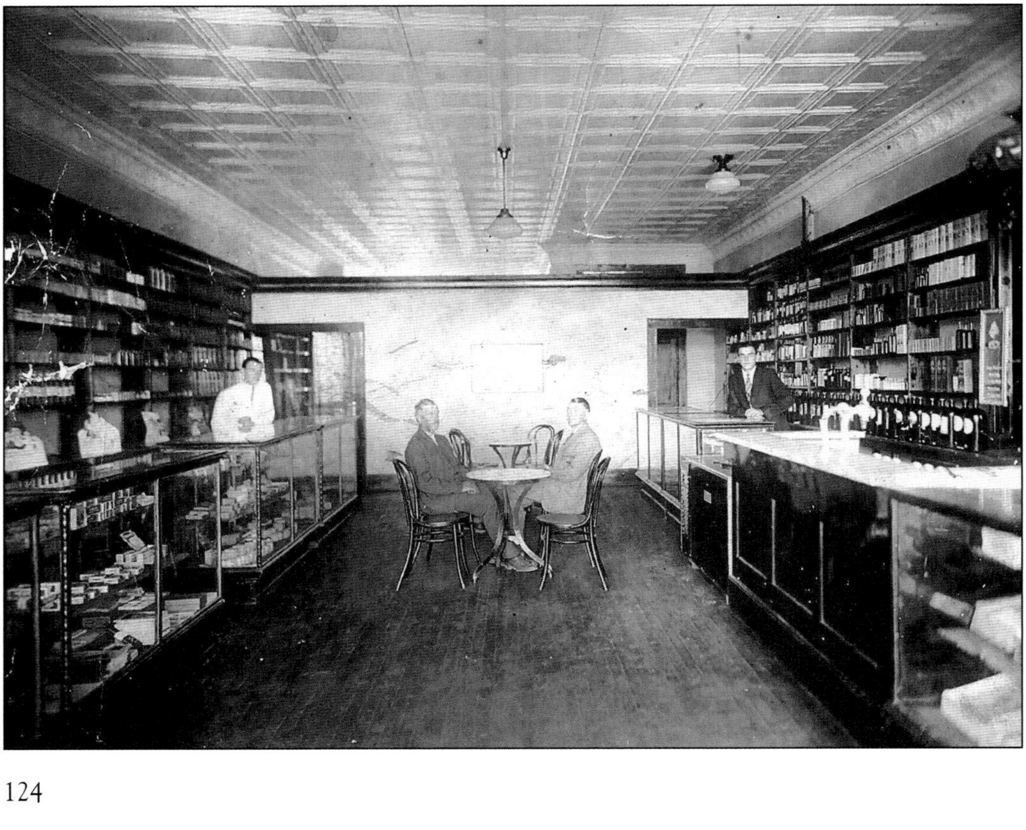

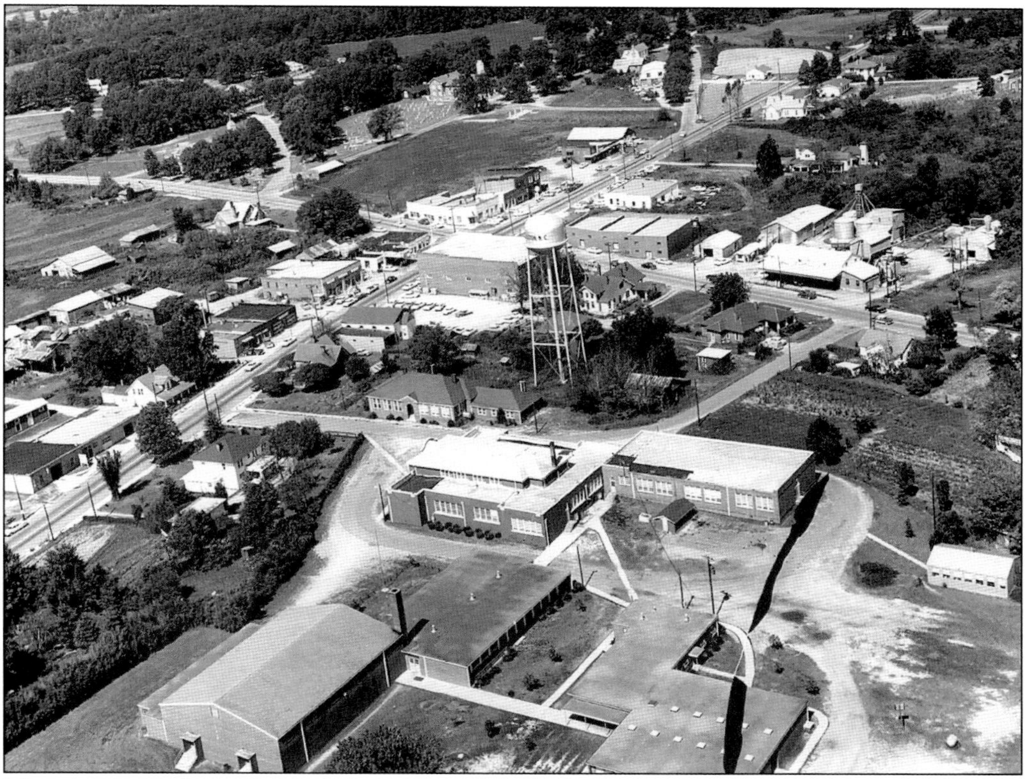

This aerial of Fallston shows the town in the early 1960s.The old Fallston School is seen in the lower half of the photo. Stamey's is to the left of the water tower and the Dixon Store was across the street from Stamey's. (Virginia Coon.)

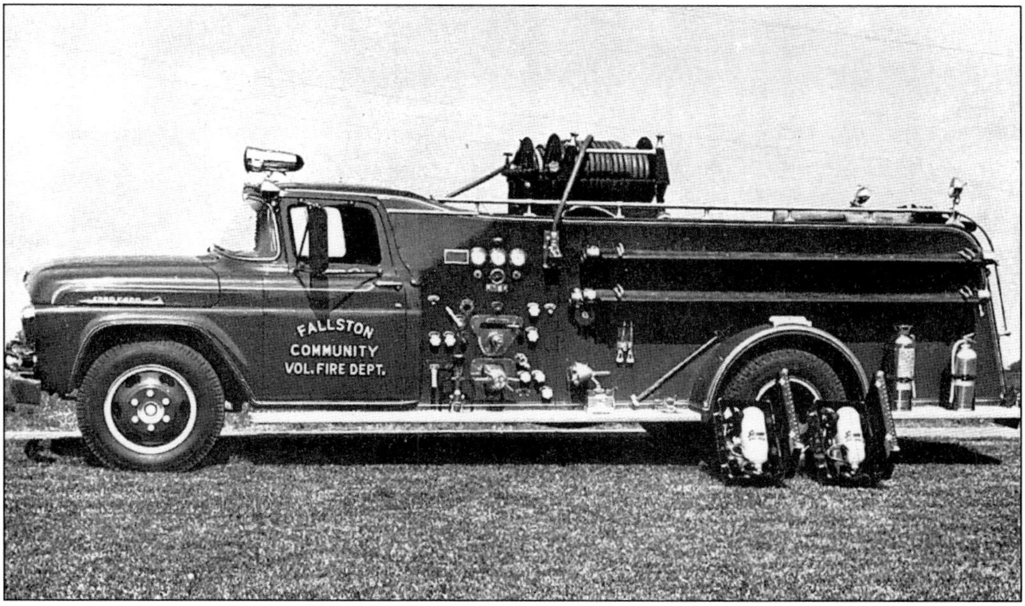

In 1958, this Ford pumper was the pride of the Fallston Community Volunteer Fire Department. The fire engine was recently donated to Cleveland Community College for use in fire and rescue training. (Ralph Dixon.)

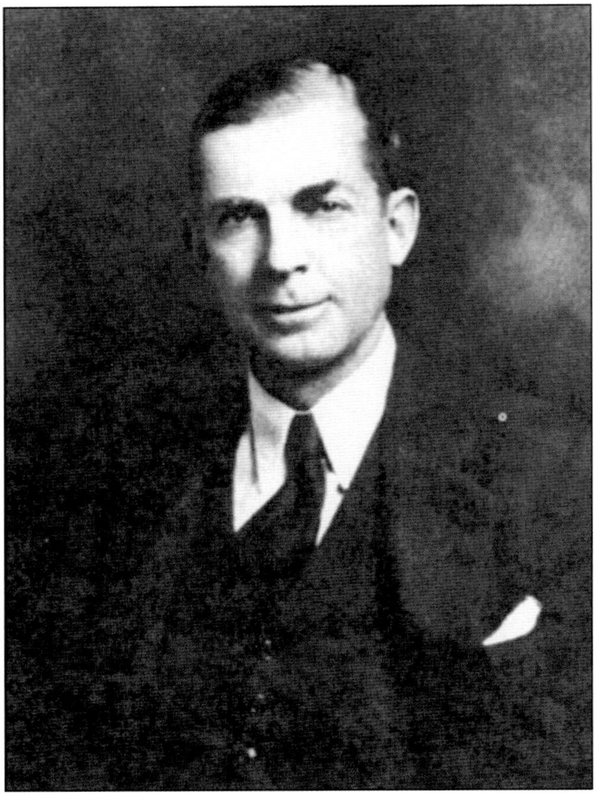

Cleveland County can boast being the home of a Pulitzer Prize winning playwright. Hatcher Hughes of Grover wrote *Hell Bent fer Heaven* in 1922, and the play was produced in 1924 in New York City.

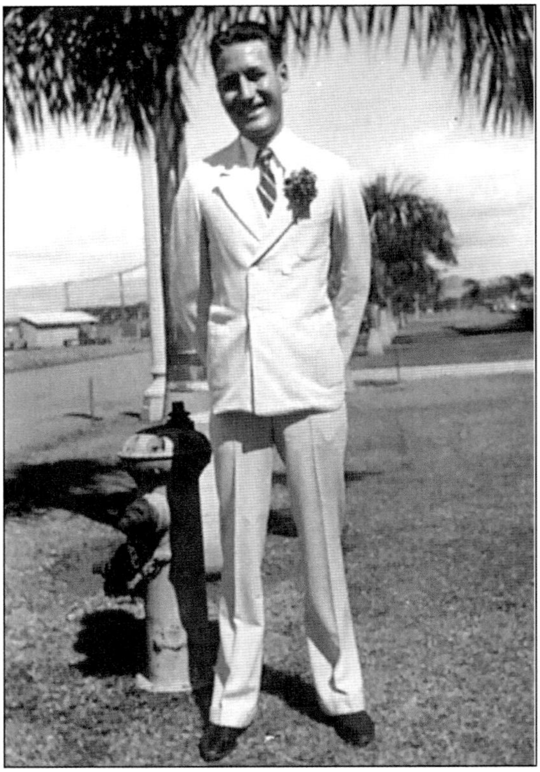

Carlson "Skip" Stewart of Grover was listed as "missing in action" after the 1941 bombing of Pearl Harbor. Carlson was known as a fine baseball player. (Tony Stewart.)

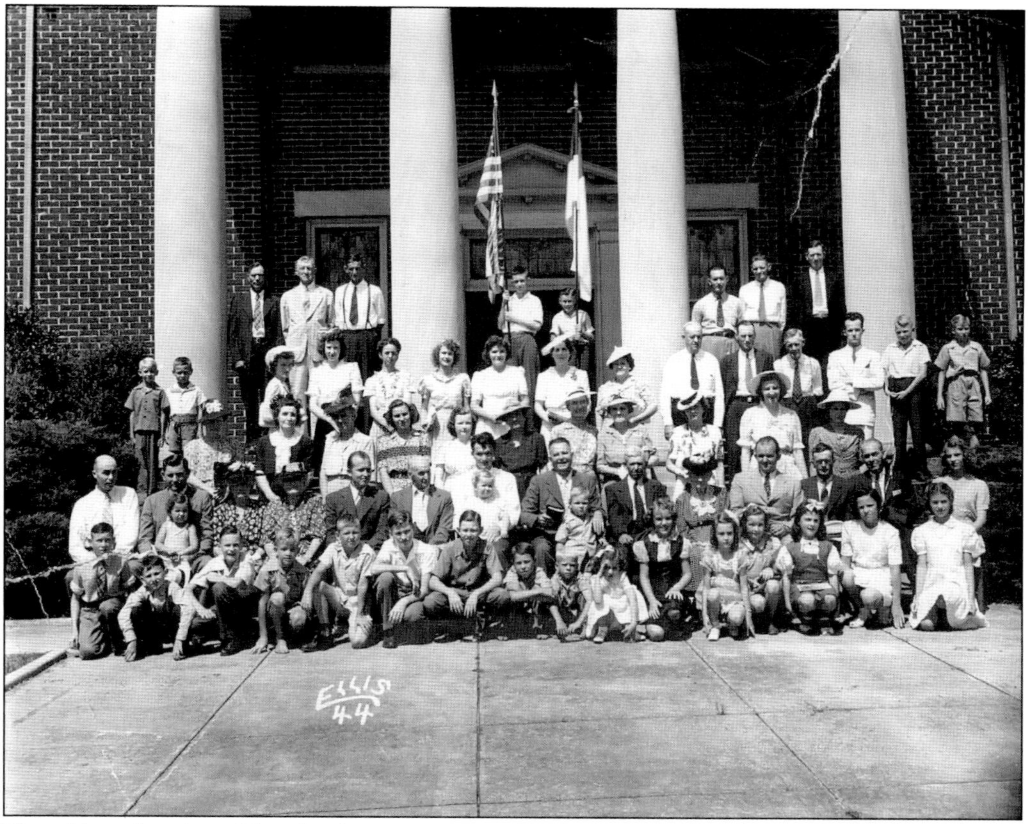

The oldest church in Cleveland County is Shiloh Presbyterian in Grover. The church was formed in 1780, just three miles from the Kings Mountain Battleground. The congregation poses for this 1944 photo in front of the church. (Jean Harry Frances.)

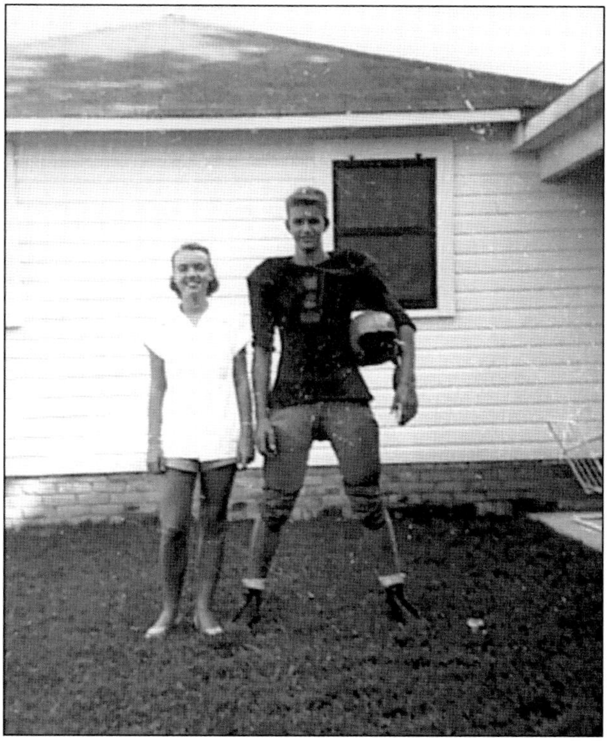

Before he was stricken with polio, C.F. "Charlie" Harry III was an average teenager. He poses in his football uniform with his sister Jean in this 1950 photo. Charlie's life was anything but average. An outstanding businessman and civic leader, he is missed by all who knew him. (Jean Harry Francis.)

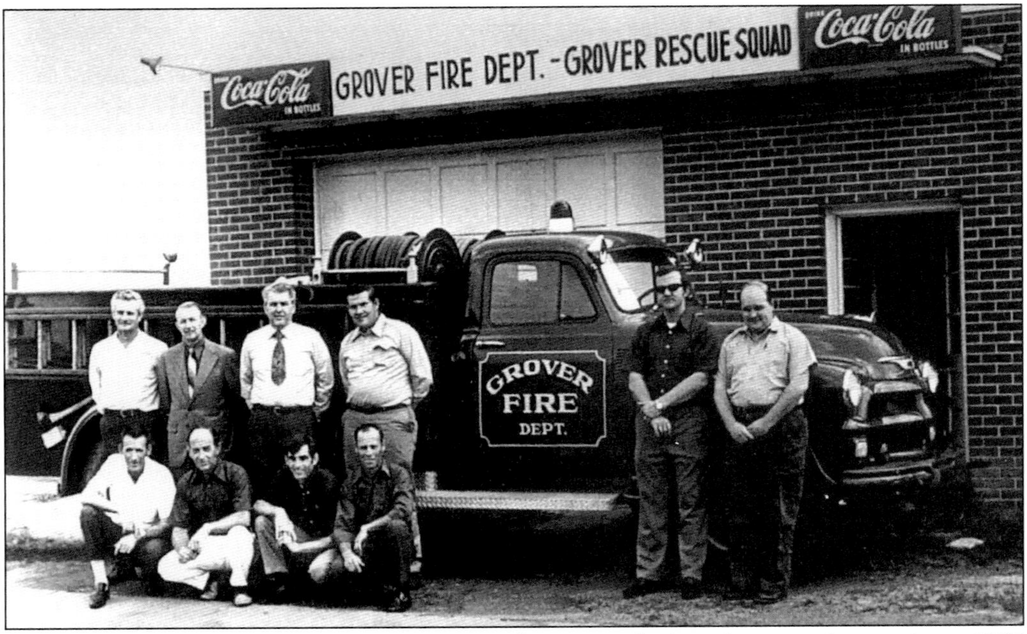

Members of the Grover Fire Department proudly pose with their first new fire truck—a 1953 Chevrolet pumper. (Dewey Cooke.)

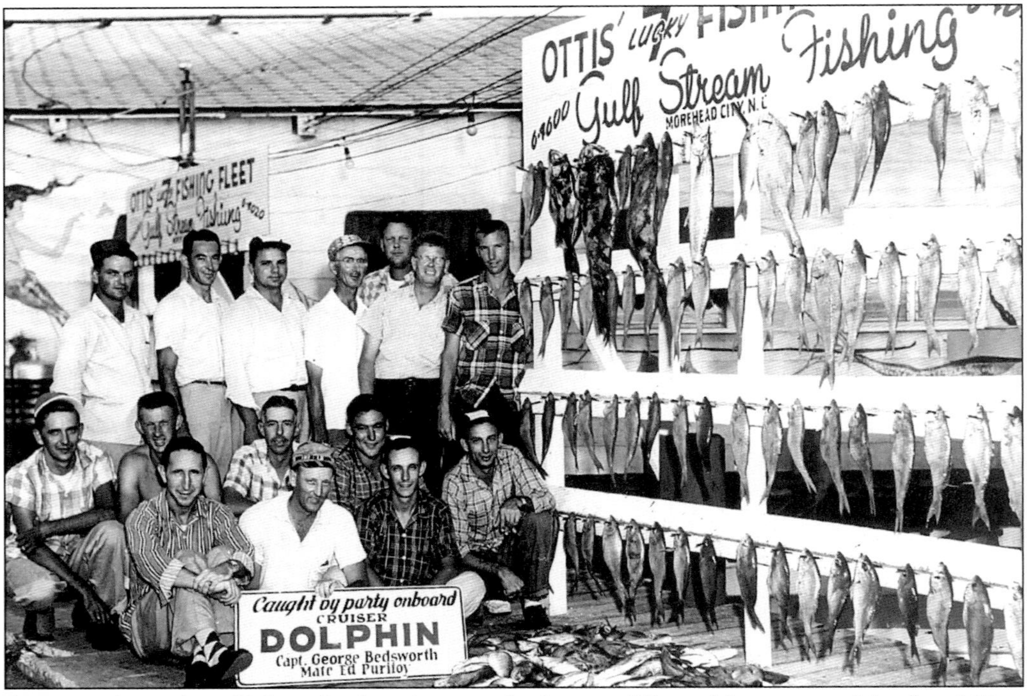

A group of men from Toluca displays their catch after an offshore fishing trip at Morehead City. Toluca lies on the Cleveland-Lincoln County line, therefore, whether one lives in Cleveland County depends upon exactly were one's house is. From left to right are (front row) W.C. Cook, R.A. Brackett, and Hugh Lee Cooke; (middle row) George Moore, John Thomas Cooke, Claude Cooke, Ray Saine, and Joe Justice; (back row) Don Putnum, Lamar Willis, Kemp Sain, A.B. Prince, Max Shull, John Sandes, and George Hardin. (Becky Sain.)